BEAR

The Hard Life and Good Times of Alabama's Coach Bryant

PAUL W. BRYANT
JOHN UNDERWOOD

A Sports Illustrated Book
LITTLE, BROWN AND COMPANY
BOSTON   TORONTO

FOURTH PRINTING

T 01/75

Sports Illustrated Books
are published by
Little, Brown and Company
in association with
Sports Illustrated Magazine

LIBRARY OF CONGRESS CATALOGING IN PUBLICATION DATA

Bryant, Paul W
  Bear; the hard life and good times of Alabama's
Coach Bryant.

  "A Sports illustrated book."
  1. Bryant, Paul W.   2. Football.   3. Football
coaching.   I. Underwood, John, 1934–   II. Title.
GV939.B79A32   796.33'2'0924 [B]   74-17177
ISBN 0-316-11325-5

Designed by Susan Windheim

Published simultaneously in Canada
by Little, Brown & Company (Canada) Limited

PRINTED IN THE UNITED STATES OF AMERICA

To Mama, who put me on my way, and to Mary Harmon, who made it a pleasant journey; and to the players, the coaches, and the fans of college football, the greatest game there is.

Preface

Among the Bear-watchers I have known is a gentleman named O. A. (Bum) Phillips, who I met on a tape recording sent from Stillwater, Oklahoma, where Bum was in the service of college football at Oklahoma A&M just before he defected to the pros. Previously, he assisted Bryant at Texas A&M.

In all the time I have spent trying to crystallize the particles that separate Bear Bryant from his contemporaries — and from just about every other man I have known — I never achieved the grasp Bum Phillips did on that little tape. He sent it in response to a request for opinions, and I imagine he sat right down and rolled it off the tip of his tongue. In other words, Bum made me look bad.

This is he speaking:

"Coach Bryant doesn't coach football. He coaches people. When I went to work for him — and I say for him because you sure don't work with him — the feeling was he could get more out of people than anybody. Others might know more about football, but I think, I *know*, I've never been around anyone who knows as much about people. Like Jake Gaither used to say, Bryant could take his'n and beat your'n, and take your'n and beat his'n. He could win with either group.

"We used to have those conferences before practice at A&M. Coach Bryant would stick his head in, and in the middle of a sentence everybody would stop and look at him. Total quiet. He'd walk in, real slow. Sit down. Take out a cigarette. Tap it on his fingernail, and light it. And as often as not he'd smoke the whole damn cigarette without anybody saying a word. We'd just sit there and wait.

"Some of these guys had played for him for four years, and coached with him I don't know how long. I don't mean they were scared of him" — some were, Bum, some were — "but they respected him, like I did. If he was going to say something they damn sure wanted to hear it. He never had to say, 'Let me have your attention.' He already had it.

"I remember one time walking out of his office, shutting the door behind me, and John David Crow was standing there. I said, 'What do you need, John?'

"He said, 'Just wanted to see The Man.' Everybody called Bryant 'The Man.'

"I said, 'Whyn't you just go on in. There's nobody with him. He'll be glad to see you.'

"Crow said, 'Oh, I'll just wait.'

"Crow was a senior then and had played out his eligibility. I couldn't talk him into going in. He just leaned against the wall. It must have been twenty minutes before the door opened and Coach Bryant came out. He said, 'What the hell you doing out here, Crow?'

"Crow said, 'Well, I wanted to talk to you.'

" 'Why didn't you come in then?'

" 'I thought you were busy or you wouldn't have had the door closed.'

"And all John Crow had done was make All-America two years in a row and win the Heisman trophy. That's the kind of respect Bryant gets from people."

The gathering apotheosis of Bear Bryant has not been easy to miss in recent years. The jokes are all cut from the same anointed cloth (an atheist in Alabama is someone who doesn't believe in Bryant; an outsized picture postcard sold at newsstands shows him walking on airbrushed water over the caption "I Believe"). An

Alabama contestant in the Miss U.S.A. contest, when asked to name the world's greatest person, responded instinctively, "Paul Bryant." And George Blanda, in a book he wrote twenty-six years later, said that when seeing that face for the first time — granite and ice, and true grit — he thought, This must be what God looks like. Blanda said when Bryant walked into a room you wanted to stand up and applaud.

All this is entertaining and image-serving, to be sure, and if you live in Alabama you might not take it lightly. The trouble is it diminishes the humanness of Bear Bryant. In the end, humanness may be his most serviceable asset. Bryant himself has been pushing a somewhat underexalted self-image lately. Taking time to be humble. People like my wife, who counts herself among the adoring, believe he is now mostly crust, with a soft, sweet center. Like a creamhorn. Those of us who deal with him know better. There is still plenty of steel at the core. But I can understand her affection.

My first real encounter with Bryant occurred at the Georgia game in Athens the season after *The Saturday Evening Post* charged him and Wally Butts with conspiring to fix the previous Alabama-Georgia football game. He stood by a fence near the end zone at the Athens stadium, a large, menacing figure in a straw hat that hooded his eyes, his big jaw in his left hand propped against the fence. He did not seem overly pleased to see me, or particularly interested in my blunt line of questioning, which had to do with what this game, especially, meant to him. Nevertheless, he invited me to come by his hotel later to continue the chat.

I got there before he had taken his sleeping pill. He was sitting by the radio in red pajamas, charting a game that involved a future opponent. The future opponent was supposed to be very good that year, and Bryant was scribbling on a tablet as the broadcast progressed. Others were there listening with him, but I suspect they, like me, were merely following the lead, with no real interest in the outcome.

The game was barely into the second quarter. But something happened that drew a growl from Bryant. He stopped charting and with deliberate strokes scrawled across the tablet: "Can't win," underscored it twice, and threw the tablet aside.

"Who can't win?" I asked, reading the scrawl upside-down. He named the future opponent. I was amazed because at the time the game was scoreless.

The next morning at breakfast I opened the local newspaper to find out if the team Bryant said could not win did not win. It did not. The score was 24 to 0. Later that year Alabama beat the same team by five touchdowns.

We have spent hundreds of hours in conversation since, mostly when I was in search of his viewpoint for *Sports Illustrated*. His candor, from the beginning, was remarkable. And unsettling. I wasn't always sure I wanted to be entrusted with the classified stuff he threw at me. Before games he would pour out the wisdom of his battle plan, explaining what his team would do to win on Saturday, and then ask, "Are you sure you understand this?" I would say, "Sure I do." And he would say, "I don't think you do. Let's go over it again."

More remarkable was his frankness in explaining himself. In that he left nothing unsaid. When he wanted a name protected, or a fact kept confidential, he simply asked it, as if trust were imperative. His ability to recall conversations, incidents, names, places, dates, yard lines, etc., was — and is — uncanny. I have on record the same stories told six years apart. Not only are his words the same but so are his voice inflections.

But what really got me was that three months or six months or a year later he would throw something back at me that *I* had said, something in passing during a gin game on a private airplane, or at poolside on the Florida Keys when he was relaxing. He would say, "Wait a minute. Didn't you tell me last June that so and so and so and so?"

Yes, I would be forced to admit, "but I thought I was interviewing you." I got by with no imprecisions.

The few arguments we have had were more purgative than divisive, clearing the air rather than clouding it. And whenever there was time between meetings he would start off by asking after a sick child, or the disposition of a personal problem he remembered from the last call. He would do this every time.

Much of what Bryant says in this book is tempered with a new appreciation for his position as the greatest living football coach.

Nevertheless, the bitter episodes in his extraordinary life — there was some bile in every cup, from Maryland to Kentucky to Texas to Alabama — have been presented intact because, as he says, that was the way it was and the way he felt. *Then.*

Lately he has enjoyed an almost romantic serenity, which makes it easier for him to be philosophical about bygone strife. The embattled Bear I knew in the early sixties has pulled around him the robes of a patriarch. The sons of former players now play for him. The words that proceed from his mouth are more conciliatory. He has been mending fences, most notably the one between Alabama and Georgia Tech, and him and Bobby Dodd. Close the wounds, hide the scars.

There are two mistakes one can make from getting too caught up in this new image (the pacified, mollifying Bear). One is believing that some of it was not there all along. Elmer Smith, another like Bum Phillips who had an ear for Bryant, told me of a time when the two of them used to go for rides in the country around Texas A&M, usually before dawn, being ex-farmboys and early risers and having beaten everybody else to the office.

Often, he said, Bryant would take him down the old Wellborn Highway to talk about an upcoming game, or mutual friends, or nothing at all. But on one particular morning Bryant suddenly turned into a driveway less than a mile from the campus. A little boy was standing outside the house, crying. Bryant said nothing to Elmer Smith, just got out of the car and went over to the boy and knelt beside him, talking to him with his big farmer's arm on the boy's narrow, birdlike shoulders.

Elmer didn't know what was going on. Finally the boy's mother appeared, and Bryant spoke to her, and then came back to the car. As they drove back to A&M, Elmer Smith's curiosity got the best of him and he asked Bryant to explain.

Bryant said he had run over a dog on his way in that morning. He wasn't sure whose dog, but before he could think about Baylor or anybody else he had to find out. What he was doing in all that commiseration, he said, was promising the boy another dog.

The second mistake is to believe that the leavening process of a more agreeable Bear has made him a more vulnerable one. Believe that and, if you are a rival coach, he will surely pin your ears back. The alternative is not to believe it. Chances are you will have them pinned back anyway. *C'est la Bear.* But if you don't have to coach against him, just relax and read him. It's easier.

One

When I was generating all that heat in the Southwest Conference in the mid-fifties, and Abe Martin of TCU was saying how I'd made the other coaches in that league put away their golf clubs, a Dallas sportswriter named Harold Ratliff asked me if I thought I was a genius. Ratliff always had the needle out. Compared with what a lot of folks were saying in those days, old Harold's twits were like love taps. I smiled — this was at a party and I was on my best behavior — and said, "No, Harold, I'm no genius. But I'm a damn good football coach."

I doubt there are any geniuses coaching football, but if you were to ask me if football is a coach's game I'd have to say it is. And always was. And if you were to ask me why some coaches are going to win more than others — why they get their players to win, and why a certain few win consistently, no matter where they coach — I wouldn't tell you if I knew. This is my book you're buying, not my blood.

When I was at Kentucky I got booed one night by a group of students who came to the train to see us off for a game with Cincinnati. I had fired some of our star players and they didn't like that. And we'd lost three of our first five games and they didn't like that either, which I can understand. I didn't like it myself. In fact, I hated it. For a young coach — which I was then — so keyed up I couldn't get to work in the morning without vomiting along the way, it was not exactly heaven on earth. The Cincinnati game took on added importance.

Cincinnati had fine teams then, coached by Sid Gillman, who has been a big name in the pros and is with the Houston Oilers now. What I'm about to say should not be taken as a lack of respect for Sid. You have to appreciate that my collar was tighter than it is now.

We got to the stadium at Cincinnati and I sensed something was wrong. When we went out to warm up for the game there was nobody in the stands. Just a few handfuls scattered around. I thought for a minute I was in the wrong place. When we finished our warm-up and the Cincinnati team still hadn't made an appearance, I said to Carney Laslie, one of my original assistant coaches, "What's that no-good conniving smart-aleck" — meaning the eminent Coach Gillman — "up to now? What the hell is that damn thief trying to pull?"

Carney just shook his head. He was as dumbfounded as I was.

I ordered the team back into the locker room — and then it dawned on me. I'd screwed up the schedule. We were an hour early.

I was too embarrassed to tell what I knew. I just walked around, up and down the aisles where the players sat waiting, my big old farmer's boots making the only noise in there. I couldn't think of anything to say, so I didn't say a word. For an hour I clomped up and down. Finally, when I'd used up enough time I delivered a one-sentence pep talk, the only thing I could think to say:

"Let's go."

They almost tore the door down getting out. Cincinnati was favored that day, but it was no contest. We won, 27–7.

For years afterward Carney Laslie and another long-time assistant named Frank Moseley used to tell the story whenever they spoke to football groups or at clinics, describing it as the greatest psychological ploy they had ever seen. I didn't let on because I was embarrassed. I finally spilled the beans to Carney fifteen years later, before he died, and I wish now I hadn't because he was sure disillusioned.

"You mean," he said, "that what I've been calling the smartest move I ever saw turned out to be dumb luck?"

I had to admit it was.

Well, if you'd rather be lucky than smart — and I've certainly been lucky — that makes a pretty good story. Bobby Dodd used to say if you think you're lucky you are, and that's probably right. I've done dumber things trying.

I had a hot appendix at Kentucky in 1952 and was in the hospital just before our game with LSU. The team was all primed to win one for me, just like in the movies. Or in this case without me. Dr. Grandison McLean, my physician, said it was no sense my begging to go because it was impossible. He removed the appendix on Thursday night, and Harry Jones, one of the Jones twins who played so great for us and went on to make a fortune in real estate, came by to see me on Friday.

As he walked out Harry said, "Coach, you'll be there tomorrow, won't you?"

Not "Will you?" or "Can you?" but "You will."

I said, "Yeah, Harry, I'll be there."

And when the time came I dragged myself out of bed and went, just as I'd seen John Wayne do a hundred times. And the sight of me being delivered to them, held up on either side by attendants, was such a shock that my players forgot all their plays and got murdered, 34–7. I had to be taken back to the hospital immediately after the game, so weak and sore I could hardly move. If I'd stayed in bed to begin with I'm convinced they would have won.

What we're talking about here, really, is motivating people, the ingredient that separates winners from losers — in football, in anything — and one way or another everything I've done most of my life has been wrapped up in that question.

Coaches always want to know how you make winners out of chronic losers, a problem familiar to all of us. You seldom inherit a warm bed in this business. Maryland had won one game the year before we took that job. Kentucky hadn't won as many as six since 1912 when we got its program going, and had never been to a bowl game. Texas A&M hadn't had a Southwest Conference championship in seventeen years when we won it there in 1956. At Alabama, the tradition was rich, and tradition is something you can tie to, as a start. But the Alabama teams had won four games in three years when we arrived in 1958.

There is no formula, no prescription I could lay out. But I wouldn't tell coaches that. I would tell them about my first season at Texas A&M. I never had a season like it. We lost nine games, and everybody was on us, and it was a matter of picking up the paper today and reading something a little bit nastier than what had been in there the day before.

Talk about gut checks. We had taken the team down to training camp at Junction to find out right off who the players were and who the quitters were, and the quitters had outnumbered the players three to one. I remember Mickey Herskowitz had come down to Junction for his paper, the *Houston Post*. He said his boss, Clark Neyland, heard there was dissension on the squad, and he came to find out about it.

I said, "Now, son, are you going to quote me on this?"

He said, "Yessir."

I said, "Well, you call your boss, and tell him I said if there isn't any dissension now there's damn sure going to be in a hurry, and I'm going to cause it."

And he wrote it that way.

We struggled along, down to the end of the season, and were getting ready to play SMU. The kids we had left had been playing their hearts out every week, and every week I was afraid they were going to throw in. But they were hanging in there all the time, losing games by a point or two or a touchdown, and all the time winning the people. And certainly winning me.

They'd been dead all week in practice before the SMU game, and I wondered, what could we do? What was left to try? I'd run out of ways to motivate them. Elmer Smith, one of my assistants, said he remembered one time when he was playing for Ivan Grove at Hendrix College. Grove woke him up at midnight and read him something about how a mustard seed could move a mountain if you believed in it, something Norman Vincent Peale, or somebody, had taken from the Bible and written in a little pamphlet. It impressed me.

I didn't tell a soul. At twelve o'clock on Thursday night I called everyone on my staff and told them to meet me at the dormitory at

6

one o'clock. When they got there, I said, OK, go get the players real quick, and they went around shaking them, and the boys came stumbling in there, rubbing their eyes, thinking I'd finally lost my mind. And I read 'em that little thing about the mustard seed — just three sentences — turned around, and walked out.

Well, you never know if you are doing right or wrong, but we went out and played the best game we'd played all year. SMU should have beaten us by forty points, but they were lucky to win, 6–3. In the last minute of play we had a receiver wide open inside their 20-yard line, but our passer didn't see him.

Several years after that, Darrell Royal called me from Texas. He was undefeated, going to play Rice and worried to death. He said he'd never been in that position before, undefeated and all, and his boys were lazy and fatheaded, and he wanted to know what to do about it.

I said, "Well, Darrell, there's no set way to motivate a team, and the way I do it may be opposite to your way, but I can tell you a story." And I gave him that thing about the mustard seed. He said, by golly, he'd try it.

Well, I don't know whether he did or not, but I remember the first thing I wanted to do Sunday morning was get that paper and see how Texas made out. Rice won, 34–7.

So if you ask me what motivates a team, what makes them suck up their guts when the going is tough, I'll tell you I don't have the answers, but I know for myself I've been motivated all my life. When we were losing at A&M — and I never doubted we would win with the boys we had left — the losing just made me get up a little earlier to get started the next day.

I still get up at five o'clock. I'd like to sleep later but after thirty-seven years in this business I find I can't. To me it's still time wasted when you sleep past six. At Alabama one morning at seven, I placed a call from my office to Shug Jordan or somebody at Auburn, and the girl said nobody was in yet. I said, "What's the matter, honey, don't you people take football seriously?"

Everybody thought that was a nice joke, but I meant it. You can get the Auburn people now at seven, or thereabouts, because they've been trying harder. To be honest, they soon copy everything we do. As an example, they were using those big, burly boys and we beat

7

'em with little quick ones. They switched to the little quick ones and we went to the big ones and beat 'em some more. Now they're back to the big ones. It's flattering, actually.

At Kentucky I was always so keyed up I didn't know what it was to get to work in the morning without having to make an emergency stop along the way. When our Alabama team bus was taking us to the game at Lexington last year we passed the little filling station where I usually left my mark. I pointed it out to the players. My private monument. I've had some terrible gut checks, too, I'll tell you and I've cried like a baby over some things. Literally cried.

I cried from Houston all the way to College Station the night they put us on probation at A&M. I had to suspend the best athlete I ever saw, Joe Namath, with two games to play at Alabama in 1963, both games on national television, and I cried over that. I cried like a big fat baby when I got up there in front of those Aggie players to tell them I was leaving to go to Alabama. And in private I've cried out of plain madness over the dirtiest journalism I've ever seen, when I had to defend myself and my program and my boys against the worst kind of lies.

It's an old story. You stick your head above the crowd and you're going to have people trying to knock it off. We've done it wherever I've been, got it up there pretty high, and they've tried, and I've had to be darned active defending myself. Duffy Daugherty used to tell me, "Bear, you may not be the best coach in the world, but you sure cause the most commotion."

Football has never been just a game to me. Never. I knew it from the time it got me out of Moro Bottom, Arkansas — and that's one of the things that motivated me, that fear of going back to plowing and driving those mules and chopping cotton for fifty cents a day. I used to think it would be nice to wind up being one of those guys who gets up on a Saturday morning and goes fishing, but I know now it'll never be. Benny Marshall, the late *Birmingham News* sports editor, asked me once, "How long can you go on like this? How long does it last?"

I said, "Why, I guess I hope it lasts forever."

I've found, over the years, that I'm not alone in my obsession. I remember that first year at Kentucky, 1946, when we were trying to determine which boys the game meant a lot to. It was difficult,

8

because so many were just coming out of the service. In our second game that year we played and beat Cincinnati, which had beaten Indiana — the Big Ten champion the year before — and I didn't know how a team was supposed to act before a game. But I knew this bunch was really fired up, really motivated.

I looked around the room, and I had a kid in there named Jesse Tunstill who had been a prisoner of war for about three years, and another named Jim Babb who's a principal of a high school in Lebanon, Tennessee, now. Babb had fought on Iwo Jima. And I got to thinking about it, looking around, and I said to myself, hell, here are all these guys and me who never fought anybody, and if they can get so emotionally worked up over a game of football after what they've been through, then football must be something pretty good.

I believe that football can teach you to sacrifice, to discipline yourself. Bobby Dodd of Georgia Tech has been quoted as saying some supertough coaches have found they can take a group of lesser boys, an inferior team, and beat a superior team by supertough conditioning. He's right about that, and I'm flattered if I fall in that category. Some teams get all those big, fine, wonderful athletes, and they play about 75 percent, and teams that live tough and play tough and are dedicated beat their fannies seven out of nine times, which our boys did with Georgia Tech. Has anybody thought to ask the boys if it was worth it?

Dodd and I were at odds there for a long time. We had been close friends before, and we have mended the fences and are friends again. Tech is back on Alabama's schedule. But for a while our philosophies and objectives were in direct, bitter conflict. I had a hate on for Georgia Tech, and the entire city of Atlanta, too, for any number of reasons, and I probably let it blind my respect for Bobby.

I said once, years before, that nobody in the country could coach like Dodd and win, as easy as he was with his training program. All those between-meal snacks and water breaks, and playing volleyball instead of scrimmaging. Jess Neely of Rice used to say he'd like to play the guy who coaches like Dodd every Saturday. Not play Dodd, play the guy who *coaches* like him. I would, too, because only Dodd

9

could get away with it. And he did during those twenty-two years coaching the Georgia Tech teams. He won.

Bobby was one of the best at-the-game strategists who ever lived, a coach who came up with the right decision at the time when a decision was needed. So-called Dodd Luck and Grant Field Luck was really Dodd Smart. He could get more out of players who had ability than anyone. Over the years I've proved less able to motivate that type of player. The player I can reach is the one who doesn't have any ability, but doesn't know it. My way, therefore, was opposite to Bobby's, and it is true that mine is also a much tougher way.

I've tried to teach sacrifice and discipline to my coaches and my boys, and there were times I went too far and asked too much and took out my mistakes on them. I've made a lot of stupid mistakes. I know that. I lost games by overworking my teams, and I lost some good boys by pushing them too far, or by being pigheaded.

I'm older now, and I hope not as dumb, and some things I would do differently because I know better, but that doesn't change my mind about the value of hard work. Hard work and mental toughness.

Listen, does your boy know how to work? Try to teach him to work, to sacrifice, to *fight*. He better learn now, because he's going to have to do it some day. Lloyd Hale was a sophomore on that first team we took to Junction, and he asked me one time what I meant by "fight." Well, I don't mean fistfight, like we used to do back in Arkansas, I told him. I mean, some morning when you've been out of school twenty years and you wake up and your house has burned down and your mother is in the hospital and the kids are all sick and you're overdrawn at the bank and your wife has run off with the drummer, what are you going to do? Throw in?

Like I say, I've done some stupid things and made some stupid decisions. I quit Kentucky because I got a mad on and made up my mind it just wasn't big enough for me and Adolph Rupp, and that was sure stupid. Rupp and I should have complemented each other. He was top dog, the greatest basketball coach of all time, and we're warm friends now. But all I could think of at the time was how much less I'd like to see of him. So I quit and went to Texas A&M.

I can tell you a lot about quitters. I used to have a sign at Kentucky: Be Good or Be Gone. Jerry Claiborne used to say he had a different roommate every day. I don't have that sign anymore. Don't believe it's necessary now, because I don't believe you can categorize every boy who quits football as a quitter. For some it's just a matter of finding other interests, just like switching courses. I still want my players to be good, but I sure don't want 'em to go. But from the time I played at Alabama until a few years ago, I believed that if you weren't a winner, if the game didn't mean enough to you, you'd probably wind up quitting.

So I've laid it on the line to a lot of boys. I've grabbed 'em, shook 'em, kicked 'em, and embarrassed them in front of the squad. I've got down in the dirt with them, and if they didn't give as well as they took I'd tell them they were insults to their upbringing, and I've cleaned out their lockers for them and piled their clothes out in the hall, thinking I'd make them prove what they had in their veins, blood or spit, one way or the other, and praying they would come through.

I used to surprise myself how quick I could get down off that tower at practice, and when the timing was right — success in anything is a matter of timing, no matter what you do — when the timing was right I'd say to a boy I was trying to reach, "Young man, you've been here three years on a gravy train and you haven't done a damn thing to earn your keep. If you don't suck up your guts, you're gone." And sometimes it worked. And sometimes they went.

You never know. When I was playing at Alabama I quit one time, and Coach Hank Crisp went to where I was staying and brought me back.

After a while I got to sulking around again, threatening to quit. Coach Hank was Frank Thomas's assistant, and he was more what I am, a field coach. I'm not much on the blackboard, but I can coach on the field. Or could. My assistants do all the coaching now. I just referee the arguments.

Anyway, I was big-dogging around, talking about quitting and going to LSU, which was one of the few schools other than Alabama that had offered me a scholarship. I threw the name out just to be popping off. Coach Hank sent for me. He was down there where we had our equipment, and he had my trunk out. I had this big old

11

country trunk. Don't know why, because I didn't have enough clothes to fill one-fourth of it.

But he had the plowline out and said, "I hear you want to leave. Well, dammit, I *want* you to leave, and I'm here to help you and see that you do. Come on, let's get that plowline out and tie this trunk up and get your ass out of here."

Well, you never heard such crying and begging and carrying on. I finally talked him into letting me stay, and I never let out a peep about quitting again.

Some of my boys I've pushed to that point, some of the real good ones. John David Crow told me he was about to quit one time. He was a sophomore at A&M and he was sitting in the shower after a real hard practice, just sitting there worn out, and the manager came in and said, "OK, Crow, come on. Coach Bryant was just getting the spectators out of the stands."

Which I was. I used to do that, and still will, if a practice is going bad. Send the team in, lock the gates after all the spectators are gone, and bring the team back out.

Crow told me he was about to quit that day. He said I came back out there, real calm, "and when you're real calm, it's trouble," he said. "We never paid any attention to you when you were raising hell. When you said, 'Now, gentlemen, we're going to put the ball down here, and we're going to get it behind the goal,' you were real calm, and we knew we were in for it."

He said it was the doggonedest scrimmage he'd ever been in, and I asked him why he didn't quit. He looked me square in the eye and said, "Because I would have killed you before I'd let you make me quit."

Two

It doesn't always work that way. One boy I remember telling I was fed up with his sulking around and I was going to help him pack, just like Hank Crisp did me, only this boy *let* me help him, and he went on to another school and made All-America and played six years or so for the Cleveland Browns.

Bob Gain is a better example. Bob had been a big discipline problem, and I finally told him he was the sorriest thing I had ever come up against and threatened him with everything I could think of. When he straightened out he was the best leader I ever had, but, boy, he hated my guts.

Bob went to Korea shortly after he got out of Kentucky, and the night before they were going into battle he sat down and wrote me a letter. It was the most amazing thing I had ever read. He told me he hated my guts, all right, *then*. But, he said, "I love you tonight for what I used to hate you for." You don't think that makes it all worthwhile?

So I say I don't know any sure way of motivating a boy. You talk about paying players. That's a form of motivation. Very popular after the war, too, but not as popular as it is today. Buying players is at an all-time high. Well, I've done that, or at least let some of my alumni do it, and if I was a young coach twenty-eight or thirty years old and just starting out I might do it again, if the competition was paying boys and I felt I had to meet the competition. Wouldn't do it now, of course. Don't have to and wouldn't anyway. I'd resign first. That's the one thing I told them when I came to Alabama. I wouldn't cheat.

But we had a couple boys at Kentucky that got something, and at A&M there were four or five, and I believe most of the time you could tell who was getting something by the way they played. The game just didn't mean as much to them.

Ordinarily you can tell what the game means to a boy just by the way he goes about things. It has to mean an awful lot if he plays for me. I tell young players who want to be coaches, who think they can put up with all the headaches and heartaches, "Can you live without it? If you can't live without it, don't get in it."

There's no doubt young people have changed, and it is a fairly recent thing. Football players have changed, too, and as a result *I've* changed. I don't pretend otherwise. For example, I let them wear their hair long at Alabama. I don't mean they go around looking like sheepdogs, but by my bowl-cut standards it's pretty darn long. Used to be I'd have personally jerked it out by the roots if a kid wore long hair.

But I'd seen Darrell Royal with longer hair, and even the late President Johnson, and when I had a meeting with a freshman group a few years ago — during a time when we weren't winning as much as my critics thought we should — I told them, "Go ahead, let your hair grow. Just keep it neat."

I had just finished giving them an ultimatum. As a group they'd been accomplishing nothing, just wallowing around. I had said, "You got ten minutes to get right or be gone." They decided to stay. Then I invited them to come see me if they had any problems.

And one freshman had enough guts to get up and say, "Coach, the only reason I came to Alabama was you, and this is only the second time I've ever seen you." You can guess how low that made me feel.

But you can learn from anybody. During that time campuses all over America were in trouble, and football teams were in rebellion. The drug problem was hitting everybody, even us at Alabama, and

I'd made the mistake of being too busy to notice, of removing myself from it rather than getting involved. Well, I *got* involved. That boy who stood up has graduated now, but you can bet he saw a lot of me the last four years.

The very next day after that meeting this one big old burly lineman came to visit, like I had suggested. He said, "Coach, that thing you did yesterday about the hair was the greatest thing that ever happened."

I said, "What? Your hair?"

He said, "Aw, coach, you know what I mean."

I couldn't believe it. It never dawned on me that a kid's hair could be that important. If I'd *known*. It made an impression on him, but it made a bigger impression on *me*. If hair meant that much to these kids, I wasn't going to raise too much hell about hair. Don't misunderstand. I still have rules, and if the hair or anything else gets more important to them than football I don't want 'em. But I was awakened. The hair issue finally got to be a joke. Now they kid me about it over at the dorm. "Coach, your hair's getting awfully long."

I didn't lose my guts during that period but I gave in a lot, and I'm glad I did because anything that is important to the kids is *important*. We were 6-4, 6-5, and then the last three years we went back to what I consider respectable — 11-0, 10-1 and 11-0, and with Notre Dame shared the National Championship again in 1973. Our fourth since 1961. (I don't consider the loss to Notre Dame in the Sugar Bowl a defeat. We just ran out of time.)

If I had a problem now I'd probably say, "Go on home, we can win without you," the way I used to. If you're 11-0 they believe you a little more and listen a little closer. If you're 6-5 they might have a doubt.

It's probably true that my kids don't pay as much attention to me as they used to. But age has nothing to do with it. You're never too old until you think you are, anyway. I never felt I had to sacrifice my authority during that period, and if I had they'd have lost respect for me in a minute. That will *never* happen. Kids haven't changed that much.

I'll tell you another thing that happened to us along in there that was good. After the Southern Cal game in 1970, when they beat us so unmercifully in Birmingham before the largest crowd we'd ever had (and the biggest payday USC ever had, according to Coach John McKay), one of our players — I'll never tell who it was — came to me and said some of the seniors had lost confidence in me. He said it matter-of-factly, that they had had a meeting at the dorm and talked about it. Remember, this was the opening game of a new year and, as it turned out, a terrible year for us. We lost five out of eleven.

I didn't fly off the handle. I just called them together for a talk. I told them I'd heard about their meeting, and that I was disappointed because they hadn't come to me. If they had, maybe we could have accomplished something. There were about twelve seniors there, in the meeting room at the dorm, and I pointed to each one and called him by name.

And I said, "Now. I'm going to tell *you* something. You're not dry behind the ears yet, and we've had teams here that won national championships and bowl games and everything else, and I want to make this plain. I'm going to give you one week. You can't do that with me, but I can with you. I'm going to give you a week, and if you aren't laying it on the line by then I'm going to fire you.

"Maybe I'm old-fashioned. Maybe I am past the ropes. But you better come talk to me first about it next time or for you there won't *be* a next time."

I got their attention that day, I'll tell you. I was so mad I was trembling. We played VPI the next week and won, 51–18, and it was a good thing. I would have fired every one of them.

I may be wrong, but I think the American young person is getting over this rebellion thing. I think it has lost most of its glamour. We never had what you would call a "rebellion." We had that hair thing, and a drug problem that we hopped on in a hurry, and I'll get to that later. But it was nothing compared with what a lot of coaches were going through, especially in the late sixties. Some of them were good friends, former assistants of mine like Jim Owens of Washington. Jim Owens went through hell, and didn't deserve it.

Part of the fault was that too many administrations around the country lost their guts. If we had had any kind of rebellion when I was coaching at Maryland, under Curly Byrd, the university president, he would have fired me and the team and the entire athletic department before he'd have knuckled under.

The big difference today is that kids are a lot more knowledgeable, and that's no revelation. More knowledgeable about money, about life — about everything. And I hate to admit it, but football doesn't mean as much to them. All I had was football, and I hung on as though it were life or death, which it was. And up until about ten years ago that's the way it was for most of our players. But *now*. Their mamas and papas can make more on relief than we could working. All of them come from something, or 90 percent of them.

The ones who will consistently suck their guts up and stick by you now are the blacks, because they don't have anything to go back to. And I've come to appreciate that in the last few years. Bo Schembechler of Michigan told me once, "A black won't ever quit you," and I got to thinking the way it had been for me, and he was right. Because I didn't have any place to go, either.

Three

So what motivated me? That fear, I guess, for a long time anyway. I can remember so well being on that old wagon with Mama, peddling milk and butter and eggs, turnip greens and black-eyed peas and watermelons and whatever else we had. In the black sections mainly.

There were twelve of us, including Mama and Daddy. Three children had died in infancy. I was the eleventh child. I don't know what kind of name Bryant is, where the family got started, but Daddy's people were from Georgia and were farmers. His full name was Wilson Monroe Bryant, and by the time I was old enough to be aware of anything he was a semi-invalid. He had high blood pressure and got out of breath real easy, so he couldn't do much.

Our whole income was those truck patches. This was in Moro Bottom, Arkansas, which is no more than it sounds, a little piece of bottom land on the Moro Creek about seven miles north of Fordyce and five miles west of Kingsland. Fordyce was our big city. It had a population of about 3,600, the same as now. Kingsland's was 900. Moro Creek ran through where we hunted hogs, but I'm not sure the formal name Moro Bottom was ever given the area. I just

18

always called it that. Metropolitan Moro Bottom consisted of six families spread over a two-mile area.

Most of the ground is rich timberland now, and our old house is gone, but back then we farmed a full 260 acres. Vegetables and cotton, mainly. By modern standards it was no more than a truck farm, of course, but I thought it was a plantation. When I fly over the area now I realize you could throw a rock across the fields I plowed.

There wasn't any highway, just an old dirt and gravel road. So I was barefoot most of the time. Whenever it rained or snowed my older brothers would hitch up the mules because somebody was bound to get stuck in the mud. They could make a buck or two pulling out stricken cars. They would be listening all the time and as soon as they could hear the grinding they'd hitch up.

My brother Jack was a real entrepreneur. He was great for riding down a road and seeing a bull in a field, going in and buying it, and selling it a week later for a nice profit. He was always loaning somebody some money at 10 percent. One year he raised a crop on an adjoining farm — sharecropping, actually — and paid me fifty cents a day to work it. He didn't have time because he was getting $2.75 a day at the sawmill.

Most of my brothers and sisters were grown and gone by the time I was old enough to pitch in. There were no athletes in the family — no time for it, really — and I include myself. But there were no loafers, either. The Bryant farmers' lineup went like this, oldest to youngest: Barney, Orie, Harlie, Jack, Ouida, Kathryn, Louise, me and Frances. Barney was the tallest, but I eventually caught up with him, and I was heavier. I was probably closer to Orie than any of them because he used to come watch me play in high school, and when I was coaching at A&M he was into oil-rig moving in Texas and was one of our best customers for football tickets.

Being the only boy left at home meant all the tough chores fell to me. My sisters didn't get out of anything; they were still out there with everyone else, chopping cotton in those bonnets girls used to wear. But besides the plowing and chopping, it was my job to draw the water for the cows, which is an impossible task because you can't fill up a cow, and to hitch up and drive Mama on her selling trips and the family wherever it had to go.

As wagon engineer I was first up every day. I had to be ready to take the kids to school, and for Mama's peddling in Fordyce. And oh, my, those winters were so cold. Mama would heat bricks to keep us from freezing to death on the wagon. We'd put sideboards up and a tarp over the top and our produce on top of that so the water wouldn't come in and ruin our business when we crossed the creek. Sometimes the wagon would actually float. I was always amazed how those old mules — a black one named Pete and a white one named Joe — could swim the Moro Creek as they pulled that wagon.

I was a mama's boy. It came naturally because we were together so much, and because she had taken over as family disciplinarian when Daddy got sick. She was born Ida Kilgore, from a family of Texas farmers, and I don't know how to describe her except that she was my favorite person in the world and that she looked great to me. Today I suppose you'd call her a handsome woman. She was a little taller than average, and her hair was already gray, and there was something about her eyes that got your attention. You could look at her and tell she had class, despite all she had been through. She'd had it tough from the day she was born.

She didn't show her depressions, even if she felt them, but, boy, I did. I hated it. I hated every minute of it, making those rounds. Whatever Mama had left over she'd take up to Uncle John's store at the hotel in Fordyce and he bought up the rest to do her a favor. Then she went in there for a good meal. But I had such an inferiority complex I was too ashamed to go with her. I didn't know whether to use the knife or the spoon or what, so I'd go to Mr. Keeton, the cattle buyer, and for a dime he'd give me a hunk of cheese enough for four people and a stack of soda crackers.

Then I'd get a quarter's worth of oats and chops for the mules and go down to Mr. Atkinson's livery stable right across from the railroad station, where there was a pump, because that cheese made you thirsty, and I'd get up on a boxcar and imagine how wonderful it would be to be an engineer or a fireman, and I'd eat my cheese and crackers until four o'clock. I could see the clock on the courthouse from there. At four o'clock I would go back and get Mama, and we'd load up the supplies she bought and head home.

My wardrobe was some overalls. Later when we moved to Fordyce, Mama bought me some khaki britches and a khaki shirt, and for the first time in my life I was dressed up. But until then it was overalls, and one Saturday in Fordyce she took me into Mays' General Store and bought me a pair of shoes.

The man said, "Do they fit?"

I said, "Oh, yeah."

They hurt my feet so bad I still have the bunions and corns they raised. I remember one time I took 'em off in church, just to get some relief, and I don't know if Mama saw me or smelled me but afterward she sure whipped me.

They had school on Saturdays then, because they said they wanted to keep the children off the streets. Actually there was nothing to run over them but a mule or runaway horse, but on Saturday we invariably wound up at old Arch Weathers's at ten to twelve, and in front of the school at twelve. I can pass that school now and hear those voices. As they let out for lunch, the kids would come along and make fun of me and those old mules. I still remember the ones that did it.

I was sensitive to any kind of putdown. To get to the school in Kingsland, where we went for the elementary grades, I had to have the mules ready at 4:00 A.M. and I was already in a good sweat by the time we got there. At recess I had to go out and feed them their oats and chops while everybody else played. We had a lady teacher in the fifth or sixth grade who was always preaching hygiene. I didn't know what she was talking about until one day after a long lecture on cleanliness she made me trade seats with one of the boys in the back. I can still hear those giggly girls, enjoying my embarrassment. I haven't forgotten *their* names, either.

When I think back, the only good thing about those mules was that they got me out of milking the cow. My sisters had to do that. After the three older boys had left, Daddy hired a man to help out. He was about 45 or 50 years old, and the only thing I ever called him was "Mr. Dukes," so don't ask me his full name. Mr. Dukes was proud to work for us, and I was glad to have him. Tickled to death, actually, though I have to say he might not have been the best influence. Up the road a piece was a family named Jarrett, who had a girl named Zora who was about 18. Mr. Dukes spent a lot of time riding his horse — we called it "Old Cow," but it was definitely a horse — back and forth in front of the Jarrett house.

But he never got to meet Zora, who was still in high school then, until he got a new horse named Button. With a fancy saddle. Mr. Dukes bought himself a Texas-style hat, and he took Button past the cemetery and back and forth in front of the Jarrett house some more. Lo and behold he and Zora wound up married. The last I saw him he was in the veterans' hospital near Little Rock. And I don't mean to imply that the two events are related.

Anyway, besides the ins and outs of sex, Mr. Dukes had other things to teach an impressionable young boy. One day a casket was driven by our house in a wagon, on the way up to the cemetery, and Mr. Dukes started telling me about hants. I had always been scared to death of hants. I thought I had seen plenty of them at different times in my life, and Mr. Dukes gave me chapter and verse on a few more.

There was a grave with a tombstone on our property then, behind the smokehouse where we had a cotton patch, and the grave was surrounded with weeds. About dusk my brother Jack dared me to go up and see if there were any hants around the grave. He said he'd give me thirty-five cents if I did. That was enough to make me swallow my fear, so I took off running, up the trail through the weeds.

And just as I got to the grave a ghost rose up from behind the tombstone. It was Mr. Dukes covered in a sheet, but I didn't stop to ask for identification. I took off back toward the house, fell down halfway there, and crawled the rest of the way. To my recollection, that was the only time Papa ever got mad. He ran 'em both off that night and threatened to run 'em off for good.

To me Mr. Dukes was still a wonderful guy. He paid attention to me and helped me do the odd errands. He took me 'possum and squirrel hunting. We would kill rabbits and hang them up in front of the fireplace in what we called the "big room," which was the only room in the house where you could keep warm, and we roasted them there, and you never tasted anything so good. It was Mr. Dukes, too, who gave me my first lessons in cussing. He would teach me a few words, then he'd go tell Mama and she'd whip me.

The thing was, though, I must have craved attention, and maybe this has something to do with shaping a man. I still like attention. Little things make me proud.

One of my television sponsors, Sloan Bashinsky, has a house on the Florida Keys at Islamorada, right on the ocean, and a lot next door that's nothing but coral and weeds, and he said he was going to call the lot Bear Bryant Field and put signs up. I went down there one day, telling a friend of mine how much old Sloan thought of me, and when we got there he had the signs up, all right, but they said Tide Field. Old Sloan was going for something more permanent. Another friend of ours named Julian Lackey eventually got him to change it to Bryant Field.

So I always craved attention. When I was a little-bitty kid, if I wanted a dipper of water I wouldn't let my sisters get it. I wanted Mama to quit her washing or ironing and come get it, and if she didn't I would hold my breath until I turned blue. She whipped me, of course. Used an old plum-orchard switch that cut bad. But I got that attention.

As I said, Mama handled the heavy stuff. Daddy slapped me a couple times when I was bad, but it made his blood pressure rise so he had to leave it to Mama. When some folks held a revival meeting at the church down at Mount Lebanon one time I took a little old cat and threw it in the window during the services, right into a girl's lap. She squealed like a stuck pig, and I got a lot of attention for it. Mama always had her own special way of making me pay. She would say, "I am going to whip you for that, son. You did wrong."

Then she would wait. And wait.

And I'd hope she had forgotten. But she never did. I bet she waited two months after I tossed that cat before she whipped me.

The area we lived in was so sparsely populated the only social life we had was the church, the Smith Chapel, about a quarter-mile from our house. If I am not mistaken it was in the Church of God group. My folks were very religious. To an extreme, really. They wouldn't go to picture shows or anything, and neither of them ever saw a football game. Years later when we took teams to bowl games I got Mama to go along, but all she did was sit with the children in the hotel. I didn't smoke in front of her until the last few years of her life, when I finally admitted what a hypocrite I was. She knew I smoked, but I wouldn't do it in front of her. I respected her too much. My sisters would come home and pull those weeds out and light up, but I never had the nerve.

I'm thankful for the training she gave us because of her religious convictions. She had to have some kind of inspiration, running twelve children through the ropes. I think, too, she would have loved for me to have been a preacher. I was the only one in the family who got to go to college, and I'm sure she thought it a waste for me to wind up coaching football. I used to tell her that <u>coaching and preaching were a lot alike,</u> but she didn't believe it.

When I was little I hated church, listening to those old long-winded lay preachers. I didn't know what they were talking about so I just sat and squirmed and got into mischief. I am a little more appreciative now. They still have those all-day singing-and-dinner sessions on the grounds the first Sunday in June, the way they used to when I was a kid, and I went over a couple years ago and had a good time. I'm always humming those good Sunday school choruses, like "Jesus Loves Me" and "Love Lifted Me." My players and assistant coaches used to say that when my humming was loudest it was at the time I loved them the least, and was about to lift them by other means.

I don't make a lot of noise about it but it has been important to me, my belief, if you want to call it that. I was reading President Truman's book where he was saying when you hear those loud prayers, and they're louder than usual, you better go home and lock up your silver. I don't feel that way, of course, but I don't think you have to go around beating your breast, either.

I know, now, I never got over that need for attention, no matter the consequences. One summer when I was playing at Alabama, Joe Dildy and I and a couple other Arkansas boys on the team rented a car and drove home to see the folks. On the way back we stopped in Meridian, Mississippi, for some dinner, and one of the guys, Calvin (Shorty) Fry, called some football players he knew who lived there. They came to the restaurant by the carloads, in old jalopies.

I said, "My fans usually drive Cadillacs." And when we finished eating and walked out front there was a can of garbage on the sidewalk. Like the big ham that I am, I announced to the group that I had not had my blocking practice for the day, and laid a block on the garbage can that made the biggest mess you ever saw. Mama would have wore out two cherry switches on me that night.

For the greater part of my young life I was not accustomed to any sparing of the rod. I got more of the same at school. I took a turtle and put it in a girl's desk one day, and when it crawled out onto her lap you never heard such screaming. At that time they had just fired a lady teacher, who we laughed at when she whipped us, and brought in this great big old guy who had played football over at Henderson-Brown, Alec Wysinger.

Mr. Wysinger got that little girl calmed down and ran off my turtle. Then he took me up front of this one-room schoolhouse, the Stonewall School, up on the stage where we recited our lessons, and he put me over his knees like a sack of flour, held me with one hand and took a paddle with holes in it in the other. Every time he hit, it raised a blister. I told him when I got old enough I was going to come back and whip him. My brothers wanted to go whip him right then when they heard about it, but Papa said I probably deserved more than I got, which was true.

Years later, when I was hitchhiking home from Alabama one summer, a fellow picked me up and when we were down the road a piece asked me if I remembered what I had promised to do when I got big enough. It was old man Wysinger. I laughed and said, "Yessir, I remember, but I'm still not big enough."

Four

I was always a big kid, and I remember one summer we walked in from the Bottom to Mr. Smith's picture theater in Fordyce. The Lyric Theater. There were several of us, I remember; the Jordan twins were with me, and Ike Murry. The Jordans — Clark and George were their names, but we called them Click and Jud — were my best friends and the best athletes Fordyce High ever had. They were both triple threats. When they went to the University of Arkansas they scored four touchdowns between them in the space of two minutes, thirty-nine seconds, of one game. It made Ripley's "Believe It or Not." I wasn't as close to Ike Murry then. We were more like friendly rivals.

Drucilla Smith was at the theater, a striking "older" girl with reddish-blond hair. She was standing by this poster that showed a picture of a bear and a guy offering a dollar a minute to anyone who would wrestle the bear. Mr. Smith was out front, and he was all excited because the man that was going to do the wrestling hadn't showed up.

Somebody said to me, "Why don't you go in there?"

And I sort of glanced at Drucilla Smith and said, "For a dollar a minute I'd do anything."

You know, big-dogging it. I think this was in the summer, because I was chopping cotton for fifty cents a day at the time and I felt I'd wrestle King Kong for a dollar a minute.

Anyway, they egged me on, and Mr. Smith lined it up with the fellow who had the bear. There wasn't anything else to do anyway, and the picture cost a dime. Mr. Smith agreed to let me and my friends in free.

The theater was a little old thin room, and the seats went downhill. At the bottom was the big stage, and if you sat right in front you couldn't see the screen for the stage. Nobody sat in those seats. When they brought that bear out Ike Murry said it was the scrawniest thing he had ever seen, but Ike wasn't volunteering to wrestle it. To me it looked 30 feet tall. I must have wanted that money real bad.

The only thing I knew about wrestling was that if you got hold of somebody and kept your body away from him, he'd have a hard time breaking your hold. That was what I was going to do. Keep that bear from rolling over on me.

The man made his speech about this big, ferocious thing and introduced me, and about the time the bear reared up to face me I charged him and in a second had him down where he couldn't move. And there we lay. After a few nonviolent seconds the man began pushing at me, telling me to let him up. I wasn't ready to do that because time was flying by. I know what he wanted, though. He wanted action. I just lay there.

Finally the bear worked loose, and I got him again, and he got loose again, and he started acting pretty ornery. And when I looked up his muzzle was off. I felt this burning on the back of my ear, and when I touched it I got a handful of blood. I was being eaten alive. I jumped off that stage and nearly killed myself hitting the empty front seats with my shins. I still have the marks on my legs where I crashed into those seats.

After the show was over I went around to get my money, but the man with the bear had flown the coop. All I got out of the whole thing was a nickname.

Don Hutson and I saw the man, and that same old scraggly bear, years later in Fayette when we were over there bird hunting. The bear-wrestling act was part of a little carnival sideshow. By then I was an assistant coach at Alabama and had achieved a certain amount of dignity, so I was able to stifle the desire to go choke my money out of the man. He probably needed it more than I did anyway.

About the time of the bear-wrestling episode Mama took a couple of rooms up in Kingsland — a little apartment — because it was so cold riding in. I'll tell you when it was: it was when the man named Floyd Collins was trapped in the cave in Kentucky, because we walked down to the railroad station every afternoon when the train came by and brought the papers. We didn't buy the paper; we just looked at the headlines to see how old Floyd was making out. Anyway, instead of having to drive those mules around and unharness them and turn them out at noon when everybody else was playing basketball and stuff, I got my first chance to play.

Of course, nobody wanted me on their side. I was a rotten athlete. None of my brothers had played anything, and the nearest neighbor boy was a quarter-mile away and he didn't know anything about sports, and beyond him were a couple mean little boys named Ewbank who I didn't mess with, and a cousin another half-mile from them. You can't get much of a game going that way. And I sure hadn't picked up any athletic technique plowing and tending those mules. I was always the last one picked, and that didn't do a whole lot for my inferiority complex. Well, I must have got a little better, because I remember there was a big bully named Jack Mosely in about the sixth grade, and one day he chose me first on his basketball team. I thought, boy, I really got it made now.

Eventually my mother rented a big house over in Fordyce and took in boarders and we moved over there, and one day I was walking past the field where the high school team was practicing football. I was in the eighth grade and had never even seen a football. The coach naturally noticed a great big boy like me, and he asked if I wanted to play.

I said, "Yessir, I guess I do. How do you play?"

He said, "Well, you see that fellow catching the ball down there?"

"Yeah."

"Well, whenever he catches it, you go down there and try to kill him."

I didn't know it then, but they were covering punts, and I just happened to get down there about the time the ball did and just kind of ran over that little boy. The following Friday I played on the team, and I didn't know an end zone from an end run.

I am embarrassed to say it, but I lived with a chip on my shoulder in those days. I enjoyed fighting. I suppose it was a way of expressing myself, and I never missed a chance. I didn't go undefeated or anything. Those mean little Ewbank boys could whip my tail when I was younger, and it got so I hated to go to our mailbox two miles up the road because one of them would always be lurking there and would start something and I got whipped every time.

When I first moved to Fordyce, Clary (Jim) Atkinson, who is sheriff of Dallas County now and is still a warm friend of mine, used to get his father's old Packard touring car and we'd ride around trying to pick a fight with somebody. Not the kind of fights they have in the big cities, with gangs and knives and things. Just one-on-one fisticuffs that didn't prove anything but didn't get anybody killed, either.

At 13 I was as big as I am now, and I actually had a fight with a grown man in Fordyce. It really wasn't much when you tell it. The man wasn't going to pay me for delivering some groceries and when he tried to shove me out of his store I hit him a few times and got him to appreciate my position. I was his best friend after that.

That summer Chink Lacewell and I hitchhiked to Cleveland where my sister Ouida was living with her husband Joe Wood. Chink was a close friend. He was a little guy with Chinese-looking eyes whose daddy was foreman at the sawmill. Chink's son Larry is defensive coordinator for the Oklahoma football team now. Chink played, but he was better at hatching big ideas. One time before our Cleveland trip he talked me into going to Texas with him to be cowboys. We hopped a late afternoon freight out of Fordyce and hid in the coal car, standing on top of a big piece of coal over the trapdoor. If it opened up, as they can do, we would have been goners. It was already half-open. You could see the light coming in.

By the time we got outside Texarkana it was past midnight, and we were hungry and thirsty and didn't want to be cowboys anymore. We hitchhiked back and were in Fordyce the next day. Nobody even knew we had left.

My sister Ouida's house was in Parma, which is a city now but then was out in the sticks at the end of the Cleveland trolley line. I got a job with the Claybrook Manufacturing Company, which made headlights for automobiles, and rode the trolley every day, an hour and fifteen minutes to work, an hour and fifteen minutes home. I didn't know it was called commuting then, but I know I would never want to be a commuter.

Chink went back to Fordyce, and I started hanging around with a kid named McDonald who was captain of the West Tech High football team. We passed West Tech every day on the way to work. McDonald was going to tell the coach about me, get me a deal so I could stay and play for West Tech. I switched jobs, to an outfit closer to Ouida's house that made spokes for automobile wheels, and I thought, boy, this is perfect.

I was stashing away everything I earned, except the six dollars a week Ouida charged for room and board and the two bits I spent for bleacher seats at Dunn Field watching the Indians play. I wasn't a baseball fan until then, but I sure became one, and am now. I still read all the box scores. I can remember the first game I ever saw as if it were yesterday. Wes Farrell pitched for Cleveland that day.

Then one Friday, which was payday at the spokes factory, I got into an argument with a big blond-haired boy. He said I had taken his girl out, and I said maybe I had, and he said he'd be waiting outside to show me why that was a terrible mistake.

I was scared, but I had to get my money, and when I came through the gate there was a circle of factory workers waiting to see the fight. I had already made up my mind what I was going to do. Like I tell my coaches, you got to have a plan for everything. I was going to get in the first lick. That's the most important one. There might not be a second.

Evidently the blond boy didn't have a plan, because he opened his mouth to say something and I put my fist in it. And then there wasn't any fight. I tore his mouth up, and my fist, and it scared me so bad by the time I got to my sister's house I was ready to pack up for Arkansas. I considered myself reformed.

Since I didn't want to waste any more money, I went down to the freightyard to catch a ride. That week a professor at Ohio State murdered a coed and escaped, and the papers were full of it, and when the train got to Columbus the yards were crawling with bulls looking for the professor. I pulled out my old engineer's cap, one I'd bought for the occasion, and I got up on one of the cars and sat there out in the open as if I belonged, like a brakeman or something.

Nobody bothered me. When we got to St. Louis I had to switch to one of the Cotton Belt trains, knowing they went through Arkansas. But I spotted a big bull I'd seen before, so I ran down below the terminal point where they were making up the train, and when it started I ran along and caught it on the way out. Even if they saw me they weren't going to stop a train for one lousy hobo. This time, though, I didn't have my pick of accommodations. I was stuck on top of a boxcar, holding tight because the train was moving too fast for me to walk forward.

And I hung there. This was September, and at nightfall it turned cold. *Really* cold. The wind was whistling and my hands were getting numb, so I took off my belt and wrapped it around the catwalk and buckled myself to it, just in case I fell asleep. I rode that way the rest of the night, held by my belt, and I don't know if I dozed or not but I know I almost froze to death.

When we stopped the next morning I scrambled down and got inside the boxcar and closed the door. Then the sun came up, and the boxcar turned into an oven, so hot I almost suffocated. One extreme to the other. And I was dying of thirst. We crossed into Arkansas, and outside some small town the train stopped by a ricefield, where I could see a little boy knee-deep in water. I got down and pushed the rice apart, and drank my fill. The water was muddy and full of junk and smelled, and it was the best drink I ever had.

My luck held until we got to Pine Bluff. When I stuck my head out there the bulls grabbed me. They took me into the dispatcher's office, to the chief dispatcher, and you talk about falling into it. The chief's son had played at Pine Bluff High, with Don Hutson, and the chief knew me.

He said, "Let the boy go on. He's had enough excitement." I was at football practice at Fordyce High the next afternoon.

My daddy didn't want me to play football. He said he'd whip me if I did. He wanted me to farm, period. But I got Mama on my side. She never said I could play, but she wasn't saying I couldn't, and finally Papa quit saying anything about it. Mama took my high-top black shoes down to Mr. Clark, the shoemaker, and had him put some cleats on them. Boy, talk about proud! I wore those cleats to football, to class, to Sunday school. I wore them in the house, everywhere, clomping around and making a terrible racket. They were the only shoes I had.

It's a funny thing about what a pair of shoes or a suit or something will do for a fellow. I'll never forget how much those high-top black shoes with the cleats meant to me, or the time Collins Kilgore, my cousin, loaned me my first suit.

Collins's daddy owned the hotel and a couple of grocery stores and a meat-packing place in Fordyce. He owned half the town, actually, and I considered Collins my rich relative. When I came to Fordyce he looked after me, and though he was smaller he was three or four years older and he gave me that suit, and dressed me up with a big striped tie. I wore it down to a basketball tournament at El Dorado. I'll never forget how good it smelled. Collins and I have been close ever since.

Years later I saw Hank Crisp walk into a room at Alabama, where one of the players, Dub Martin, was wearing a pair of torn-up old shoes — a poor boy like me — and Coach Hank kicked off his own shoes, a brand-new pair, and told the boy to try them on. "How do they fit?" he asked. "Well, you just keep those. I can get more."

How much could that mean? I don't know, but I know what those shoes meant to me, and I know what they meant to that boy at Alabama. And I'll never forget at Kentucky when George Blanda was my quarterback. He had been like I was, never had anything, and always easing around, easing around, staying out of the way like he didn't want to be seen. For the first year or so I didn't get anything out of Blanda. He didn't go for that driving. Hollering, "Let's go!" and slapping him on the butt didn't mean a thing. I just couldn't reach him.

Well, the students had gotten on him pretty good. Mississippi had beat hell out of us, and they were on him because he was the quarterback. I saw him on the campus one day and I put my arm around him and told him it was all right, they'd be cheering for him before long, and I noticed he had cardboard in the bottom of his shoes.

I was stupid not to have noticed it before. If I had been more mature I would have. His record speaks for his ability. I don't mean just

32

as a placekicker for the Oakland Raiders, at forty years plus, but as one of pro football's all-time quarterbacks.

I called him into my office, and I said, "George, I want you to go down to Graves-Cox and buy yourself a new outfit, head to foot, and charge it to me."

You could do things like that in those days. It was a more liberal time. He went and you could just see him brighten up. He was a different guy after that. We didn't lose another game, either.

Five

For a little school like Fordyce we had terrific football teams my three years there. I played offensive end and defensive tackle, just an ordinary player, but I was in hog's heaven. I could run pretty fast and I loved to play. I loved to practice. And I was a big kid, so I played regularly.

I remember the biggest thrill I ever had was playing in Little Rock the first couple of years. Never had ridden on the inside of a train before, and I rode an elevator for the first time in Little Rock. We went up there my junior year and beat them, 7–0, for the first time in history. The next year they had lights and we beat them, 34–0. Dave Cash, who was kin to Johnny Cash, the singer, rode the train with us and won several bales of cotton on the game. The Cashes lived in Rison. When we got home we were treated to country ham and hot biscuits at the hotel in Fordyce.

My big thrill that night, though, was catching a 70-yard touchdown pass. It's difficult, even now, to imagine anything more thrilling than that. Click Jordan called the play, and I ran right under and caught it, closed my eyes, and kept running. Ran right through the end zone fence.

Nobody had much to do with me until I started playing football, and I loved the attention. I didn't need Mr. Dukes to tell me that girls were God's chosen people, and I soon made up for lost time. Chink Lacewell had a little girl named Mildred Byrd who came from Camden to watch us play. Her daddy had discovered oil on his land, and they drove a Cadillac, and Chink thought she was terrific. So did I. When Chink went to summer camp he asked me to look after her, which I did. I looked after her pretty good.

Every night I'd hop a freight to Camden, which is 27 miles southwest of Fordyce, and Mildred would meet me at the train. Sometimes with her mother. I went to the hotel to wash the smell off my hands, and we'd go to her house and sit. I didn't have any money to take her any place. At 12:08 A.M. the passenger train came through and I'd blind it back to Fordyce.

The way I did it, I'd hop on and scrunch down next to the door rail of the first car after the coal car, usually the mail car. Sometimes I couldn't make that one and it got pretty hairy. I had to hold on outside a passenger car door one night, my body sticking out the side of the train the entire 27 miles. When we crossed the Ouichita River I could feel the trestle beams whizzing by my head.

Mama would have whipped me if she knew I was blinding those freights. She never found out because I could get sort of unaccounted for, spending time as I did with Collins and his brothers in Fordyce and working at the Kilgores' hotel. Collins was my mentor. When I first started coming around I was so bashful I'd run from him, but by then I was older and he had me under his wing.

None of my true loves ran smooth. I couldn't seem to find one that no one else wanted. Ike Murry was the center on our team, and he was in love with a little girl who was just my style. She soon recognized my feelings. So did Ike.

We were playing the school from Warren, and winning 58 to 0 with a couple minutes to play, and had the ball on the Warren 2-yard line. Click Jordan, my buddy, announced in the huddle that he was gonna "let old Bear score a touchdown." He was going to switch positions with me so I could carry the ball. He knew I craved the limelight.

Ike Murry said, "Like hell. That sonofabitch is not scoring any touchdowns while I'm centering."

But Click shut him up, and called my play, and as we broke to the line Ike growled at me under his breath, "If you score, you'll be the first to do it without the football."

I lined up with my arms outstretched, ready for glory. And Ike snapped it ten feet over my head. By the time I ran it down it was on the 40-yard line.

There's a sequel to the story. Ike won the girl, with my reluctant blessing. He ultimately became attorney general of Arkansas, and he must have forgiven me because when I was inducted into the Arkansas Hall of Fame in 1964 he made the introductory speech.

I know, now, I was a trial for my high school coaches. Bob Cowan was both the head football coach and head basketball coach at Fordyce, and he had to be good because we won so much. There wasn't much technique involved. He just showed us how to line up, and taught us some single-wing and Notre Dame box plays, and we went to it. But he had our allegiance, no doubt about that. He was the kind of guy you could tie to.

I look back, realizing how much he tried to help me, and if I could do it over I would appreciate him more and take advantage of his guidance. I know I respected him. We got real close after I got out of school. The Jordan twins and I used to go to his house and eat quail, and Mrs. Cowan would serve us homemade biscuits and gravy till the supply ran out. And when I was coaching at Kentucky, Coach Cowan visited me a few times.

But at Fordyce High I was no bargain.

The school superintendent, Dan Clary, suspended me one time because I missed a couple weeks of school. It was in early October. He came down onto the field at the half of one of our games, down to where we were gathered around Coach Cowan. We didn't have a dressing room so we gathered at one end of the field and all our buddies would eavesdrop on the pep talk.

Mr. Clary butted right in. He said, "Boy, you haven't been to school!" He was pointing at me.

I told him I had been picking cotton.

"Well, you're ineligible."

I didn't know what ineligible meant, but Coach Cowan kept me out the second half of that game. The next week he got things squared away.

I know Coach Cowan liked me. He was a short, balding man,

36

rather ordinary-looking, really, but he had been a fine athlete at Ouichita College, and when he talked, I listened. I must have been reasonably coachable because I made All-State as a sophomore. I didn't have any doubts that what he said was right because I had no illusions about my own intelligence, and that was something that carried over into my playing days at Alabama. I always got along good with my coaches, probably because I was scared of them.

The thing was, I wasn't scared of much else. I still had that chip on my shoulder. I caused a full-scale riot after a basketball game down at Camden my senior year. Camden is in Ouichita County, and we used to go there by bus. They had these two big tough brothers, the Mendoza boys. Another of their players had stolen Mildred from me, and that year they upset us in football, so I was spoiling for trouble. We started shoving and pushing from the opening whistle, and just when the game was over one of them cussed me and I hit him in the mouth.

The gymnasium was like a handball court, with seats close in but a little above the floor, and the fans started spilling onto the floor like paratroopers. I'll never forget this big old boy in a red turban, a ringer they had brought in from Texas to play football. About the time they had us separated and the fight stopped and were holding us, I saw him coming, pushing his way through and saying, "Let me at that sonofabitch!" And I just kinda squared around, and when he stuck his head over the guy's shoulder in front of me and pushed his lip out I ran my fist past the shoulder into his teeth.

That started the fighting all over again. I must have fought everybody in the gym that night, and when we went to get on the bus the police had to line up to make sure we got out alive. They were throwing bricks and everything.

As I recall, the two schools terminated the series after that and didn't resume it for three or four years. And I have to think it was my fault. Stupid, really. I don't remember whether Coach Cowan defended me or not, but I know he wasn't nearly as severe as I would have been. I know, too, that the Camden coach would have relished a few whacks at me himself that night.

The year after my trip to Cleveland we played down in Hope, Arkansas, near the Texas line. They grow watermelons down there that are the world's largest, according to their publicity. The day we played Hope the Philadelphia Athletics scored eight runs in the ninth inning to beat the Cubs in the World Series. I had become an Athletics fan — still am, really, with Charlie Finley making it fun again — and we were sitting outside the bus listening to the game on the radio.

The Jordan twins scored three touchdowns that were called back that day, and we almost mobbed the officials. When we finally won, 20–0, we polished it off with a brawl at midfield, and I got my knee hurt. Back in the Hope dressing room I sat there for a long time, holding one shoe in my hand as a weapon in case any of their guys came in.

The knee was still bothering me when we played up at Pine Bluff the next week. Pine Bluff was Don Hutson's school, and Charlie Marr, the big tackle who went with us to Alabama and made All-Southeastern Conference, was on that team. He came over to where I was sitting before the game and started probing around with his fist, punching my knee and saying, "Bear! How's the old knee, Bear?"

I said, "Get away from me, you bastard." But I wasn't dumb enough to mess with old Charlie.

The reason I mention it is that Marr and I got into our first college game at Alabama together as sophomores, against Oglethorpe in 1933. He fell down trying to defend against an end sweep and I hit him in the head with my bony knee. He had broken through and dove for the ball carrier, and when I jumped over him trying to catch up he raised his head and I knocked him cold. Only time I'd ever seen him out. Charlie was a very solid 225 pounds, and so damn tough. He broke his neck one time and never lost consciousness.

I didn't say anything afterward because I was afraid he'd kill me. Two weeks later I confessed.

"Charlie," I said, "it was me."

He said, "You bastard, I'd rather play against you than with you."

Well, he must have forgotten that we beat Pine Bluff, 7–0, that first year we went up there. And the next year we poured it on Don Hutson's team, 50–12. Hutson caught both touchdown passes. He was something to see even then. We'd hitchhike to Pine Bluff just to watch him play. He was already a great all-around athlete, an excellent baseball player and a basketball and track star as well, and we became friends even though we were rivals.

I tried all the sports, too, but outside of enthusiasm I didn't bring much to the others. The pinnacle of my basketball career was a 13–12 victory over El Dorado in the district tournament. I was high point man with four points.

That was the time I had Collins Kilgore's old suit and striped tie, and we went down and stayed with Schoolboy Rowe, who later became a star big league pitcher. I'll never forget Superintendent Clary. The El Dorado gym was also the school auditorium, the court being the stage. Mr. Clary was down front with the El Dorado principal, and when we came out in our red and black uniforms the principal said, "Dan, you got a fine-looking group here." And about that time our seventh guy walked out in a long black overcoat and a hunting cap. Mr. Clary took it calmly, though. He knew we were a bunch of rowdies.

If I had lost more fights than I won I suppose I would have gotten over that scrapping business earlier. I remember a guy whipped me pretty good at a dance at Hot Springs one night. And after the game at Warren I was telling you about, when jealous Ike Murry deprived me of my touchdown, I got into a fight with a big red-headed guy and he gave me the worst licking I ever took, man or boy. He runs a filling station near Fordyce now and I make it a point whenever I drive to Arkansas to stop in and let him fill 'er up. I especially enjoy it when I am driving a Cadillac.

There is one more fight I'll tell you about, then I'll get off the subject. It was my last. Or should have been, if I had had any sense.

I was a sophomore at Alabama, home for the holidays, and just before it was time to go back a black boy named Bit Roland, who had been a close friend since childhood, got the idea we'd hire a band and put on two dances for profit. One would be at the white country club, the other at the social club where the blacks hung out. Bit said we'd clean up.

Collins Kilgore backed us because we didn't have any cash. The plan was to hold the first dance Friday night at the social club, which was a big old building on the side of a hill. On Saturday we'd move the show to the country club. I handled the tickets. I asked T. R. Galloway, the chief of police, to loan me his pearl-handled .38 as insurance, which he did, and which was dumb because I knew nothing about pistols. I stuck it in my bellyband and went to the club. I take full blame for what happened next. This guy came up to the little booth and put down a dollar. There wasn't much light and I couldn't see him. We'd advertised the dance at 99 cents a couple.

I said, "Thank you."

He said, "What about my change?"

I said, "Ninety-nine cents plus tax."

He said he wanted his penny. He said he wasn't moving until he got it. And he cussed me.

I had to go around the little booth to get to him, and when I could see good I recognized him as about the toughest guy in town. And when he said something else about getting his "goddamn money" I knocked him down the steps, backward. When he came back up he was reaching in his pocket for something, but I was in position and had the advantage. And I hit him — *really* hit him this time — and he kind of sailed down those steps and landed on the back of his head. Out cold. I thought he was dead.

Collins Kilgore was sitting in his car listening to the music. When he saw the commotion he came running and grabbed me and got me out of there to the hotel where I was living.

He said, "Paul, you're in big trouble. We gotta get you out of here."

I ran upstairs and got an extra pair of britches, and he piled me in his car and started for Little Rock. Then we switched to the Pine Bluff road. I decided I'd stay with Hutson.

I holed up there for three days. The guy was still unconscious. Every hour I was awake, for three days solid, I promised the Lord if he let me out of this mess I'd never have another fight. And I believe that's right, because I don't recall having another one. Which is convenient because I'm a coward at heart anyway.

On the third day he finally came to. I was afraid to go home after that, though. To get to Mama's house I had to pass through that black section. But if I slipped around to avoid it they'd think I was scared. Which I was. Collins was the wise head. He said, "If you hit him hard enough you won't have to worry about him bothering you again." Collins must have been right because I walked through there a dozen times after that and never saw the guy again.

Well, I wasn't very smart in school, and lazy to boot. Of all the people who might do something in life, I was the one folks figured would do the least. I was always involved in something, and my brother Harley had gotten the family in a sort of feud with another family when he caught one of the boys slaughtering one of his cows. Actually it was a near shooting feud. There were threats to kill, and gun-toting and everything. Stupid. And I had busted up those boys in Camden at the basketball game, and word spread about that. So I was the last one you would figure to go to college and get a degree.

There was good football played in Arkansas in those days, at Henderson-Brown and Arkansas Tech as well as the university. But we read and heard more about Alabama, and that's where I wanted to go. If you were any kind of football fan you knew about the Crimson Tide, and Wallace Wade, who had been head coach there since 1923 and took them to three Rose Bowl games. He left the year before I arrived to go to Duke, where he fielded another Rose Bowl team, and Frank Thomas took over.

I remember going down to a college all-star game in Dallas with Fred Thomsen, the Arkansas coach. He wanted me to come there. And at the half I slipped off and rode a streetcar back to town to listen to Alabama beat Washington State 24–0 in the 1931 Rose Bowl. Wade's last Alabama team. So when they came over to ask the Jordan twins, our best players, about coming to Alabama, they didn't have to recruit me. I was ready.

There were always a few Arkansas boys on the Alabama team because of the influence of Jimmy Harland, who ran a poolroom in Pine Bluff where the school kids hung out. He had adopted Alabama. A self-appointed scout. After Huey Long came to power in Louisiana, Harland did some recruiting for LSU, too, but when Long got shot he went back to pushing Alabama full-time. Our 1935 Rose Bowl team was loaded with Harland recruits — Don Hutson, Charlie Marr, Bill Young, Happy Campbell, Leroy Goldberg, Joe Dildy, Dutch King, me. Harland wasn't infallible. The Jordan twins opted for Arkansas.

I was only 17 and hadn't received my high school diploma when I arrived at Alabama in the fall of 1931. I needed a language to finish up, so I attended Tuscaloosa High while I practiced with the

Alabama team and lived with Charlie Marr, Frank Moseley and Johnny (Hurry) Cain in a little old upstairs room at the gym.

You had to have a job to go with your scholarship in those days, and Cain's job was to get me up and on my way to school every morning. I always made it at least to the Supe store, which is what we called the snack bar at the student union.

I was not the Joe Namath of my time, all worldly-wise and aware. I remember hearing somebody talking about the team's itinerary that fall. I didn't want to miss out on anything, but I didn't want to seem brash, either, so I casually asked one of the assistant coaches, "What size itinerary does Hutson wear?"

I practiced with what we call red shirts now, the guys who were being held out a year, and the way Joe Dildy tells it I had Coach Thomas's eye.

Joe was a freshman end, and another Arkansas boy, and one day the freshmen were scrimmaging the varsity and Coach Thomas was trying in vain to get the varsity line to block freshman punts. They were doing a sorry job. Coach Thomas called across the running track for me. He said, "All right, gentlemen, let this little high school boy show you how." He bragged on me pretty good, trying to embarrass the varsity.

We lined up and at the snap I gave the end a forearm and got by him and just threw myself in front of the kicker. The ball caromed one way and the kicker another, and I never broke stride, just kept running back across the track to where the red shirts were.

Dildy was walking in with me after practice, telling me what a great thing I'd done. I said, "Listen, Chief" — Joe was part Indian — "anybody brags on me the way they did today, I would kill myself to block a kick." I would have, too.

But nobody in Fordyce thought I would stick it out. I remember years later I'd go back just to take a walk downtown and nod and say hello and how are you and good to see you to those slickers who laughed at me on that wagon. I don't get the kick out of it now. I have very warm feelings toward the entire state. I go back to see the folks two or three times a year.

But I'll tell you how close they came to being right. It was during the Depression. Daddy had died eating watermelon — got poisoned or something — and Mama was having a tough time. Daddy shouldn't have died, actually. But neither one of them believed in doctors. No dancing, no movies, no sports, and no doctors. I think Daddy would still be alive if he had. One of his brothers lived to be about 90.

Years later Mama got sick with cancer, a tumor in her throat that was choking her to death. We just had to overrule her and my brother Barney. Barney had become a lay preacher in the church, after a long bout with alcohol, and he said he wasn't going to let Mama have a doctor. She was laying there dying in Texarkana. My older sister Ouida could bulldog anything, and we went down there and just overruled everybody. We told Mama God wouldn't put doctors on earth if He didn't want them, that it was a greater sin *not* to use them. She finally went to the hospital, and lived six or seven years after the operation. She used to say she thought that doctor was some kind of angel because she was finally rid of all that pain. She had never complained.

Anyway, with Daddy gone and most of my brothers and sisters living elsewhere, in Cleveland or Texas or someplace, if I was looking for an excuse to go home I had one.

I wrote Collins Kilgore, my cousin, and told him I was going to quit school and get me an oilfield job in Texas. In no time I got a wire back from Collins. I remember so well, I was walking between the Supe store and where the stadium is now when I opened it up. It said, GO AHEAD AND QUIT, JUST LIKE EVERYBODY PREDICTED YOU WOULD.

I wasn't about to quit after that.

Six

We thought then, and I know now, that Coach Thomas was ahead of the game. There wasn't a whole lot he didn't know about it, and there sure isn't much we do now that he didn't know then. If it bothered him succeeding Wallace Wade, the pressure that must have created, he didn't show it. His first four Alabama teams lost a total of four games, and our 1934 bunch went undefeated all the way to the Rose Bowl.

I don't know what a football coach is supposed to look like, but Coach Thomas probably wouldn't get a movie role for it. He was a short, chubby Welshman, born in Muncie, Indiana, the son of an ironworker, and he had a spark in his eye that you could catch 50 yards away. He hated the cold. I'd see him in the shower with that white belly sticking out, just shivering.

We all respected him, but we weren't particularly crazy about him. Since he came from Notre Dame we considered him a Yankee, which was not an affectionate term in Alabama. Until I became one of his assistant coaches I didn't realize that underneath he was like most coaches who have a reputation for being tough; he was a sentimental old man, just like me.

His background may have had a lot to do with it. He was a punk kid raised in East Chicago — I use his terminology when I say that — who beat up the truant officers whenever they came around, and he had that midwestern twang when he talked. He called me "Bry-annt."

He wasn't a big hell-raiser at practice. I don't think anyone is, consistently, if they're effective. If you whoop and holler all the time the players just get used to it. I have gone to the opposite extreme in my later years, been too restrained, and I'm trying to go back the other way a little. I am up on that tower most of the time. If things go bad I come down and make something happen, but you can't throw a fit once a month, go down and shake somebody, and impress him very much. They think, who the hell is this? You're like a shower coming down. Just wait and it goes away. If you're in the trenches with them every day, they'll do anything you want.

When Coach Thomas did raise hell, he got your attention. He had played under Rockne, and he had a kind of aloof, imperious way. Before a game he would say a few words, then call on Coach Hank or Red Drew, one of his assistants, and they handled the real preaching. Where Coach Thomas was great was *during* a game, the way Dodd was. He could see things, adjust to things. Not many people can do that, even now. It's so tough to see anything on the sidelines. And in those days you didn't have men in the press box telephoning information down. Films weren't used like they are today, and the ones we had were of poor quality. We didn't break them down at all, just ran them through the projector a few times.

You talk about geniuses. There wasn't much Coach Thomas didn't know about anything. He could have been a great baseball manager. I think he was one of the first to discover Willie Mays, playing in the sandlots around Birmingham. And, of course, he had a terrific football mind.

In 1933 he put in a corkscrew play off a punt formation. That's what the press called it. The ball went to the left half who faked to the fullback and gave it to the tailback coming up the middle, with the quarterback and the guard trapping. We beat Tennessee with it the first time we used it, in Knoxville. Bubber Walker ran for two touchdowns in a 12–6 game, and Don Hutson blocked two men on the first one.

Thomas used to rise to the occasion against Tennessee. He had that same feeling I later did, that to beat General Bob Neyland you had to be double good. He got the willies playing Tennessee. One story had it that before that 12–6 game he stuck the lit end of a cigar in his mouth.

In those days you almost knew where everybody was going to line up on defense. Defenses weren't as sophisticated as they are now. And Coach Thomas came up with an outside trap, where the wingback blocked down on the guard, that we got an awful lot of mileage out of before people found out what we were up to. It was the first time I'd ever seen anything like it. We called it "No. 29," and against Tulane Joe Riley must have gained 200 yards running it.

The thing about Coach Thomas, like every fine coach, was that he was sound. He beat you with the things he did best. Occasionally he would have one little new play for the opponent, but basically he preached blocking and tackling and executing. His kicking game was always great, and that taught me something. I remember Dixie Howell kicked four times from behind our goal against Saint Mary's in 1934, and every one of them sailed past midfield.

Despite his record, everything worried Thomas. He'd look out the window a jillion times to check the weather before a game. He never believed weather reports. He worried more about the coaches who *weren't* sound than those who were. Ones like Neyland he could count on doing certain things. In my last year as an Alabama player Vanderbilt beat us, and that wasn't good because Vanderbilt had a very ordinary team. In those days we didn't use rule blocking. The tackle blocked the guard, or whatever the play called for, and every man knew who to block beforehand. We were usually set up for a six-man line, or an overshifted six, but that day Vanderbilt used a *five*-man line. We had never seen one. And we never did figure out who to block.

Coach Thomas was not good company afterward.

The worst I ever saw him was after the Fordham game in New York my sophomore year. Hutson was wide open a couple times; we didn't get the ball to him and we lost, 2–0. I remember sitting on the bench when a drunk ran onto the field at the Polo Grounds and two big old fat policemen chased him to our side, where he hid behind Coach Thomas. It was that kind of day.

He was unpleasant the next week, I'll tell you. We got the full treatment. If I heard "Bry-annt" once that week I heard it 40 times. Scared of him? You're damn right I was.

Well, how much can a man influence you? I tell my coaches, when they go out on their own, to be themselves, but that doesn't mean not to learn from people who have something to teach you. I used to call long distance to get Coach Thomas's advice years after he quit coaching. Even after he got sick — and I hated to see him that way, so scrawny and weak from fighting high blood pressure — I chartered a plane just to go spend a few hours with him. He had asked me to come back and be his successor after the 1946 season, his last, but I couldn't do it at the time. When I was at Kentucky I visited him every chance I got. Just being around him could help you.

He wasn't bedridden. We sat out on his porch behind the Sigma Nu house in Tuscaloosa and visited. In 1951 when I was going to Europe for a clinic with Fritz Crisler, Biggie Munn, Herman Hickman and a few others I called to say good-bye and he said, "Aren't you going to see me before you leave?" As if he might not be there when I got back. So I chartered the plane, and came and went the same night.

I felt the same attachment to Hank Crisp and Red Drew, men I could go to. Especially Coach Hank. I burdened him with just about every problem I had until he died a few years ago. There's a tipoff for you. Surround yourself with good people.

Coach Hank didn't know a whole lot about fancy techniques, but he had more of what it takes to win. Techniques alone won't win. He had that other thing — he could get you to play. He had lost a hand in a cotton gin, and he had that nub wrapped in leather, and he'd get down there with you and flail away. We loved it. It was like patting you on the back.

Coach Hank was one of six assistants on Thomas's staff, a big staff in those days. I've got fourteen now and John McKay jokes about it all the time. He's only got nine at USC. But he's smarter than I am so he should have to make do with less. Anyway, everybody loved Coach Hank. He looked like he popped right out of a Marlboro ad, that steel-gray hair and leathery face, and eyes that went right through you. I thought he was beautiful.

He was an average size, but he had so much class you thought of him as a big guy. He had been a four-letterman at VPI, and he could do or coach anything. At one time or another he was the Alabama basketball coach, baseball coach, athletic director and assistant football coach, sometimes all at once, and he could fix the truck and plow the garden. He was always doing something. Why he never wanted to be a head coach I'll never know. He had no ambition for it. He turned down a flock of jobs.

Coach Hank handled the purse strings in those days and he was always slipping you a couple bucks. There weren't any rules against it then, and he carried a big roll around, and he might give you anything. Or nothing. Pin money, actually. Some scholarships were better than others, and some schools made it sound like theirs were better, but it all pretty much balanced out. Alabama's would be no different than, say, Arkansas's. As I mentioned, you were supposed to work — cut the grass, clean the gym — along with your scholarship, and there wasn't much to spend money on anyway so you didn't need much. If you had the shorts, you'd go seek Coach Hank. He'd dig out that roll and peel off a couple of ones and say, "Here, get yourself some toothpaste."

Off the field he was a marshmallow, but on it he was awfully tough, scaring everybody. You could win him just by trying like hell, fighting as hard as you could. If you didn't, he had no use for you. He could get me to play. Some people have that and some don't. Carney Laslie had it. And Pat James, who played for me at Kentucky and then coached for me at Alabama. Coach Hank didn't exactly have pets, but he almost did, and I was one of them.

We were playing Tennessee in Knoxville in 1935, and the week before against Mississippi State I had broken the fibula in my leg. The night before the Tennessee game Dr. Sherrill came by the hotel and took the cast off. He said if it felt all right I could dress for the game, if nothing else.

I said, "Is there any chance of a bone sticking out anywhere?" He said no.

So we go out there, and I dress, and Coach Thomas made his little pitch, his pep talk, and then he asked Coach Hank if he wanted to say anything. Coach Hank said he did.

He had a cigarette dangling from his mouth (I was kinda looking at him sideways from around Riley Smith), and he said, "I'll tell you

48

gentlemen one thing. I don't know about the rest of you, you or you or you, I don't know what you're going to do. But I know one damn thing. Old 34 will be after 'em, he'll be after their asses."

In those days they changed the players' numbers almost every week. Hutson and Howell kept the same ones, being the stars, but Coach Hank swapped the others around so that when the programs came out the fans would have to buy them to tell who was playing. I might be 26 one week, 18 the next. Coach Hank wanted to sell those quarter programs.

So he's up there talking about old 34, and I look down, and I'm 34! I had no idea of playing.

So we go out there, and cold chills are running up my back. He done bragged on old 34. Ben McLeod, whose son played for us at Alabama a few years ago, had never started a game in his life, and he was starting in my place. They lined up for the kickoff, and Coach Thomas turned to me and said, "Bryant, can you play?"

Well, shoot, what you going to say? I just ran on out there. McLeod was so mad he could spit.

I played the rest of the season with that broken leg, but that day I was lucky as a priest. On one of our first plays, Riley Smith and Joe Riley — they knew I was hurt, so they were going to fix me up fast for big-dogging — called a pass. I hobbled downfield, and when it came everybody was there to get the ball, and it just fell into my hands, and a couple of them fell over, and I ran a little piece before they caught me.

On about the third play we did the same thing, a little old hook pass, and I lateraled to Riley Smith, the All-America back, and he ran for a touchdown. We won the game, 25–0. And I probably shouldn't say this, but it's true. The night before the game we anted up our nickels and dimes and quarters, accumulated the grand total of about five bucks, and bet it on ourselves. We were big underdogs. We made a killing, about a buck apiece.

The next week Ralph McGill, sports editor of the Atlanta paper then, came over to Tuscaloosa and demanded to see the X rays of my broken leg. We were going to play Georgia that Saturday and he wanted proof that we weren't pulling a fast one. He saw the proof and wrote the story, and when I went into the Georgia game that Saturday I got a big hand, the only one I can ever remember getting. We won that one, too, 17–7, partly because a Georgia guy slugged James Whatley, our 6-foot-6-inch tackle, and old Jim was so mad he kept charging in there slapping passes away before the Georgia tailback could get them off.

I think we probably had more fun in those days than the boys do now. None of us had any money or anything. I didn't have a stamp to write home with, and there was no such thing as a player having an automobile. I think there were about three on the entire campus.

We seldom went home, except hitchhiking at Christmas and once in a while during the summer. Most of us had summer jobs with the university. Joe Dildy was the straw boss of our grass-cutting crew. It was always so hot you'd strip down to practically nothing. We were at it hot and heavy one day, sweating and stinking, and I looked up, and here comes Joe in a big black overcoat and a black stovepipe hat, and barefoot, walking real slow to where we were cutting.

"Whatsa matter, boys," he said. "Don't you like this cool weather?"

Hutson and I eventually became roommates with four other boys in double-bunk beds in a first floor room at the gym. They had partitioned three rooms out of what was an old dressing room, and there were three more rooms on the second floor where they had the basketball court. Near our room, number 10, they had the so-called A Club Room, for lettermen, with a pool table and some benches and a couple of chairs for hanging around. That was the entertainment portion of our deal.

Fifty or sixty of the athletes lived in a rundown smelly old building we called the B. O. House. The ones the coaches had to keep their eyes on were quartered at the gym. I don't say they were worried about me particularly, but they kept me busy. One of my jobs was to clean the toilet and showers on our floor.

We didn't have to study a great deal because the academic standards were not as high as they are now, so we practiced a lot. Spring practice would begin in February, and it wouldn't end until we got enough, which would be about the middle of April. I was majoring in physical education, but I wasn't studying anything. Heck, I didn't know how to study.

Hutson breezed through school. His mother was a schoolteacher and he knew how to study, and the value of it. I wouldn't swap my mama and papa for anybody's, but neither one of them had been to school, there were never any books around the house, and I was a lousy student. But then it didn't matter so much. Today these boys have to fight for their lives in the classroom. My son Paul was a Beta Gamma Sigma, and all Mary Harmon had to say was "study" and he'd go to it.

Maybe it's true that the times dictate the degree of pressure, and therefore the trouble, you have in life. Ours was a simple time, and the discipline problems were simple. A crisis consisted of a couple guys getting caught smoking, or drinking some beer or something, that kind of thing. We all wanted to win so badly we never strayed too far off the line, and those who did would hide it from the other players.

We didn't get into any big trouble or anything, but we used to like to "go riding around," as we called it, which was no more than walking around to the sorority houses before eight o'clock, when the girls went out on dates. We didn't have any money to take them out, so we'd drop by and let them bring food out of their houses so we could sit around having picnics and holding hands.

Our world pretty much centered around that quadrangle where the sorority houses were. Mary Harmon says the football players had a reputation for being the best dancers and the worst risks. Twenty minutes after a dance the girls had to be in their rooms.

We had ourselves a club, Hutson, Riley Smith, Hillman Walker, Dildy and me, with big secrets that didn't amount to anything. And I never had more fun in my life. A kid named Sam Friedman had a place out in the country, and Smith, Hutson and I, and a few others we rounded up, got our dates and bought some baloney and bread and went out there in rented cars for an afternoon. We didn't make the curfew. We had two flat tires, and when we went to check the car in we couldn't come up with enough cash. So we kept it, and it was a week before we could raise enough to turn it in. Every day the bill got higher. And every day we drove those girls around.

Finally Coach Hank got tired of it. He was Coach Thomas's disciplinarian, along with everything else. We were caught one night in our rooms with a gallon of old corn likker we paid six bits for, and another night over at the Chi Omega house after hours there were about ten of us saucering around. The girls had the music going and we were dancing and having a time.

Coach Hank had a way of finding out things, and we weren't too quiet about it. When the housemother started down the stairs to find out what was going on, we tried to escape. Charlie Marr grabbed the door handle to pull it open, and the son of a gun was so strong he pulled the knob off. We were trapped. Coach Hank got the word.

His favorite punishment was to make us run laps at 4 A.M. But this time he took us over to the track, where they were having a meet, and all the students were there, and he made us run a hundred laps. Run them, he said, or pack up and get going. We finished up about ten that night.

Hutson was the class of the outfit. His daddy was a railroad man, working steady, and he had twin younger brothers whom I eventually recruited for Alabama when I became an assistant coach. The Hutsons were a very close-knit family, with great personality. Don was everybody's friend, and though he didn't have to, he waited tables and took jobs just like the rest of us.

As I said, he had been all-everything in high school. He used to wear his track suit under his baseball uniform so he could run the dashes between innings. At Alabama he got up to about 194 pounds, though he wound up playing for the Packers at about 175. He could eat like a horse and not gain weight. He was, in every respect, a complete football player — a good defensive end, a fine blocker, and an intelligent player.

But oh, my, could he catch passes. In all my life I have never seen a better pass receiver. He had great hands, great timing, and deceptive speed. He'd come off the line looking like he was running wide open, and just be cruising. Then he'd *really* open up. He looked like he was gliding, and he'd reach for the ball at the exact moment it got there, like it was an apple on a tree.

I saw him catch five touchdown passes in one game in high school. At Alabama he had all the records, and was the leading receiver in the pros during his day. If they had had the passers and the formations they have now he would have set records to last forever. The pros were always in those tight formations then, and he played what is virtually the tight end position today. Every defensive team doubled on him and tried to tie him up and keep him inside.

In the spring of his junior year Hutson wanted to get off from football practice to play baseball. Football was liable to go on forever, and he could see the baseball field across the way, where the boys were tossing the ball around and playing pepper, and he and some of the others began to get antsy. I didn't have anything else to do so I didn't care if we ever quit practicing football. I loved it.

The only other guy I ever knew who loved it as much was Jerry Duncan, an 180-pound offensive tackle on our 1965 National Championship team. Duncan would beg to practice even when he was hurt. I've actually seen him cry because the trainer told him he couldn't scrimmage. We finally instituted a "Jerry Duncan I Like to Practice Award" a few years ago, and if we'd had it when I was playing I think I might have had a shot at it myself.

Anyway, we were going to have this big intrasquad scrimmage on Saturday, the first team against the second. Coach Thomas announced that those who did well would be let off for baseball. Football had already been going strong for six or eight weeks. Those who sluffed off would keep on practicing.

Hutson, Hillman, Walker, Riley Smith and I all had girls at the Chi Omega house, and the night before the intrasquad game the Chi Os held a dance. And I don't know how he did it, but T. A. (Son) McGahey, who was on the team, hired a riverboat and told us he was going to spike the punch so it would be easier to get the girls to go with us up the river.

I said, "Boy, that sounds great."

Hutson said, "Oh, no. Not me. I'm going to bed. I'm going to be ready for that damn game so I can play baseball."

McGahey was a man of his word. We had the punch, laced with wood-grain alcohol, and the riverboat took us way the hell up the river and back. After that we all went for some chili or something and by the time Riley Smith and I sneaked in it was about 7:30 in the morning.

Hutson was up dressing and prettying up. He said, "Oh, you poor sonsabitches, I feel sorry for you."

He was laughing at us.

We tried to get some sleep but it seemed like no time before we had to go down and get dressed for the game. We went out there and it was stifling hot. I mean *really* hot. I thought I was going to die, or, worse, fall asleep on the field.

The second team kicked off over the goal and we took it on the 20. On first down Dixie Howell, the tailback, faked to the fullback on a half-spin, raised up, and hit me with a little pass over the line. A "No. 24" we called it. I took a couple of steps and broke to the side. When I did Hutson came across and in one block took the halfback and the safety out of the play. They all went down in a heap. All I had in front of me was grass, and I could run pretty good even hung over. I barely made it to the end zone.

And with that one play Coach Hank, who was in charge of our team (Coach Thomas gave him the first unit and Red Drew the second), took me out of the game. And forgot about me. I got down to the end of the bench and stayed there. At the half I had still been in on one play, the game's only touchdown.

When we went into the dressing room Coach Hank had that cigarette in his mouth, and he really chewed us out. He got on Hutson worst of all.

He said, "Yeah, you think you're going to get off to play baseball. But the way you're wallowing around there won't be any baseball. You'll be practicing football till school lets out.

"Now, take this one over here" — and he pointed to me, "the way he's hustling. If you hustled like *him* —"

Hutson and Riley Smith nearly threw up.

"Son," he said to me, "you go ahead and dress."

And I didn't even go out for the second half. Hutson played the whole damn game.

I have to say this. Coach Hank wasn't blind. The following Monday he let Hutson out for baseball. Fortunately he never found out about our boat trip.

But I'll tell you. The clincher with those girls (they were about the only real distraction we had from football) was one night when Coach Hank called a meeting of all the athletes up at the A Club Room. He came in and everyone got scared because we knew somebody's tail had had it. He had a sackful of something, and all he did was start pulling things out of that sack — silk underwear and scarves and things — and throwing them around the necks of about five of us.

He straightened up finally and said, "Well, dammit, that's all you think about anyway," and turned around and walked out.

Now, when Coach Thomas called you it was something really special, and you didn't ever want that. He stopped Don Hutson and me on the street one day and had us get in the car with him, and we knew something was up. We rode along for a while, and he said, "I understand you boys are pretty big with the ladies. Well, that doesn't mix too good with football. You better make your minds up whether you want to play on this football team or not," and he put us out.

That afternoon the local newspaper said that "Alabama will probably have two new starting ends" for the Sewanee game at Montgomery. I told Hutson it was impossible. I said, "He may not start me, but I know he's going to start you."

On Friday we went out to practice, and when he called out the starting lineup for the game he named Gandy and Walker as the ends. I still didn't believe it.

On Saturday in Montgomery the paper came out at noon with the lineups, and we weren't starting. I wanted to crawl in a hole. He finally put us in the game after about four minutes, but the message was clear, and we passed it on to those little girls the next week. Coach Thomas meant business, and what he was really doing was getting us ready for Tennessee, which was only two weeks away. And we sure were ready for Tennessee. We won, 13–7, the closest game we had all year.

(Coach Hank was there with his roll of bills after that one, passing out tens for us to "see the town." I must have figured I was worth more, or was just overflowing with myself, because I gave it back to him. I said, "You need this more than I do," which was a pretty cheeky thing to say. Coach Hank got real miffed at that, but sometime later he came around and peeled off four ten-dollar bills and handed them to me. Boy, I'll remember *that*.)

Coach Thomas knew what to say and when to say it, and that's the secret. Timing is everything. I'll never forget, we were going out for the 1935 Rose Bowl game. I went into the men's lounge on the train. Coach Thomas was sitting there with some of the coaches and

Red Heard, the athletic director of LSU, and two or three news-papermen.

He said, "Red, this is my best football player. This is the best player on my team."

Well, shoot, I could have gone right out the top. I mean, he didn't have to say anything else. I know now what he was doing, because I try to do it myself. He was getting me ready. And I was, too. I would have gone out there and killed myself for Alabama that day.

Seven

The Sewanee game and the Rose Bowl game may not sound like much of a quiniela to you, but to me they represent two of the most important times of my life. And the Sewanee game ranks first, not because I remember anything about it, but because I remember something after it.

Mary Harmon Black was a campus beauty queen. She came from a very prominent Birmingham family, and she was just about everything a girl could be at Alabama in those days. Miss U-A, a Cadet colonel, the sweetheart of one thing or another. You name it, she was it. Plus that she was the best-looking gal you or I have ever laid eyes on. And plus that she had an automobile.

I didn't even know her. I knew *of* her, but I had never met her. I was hanging around the soup store the Monday after the Sewanee game, walking out, actually, and she stopped me.

She said, "How are you feeling, Paul?"

I was flattered she knew my name.

She said her daddy had taken her down to the game at Montgomery and she saw me limping around on the sidelines.

We visited a while, and I screwed up my courage and asked for a date. She reached into her purse and pulled out this little black book, and began thumbing through it.

"How about January twenty-third," she said.

I didn't need a calendar to know what that meant. I got my back up and said, "Shoot, honey, I'm talking about tonight," and walked away.

We had one phone at the gym where we lived, in the coaches' offices, actually. Nobody got any calls on that phone. But later that day I got a call. It was Mary Harmon. She said she had arranged to change some dates around, and I could see her that night. And I've been seeing her just about every night for 40 years.

People ask me if I remember much about the 1935 Rose Bowl game. I remember *everything* about it.

I remember we were ready to play Vanderbilt in our last game of the season, at Legion Field in Birmingham. Just before the game Coach Thomas sent everybody out of the dressing room but the starting eleven. (Eleven is right. There was no such thing as offensive and defensive teams.)

And he read us a telegram from the graduate manager of Stanford, Al Masters: "IF YOU WIN DECISIVELY TODAY WHERE CAN WE REACH YOU AFTER THE GAME?"

I remember how the cold chills ran up my back, and still do thinking about it. It meant the Rose Bowl. Vanderbilt didn't have a prayer. We won 34–0. Howell and Hutson played great, and I got in the way of Vanderbilt's All-American tackle, Dick Plasman, enough times so as not to be embarrassed. And it just happened that when Coach Thomas took me out in the fourth quarter the band was playing "California Here I Come." It sounds too corny to repeat.

I think what won that Rose Bowl for us was the way Coach Thomas prepared us. I surely remember *that*. We were going to California by train, and the day before departure we worked out in the stadium. Evidently we weren't pleasing him much because he blew the whistle and ordered head-on tackling for the last half of the practice. Bill Lee, our captain and a big All-America tackle, passed some sarcastic remark that Coach Thomas overheard. When the practice was over he ate us all out.

He said, "The train leaves at eleven. But I want you on this field in full gear tomorrow morning at eight." They had to hold the train for us until Coach Thomas was satisfied he had made his point.

I remember the train trip cross-country. How long it was. And all that free food. I'd worked that summer as a roughneck in the oil fields around Houston, and when we made a stop there at 7 A.M. the foreman of the oil drilling team, a guy named Big Boy Williams, and some others were down there to say hello. I remember them having to take one of our players, Bill Young, off the train at Del Rio, Texas, when he suffered an appendicitis attack. And stopping to practice in Tucson, where we ran wind sprints for an hour and almost collapsed in the thin air.

I remember falling in love with California. Alabama officials and dignitaries met us, and we stayed at the Huntington Hotel, where all the movie stars congregated. A lot of name writers were there, Grantland Rice and Henry McLemore, and so forth, and there was a cub reporter named Ronald Reagan, working for the local papers and radio stations. Reagan was out to our practices at Occidental College every day, getting interviews.

Hank Crisp finally got fed up because there were so many people crowding around the field we couldn't run pass patterns. He came back to the huddle after one foul-up and snapped, "The first man who runs over one of those suckers gets two dollars from me."

So Howell called a pass and threw me one deep, and I barreled into some poor little guy and knocked him down. After practice Coach Hank gave me two dollars.

That night at the hotel Dixie Howell said, "Give me my dollar."

I said, "What for?"

"Half what Coach Hank gave you."

"Shoot, Dixie, *I'm* the one who ran the guy over."

"Well, I threw the ball. You couldn't have done it without me."

"Like hell, I ain't sharing."

He said OK, if that's the way I wanted to be about it. The next day at practice he didn't throw me a single pass. Not one. That night I gave him his dollar.

I remember there were movie stars all over the place. Dick Powell had his picture made with the Arkansas boys, and Jack Oakie was there, and Mickey Rooney. A couple guys had cameras, and posed me with this good-looking, big-bosomed blond in a tight sweater.

The blond was very attentive. She said her name was Lana Turner and she was just getting started in pictures. A starlet. She asked me what my plans were, but about the only place I could have taken her was to church because I was broke again. I still have that picture.

I don't know how we kept our minds on business, which was to beat Stanford on New Year's Day. The festivities boggle you at bowl games. I ought to know something about that because our Alabama teams have been to fifteen in a row. With the four we were invited to at Kentucky, and the one at Texas A&M, that makes twenty, and I've approached them in so many different ways that I'm still not sure which is the best. My inclination lately has been to allow the players as few distractions as possible. Arrive at the site at the last minute, and have fun *after* we win. I can't be sure I'm right because Bob Devaney let his Nebraska team run loose in Miami a couple years ago and they still whipped us good in the Orange Bowl.

Coach Thomas kept a pretty tight rein, but all this glamour was new to a bunch of country boys and the excitement got to us. Every time there was an opening we took advantage. Kid stuff, mainly, like sneaking off to get some ice cream. One afternoon we were in this little ice cream store, Hutson and Joe Dildy, Hillman Walker, Kay Francis and I, all ends, and Coach Thomas, Coach Hank, Coach Drew and Coach Paul Burnum walked in. They didn't say anything, but we were worried, especially Dildy. He thought they were going to send him home.

I said, "Joe, you must be stupid. If they send you home, they have to send Hutson home, too, and they ain't gonna do that. And if they send us *all* home they won't have any ends left. Use your head." I was whistling in the dark. They never said anything, but I wasn't all that sure they wouldn't send us home.

We had a craps game going in Hutson's room one day before practice. Charlie Marr was fuming around because a guy he got tickets for, some boxing champion, didn't show up with the money, and he was trying to recoup at craps. Selling your game tickets was always a way for college players to make walking-around money. Over the years, the prices went up considerably. A star player could get a small bundle from an alumnus or somebody who wanted to brag that "I got my tickets from Joe So-and-So." In 1934, however, we were just coming out of the Depression and money was tight and we were happy to just get face value, which at the Rose Bowl was $5.

So Marr was working at it, rolling them bones, and he was a couple of bucks ahead when it was time to go down to the bus waiting to take us to practice. Only a few of us were left in the room, and darned if Coach Hank doesn't come busting in.

He didn't blow up. He just informed us that if we didn't get our tails in gear and down to that bus he was going to kick a few. I was convinced that was the last straw, though I should have known better. Charlie Marr didn't much care at that point. He was so mad when he got on the bus he kicked the seat out in front of him.

"I'm not going to play!" he said, not quite loud enough for Coach Thomas to hear.

I had some tickets to eat myself, two I'd bought for Mary Harmon. I didn't find out until the day of the game that she already had hers. I'll never forget Coach Thomas. We were on the bus to the stadium, sitting across the aisle from each other. Our center, Kay Francis, sitting on my right, gave a stage whisper you could hear a city block: "Tell Coach Thomas you're going to get stuck with your tickets!"

When the bus stopped at the Rose Bowl, Coach Thomas turned to me and said, "You get caught with your tickets, Bry-annt."

"Yessir."

"Give 'em here."

And he handed them to this big red-haired cop who always traveled with us as our guardian and said, "Sell 'em for him." And he did.

Some West Coast people really weren't tickled to death that we were the Rose Bowl choice. Bernie Bierman had one of his best Minnesota teams that year — Bud Wilkinson was on it — and had gone undefeated in the Big Ten. We heard some "We want Minnesota" cries when we got there, and that probably riled us up a little.

But I had my own worries. Stanford was undefeated, under Tiny Thornhill, and had allowed only two touchdowns in ten games, and no small part of it had been played by a big All-America tackle named Horse Reynolds. I was having nightmares about facing Reynolds. Finally, a couple days before the game, Bill Lee, Don Hutson and Dixie Howell went to a press luncheon, one of those special deals where only the star players are invited. When they got back to the hotel Hutson could hardly wait to tell me.

"Listen, Bear. That Reynolds was there, and he is *nothing*. He looks like Ichabod Crane. I wish he was playing in front of me."

That relieved my mind a little bit, and gave me some courage. And a little sleep. But when we went out there to play and I got my first look at Horse Reynolds, I knew I had been had. I was 6–3, 196, at the time. Reynolds was 6–4, about 250, and had arms and hands like a blacksmith. I don't think I blocked him all day. I held him one time, for Howell to make a long run, but I don't think I ever blocked him.

I remember every minute of the game. I remember Stanford had a double-wingback formation, and pulled a guard to block with the fullback, and they double-teamed and knocked me flat on my back two or three times in front of all those people, 100,000 plus. That had never happened to me before. Kay Francis couldn't see without his glasses, and I remember being on the bottom of one pile and Kay struggling to get up with mud caked in his eyes. He pawed at his eyes and said, "Pal" — he called everybody Pal — "Pal, could you get rid of some of this interference for me?"

And I remember Bobby Grayson, their great tailback, running for a touchdown in the first quarter to put Stanford ahead, 7–0. And the strong reaction of our players. Will Rogers said later that it was "like holding up a picture of Sherman's march to the sea in front of them Alabama boys."

I remember Howell hitting off me and spinning out and running for the touchdown that should have tied the game, but Riley Smith missed the point after. A few minutes later we were back down there again and Riley was ordered to kick a field goal. Bill Lee and I were talking during the time out and one of us said, "He can't kick the damn field goal."

Riley Smith heard us and got mad as hell.

"You sonsabitches should have more confidence in me than that," he said. And he kicked the field goal, a 22-yarder.

Grayson and Bones Hamilton were terrific for Stanford, but Dixie Howell gained more ground than their entire team. Hutson caught two or three long passes and some short ones, and I caught a couple of short ones and missed a chance for a touchdown on an end-around play. I was supposed to break it back inside but the defensive end came in tight and I bellied out and got too close to the pile, stumbled, and lost 6 yards. If I'd run the play right I could have walked into the end zone.

We had it won by the fourth quarter. By then it was 29–13, and the Stanford people who had been calling for Minnesota were quieted down considerably. It had all seemed like a dream come true to me — the thrill of being invited, of going, of getting to play in front of all those people — an ordinary football player among great players. All those things are rich in my memory.

Then just before the game ended, and Stanford was back in a huddle, I looked down and on the field right next to my knee is a big pile of silver. Dimes, quarters, half-dollars. I don't know where it came from, but I knew for sure that somebody up there not only liked me but was leaning my way. A lot of money. About three dollars in change.

I scooped it up real fast and was holding it to take to the bench between plays when, lo and behold, here comes Grayson on a sweep around my end. It was the only decent tackle I made all day. And I lost my money.

There's one other thing I'll remember about that Rose Bowl trip that I'd just as soon forget. As I said, I had begun dating Mary Harmon that year, but she was so popular I had to spread myself around a little just to keep the scales balanced. And I invited a good-looking girl from Pine Bluff named Barbara Del Simmons to be my Rose Bowl sponsor. Each player could choose a sponsor, and from those chosen would be picked the game sponsors, the girls who walked out to midfield for the cointoss carrying a bouquet of some kind. Barbara Del Simmons had been my sponsor for the Kentucky game that year.

When we got the Rose Bowl bid I wrote her and asked her to come out. Her daddy was a doctor and I figured they could afford it. She wrote back that I'd have to write her daddy. I did, but I didn't get a reply.

In the meantime, I was putting the pressure on Mary Harmon and she told me she could go. She would be my sponsor. When we got out there and they elected game sponsors, Mary Harmon and another girl named Grace McGhee won easily. Mary Harmon got

63

all the votes but two. And darned if that day Barbara Del Simmons doesn't show up. Talk about shocks. Barbara Del wound up having a good time, squired around by Happy Campbell and some of our Arkansas boys. But we didn't say two words to each other the whole time.

On the train ride home Mr. Harland, the man responsible for my being at Alabama in the first place, chewed me out a hundred miles or more for "inviting Barbara Del out there and then ignoring her."

I said, "Gee, Mr. Harland, I didn't know she was coming." And I didn't. But he wasn't satisfied.

It was almost forty years before Barbara Del spoke to me again.

Eight

The first thing a football coach needs when he is starting out is a wife who is willing to put up with a whole lot of neglect. The second thing is at least a five-year contract. He needs five years so he can set up his program and surround himself with people who are winners, people who believe in what he is trying to do. And so he can weed out the hangers-on and the politicians who can't help him, the ones who just get in the way. If the program is sound and he can say the hell with the grumblers and go about his business, then he'll win and he'll teach his players lessons that will make them better men.

All right, so he needs a contract that gives him time, and a lot of people are going to say, "Well, Bryant is a good one to talk about contracts, because he knows how to break them." But let me tell you what a contract is for. It's for the protection of the university president against the alumni or whoever else might not like it when the coach doesn't win the championship that first year after everybody has been bragging on him, because then the president can say, "Well, he's got a contract."

It doesn't always work out that easy, of course, which you can see by the coaches that get bought off every year. Not by the presidents, but because of the pressures from one group or another *on* the presidents. Chances are, sooner or later, you will get fired. It hasn't happened to me, it's not going to happen now, but it's happened to many of my people and close friends. And as I said, the only way I would recommend a young guy getting into coaching is if he can't live without it. The monetary rewards would be greater elsewhere for most of them and there's no such thing as job security.

Timing is everything. I was lucky in that my timing was always good. Bebes Stallings got fired at Texas A&M. His timing was bad. When he played for me there, and coached under me at Alabama, there was no doubt in my mind he'd be a great coach, which he is, and when he beat us in the Cotton Bowl in 1967 I thought he was on the way, but they weren't satisfied. Some folks never are. Bebes is now an assistant with the Dallas team in the NFL. Charlie Bradshaw was another. I thought he could make it at Kentucky. He's out of coaching now.

Some of my guys took impossible jobs. Phil Cutchin was getting to an age where he figured he had to get a head coaching job or else, and he took the one at Oklahoma State. There's no way Oklahoma State is going to outrecruit Oklahoma, but evidently you can't convince the Oklahoma State people of that. Phil got fired. But he had a nice contract, and they had to pay him, which enabled him to take his time getting into something else.

I don't have any sympathy for universities that moan about their coaches "quitting us" and going where the grass is greener. Anybody — the publisher of this book, the president of a school — *anybody* is going to consider moving to a better job if he thinks he's found one.

I left Kentucky with nine years on my contract. I left Texas A&M with seven years to go, and Maryland, too, when I didn't have a contract. All in all I've had more than seventy years of contracts in twenty-nine years of coaching. I'm not particularly proud of it, but I'm not ashamed of it, either. Since that first one we haven't been very hungry. Some coaches starve.

I feel now I wouldn't leave Alabama under any circumstance, but I've said that before.

The only way I could ever feel bad about leaving a place is if I'd failed to win, failed to have done what I went there to do. At Texas

66

A&M, if I could have guaranteed them in advance the conference championship we won in three years they would have given me a million dollars and a three-year contract and said, OK, go to it. What do you think they'd have said at Kentucky if I could have assured them four bowl teams in eight years? Kentucky had never won anything in football.

Sure, some of the folks I left behind were hurt, really hurt, and disappointed in me, and I don't blame them. Once or twice there I wasn't bettering myself at all, but I have no regrets. I went out and bled and worked and got them something — our boys got them something — they would have given their lives for.

By the same token, if I'd gone to Texas A&M, say, and finished 5–5 every year, I wouldn't have felt I could leave. Paul Dietzel called me before he quit Army to go to South Carolina. He said he was in a predicament, that it was all downhill at West Point, and I could sympathize with him. It's rough at the academies now. When Paul was my assistant at Kentucky he asked me if I thought he'd make a head coach. I told him I didn't think he was tough enough mentally, and he proved me wrong by doing so well at LSU where he won a National Championship in 1958. But had I been Dietzel I would have felt wrong about leaving Army if I hadn't done the job. If I hadn't won.

When I was playing at Alabama I knew it was just a matter of time before I'd be coaching, and once I got into coaching I knew the only kind of coach I wanted to be was a head coach. I tell all my coaches you have to have a plan for everything, an objective, you just don't go out day to day and coach. You have a plan you believe in, and you have to be strong enough not to compromise.

The people you tie to have to be the same way, people a winning endeavor means a lot to. Right now at Alabama I don't want anybody in my department, whether it's a coach or a secretary or the man who does the gardening, who winning a National Championship doesn't mean something to. Who doesn't believe that we can do it with my plan.

When I first started I might not have been thinking on so lofty a plane, but I was thinking of being a great coach. A great *head* coach. That was my objective. I wasn't a good football player. I played on good teams at Alabama — great teams, as a matter of fact.

We went to the Rose Bowl and we had great players, and I was just a guy named Joe on the other end of the line from Don Hutson. But football came easy for me, and I've always been a student of the game. I liked to play and to win. I get a thrill just going on the field to observe. When it's no longer that way I'll get out. Nobody will have to tell me.

Without my even realizing it Coach Thomas was grooming me. My junior year he and Coach Drew held a clinic up at College of the Ozarks and took me along to demonstrate. Catching passes, covering punts, running dummy plays without pads. The Ozarks coach was named Brown, an old country guy and a good fellow, and he had this big tackle named Godwin he was proud of, and they were standing there listening as Coach Thomas lectured on the way our ends blocked the tackles, which was almost impossible to do under the conditions we played then.

Old Man Brown was standing there shaking his head, looking skeptical. After a while Coach Thomas got peeved. He said, "Well, by God, get the pads!"

I nearly choked. One thing I wasn't interested in doing was trying to block that Godwin. I'd have preferred to theorize.

Coach Brown got the pads anyway, and we suited up. I knew I was no match for Godwin one-on-one, but I could sense he was going to try to split the gap between Dub Martin and me and just run over us. Coach Thomas called signals, and I shifted. And I happened to hit the guy perfect. Knocked him about 6 yards.

Coach Thomas said, "That'll be all, Bry-annt." There was no doubt he was pleased.

After that whenever he made any kind of trip like that he took me along, and I'd get to ride in the car with him and Coach Drew and listen to them talk. The more I listened the more I enjoyed it. We went to Indiana, and Chattanooga, and every mile was a revelation.

At midterm my senior year, the coach at Union College in Jackson, Tennessee, asked Coach Thomas for somebody to come up and help him put in the Alabama offense. I went, for $170 a month. I worked with the line and the backs and on everything else, and the coach didn't come to practice very often so I had my way. The only bad thing about it was they didn't pay me on time. I was always waiting for my checks.

Partly because I was already into coaching, and partly because I didn't think I was good enough, I passed up pro football.

Don Hutson had gotten out a year ahead of me and was an instant success with the Packers. He caught an 80-yard touchdown pass on the first play of the first game he was in, against the Bears. If he were playing now there wouldn't be enough money in the bank to pay him, as good as he was.

The Bears offered me $85 a game to sign with them, and Detroit came up with a $125 offer, but I wasn't interested. Then just before school started the next year B'Ho Kirkland, Bill Lee and Jim Whatley, who were all playing with the Brooklyn team, wired me to come up. They said they were running short of ends and if I joined them I could make $170 a game. I went in and talked to Coach Thomas and he didn't waste words. He said to forget it. That I could learn more trying to coach than trying to play pro ball. "If your ambition is to coach, then coach," he said.

Later that year the Union coach brought me back through Tuscaloosa on a recruiting trip, and while I was in town Coach Thomas asked me to go to a baseball game with him. We were sitting out in the bleachers in the hot sun — I can still feel it — and he said, "How'd you like to come back to Alabama?"

I thought he meant as a student assistant, at $30 a month or something. I said, "Do you mean full-time?"

"Yes. Do you think you could coach the varsity guards?"

"Yes*ir*." I thought I could coach anything. Well, I was young. I had a lot to learn.

"OK. I'll give you $1,250 a year."

That was more than I deserved so I didn't quibble.

There wasn't much I could screw up coaching the Alabama guards. I knew them all, I'd played with them, and they made it easy for me. Tarzan White made All-America that year, and Leroy Monsky made it the next, and I couldn't take any of the credit because they were great, but I was in hog's heaven.

By that time Mary Harmon and I were married, and I was anxious to make my fortune. Hutson was in town, in the off-season, helping Coach Thomas during spring training and getting himself in shape. We decided to pool our resources and become business tycoons. I borrowed a thousand dollars for my share, and we bought us a cleaning-and-pressing place called the Captain Kidd Cleaners. Hutson's wife, Kathleen — everybody called her "Temp" but don't ask me why — helped out at the desk, and we had two scrawny old guys who did the cleaning. It was a sorry-looking shop but we captured most of the business.

We had a girl in every sorority touting for us, and Hank Crisp put me in charge of equipment. Naturally he gave me the business of cleaning the team's uniforms.

If we could have collected for all the business we did, we'd have made a lot of money. But if we had had to pay for everything we ruined we'd have gone to jail.

I'll never forget Coach Hank. We had new uniforms in 1938, and after the first game at USC, which we won easily (I say that for John McKay's benefit), I sent them over to our place for cleaning. The boys must have used hot water or something, because when the jerseys came back they had shrunk — the sleeves didn't even reach to the elbows. They looked like doll clothes.

I was sick. Coach Hank threw a fit, and it was a good thing I was his pet. He covered for me and ordered new jerseys.

I remember so well, they were having this ROTC day, when the governor was coming, and Hutson and I had all the uniforms to clean. The ceremony was for one o'clock. At about twelve we came into our place, and there were stacks of dirty uniforms in the back room, I guarantee you halfway to the ceiling, and outside a line of ROTC cadets three blocks long.

We served 'em one at a time. Like short-order cooks. As fast as a uniform was pressed we gave it out — and if it wasn't pressed we gave it out anyway. "Here, son, try this on. Oh, yes, it fits perfect. Perfect fit. You look good. Next."

We ran the Captain Kidd Cleaners for two years before we bailed out. We did a ton of business, we just didn't collect much money. Temp Hutson was about five months pregnant when we started and she'd stand around on that hardwood floor guarding the cash register. I don't know how she took it. Mary Harmon found an old yellow bill just the other day that had Temp's handwriting on it, an old Captain Kidd receipt we hadn't collected on. I sent it to Hutson.

Nine

Our 1937 Alabama team went to the Rose Bowl, and lost to California, and I mention that only because I want you to know all that glamour I'd wallowed around in in 1935 had definitely turned my head. I hadn't forgotten it for a minute.

When we got out there after Christmas Johnny Mack Brown, who had been an All-America halfback at Alabama and was then playing cowboy roles, and his wife Connie showed me around and somebody — probably Fred Russell, because he's a great practical joker — got me a screen test at Paramount Studios through an agent named Don Gilliam. The day of the test I was supposed to go to the racetrack with the team. I said I couldn't make it because of some errands I had to run, and I slipped out to the studio. Even Mary Harmon didn't know what I was up to.

I had lunch with Ray Milland and Dorothy Lamour, whose father went to Alabama and was one of our original Sigma Alpha Epsilon — SAE — brothers. Then they took me to the set where they were going to have the screen test. I'm not sure what the test consisted of because I was too bewildered, but Mary Carlisle, a pretty little actress who looked like the typical college coed, sat on the side of my

71

chair, and Buster Crabbe, the Olympic swimmer who played Tarzan, was there. We talked and they took some pictures.

Nobody else was supposed to be in there, but right in the middle of it a guy named Farmer Seale, who was an Alabama campus newspaper writer, and a bunch of Alabama coeds opened the door and peeked in. They were on some kind of tour and I don't know whether Farmer Seale had been tipped off or not, but I was exposed.

When I got back to the hotel there was no secret about what I'd been up to. The agent had offered me $65 a week to stay in Hollywood and let him try to sell me. Mary Harmon helped me see the light, in no uncertain terms. I knew then, too, that they were trying to make a silk purse out of a sow's ear. They couldn't have cured my mumbling drawl if they'd given me $65 a minute. The movie industry was spared Bear Bryant.

So it was clear to me, as it always had been, that there weren't going to be any shortcuts, that I was going to have to work darn hard to be a success at anything, and the thing I worked hardest at in those days was recruiting. As a result, I have a reputation for being a great recruiter, although my assistants do all the work now, and they do a heck of a job, let me tell you, because good football players don't come knocking. I bet I don't see more than six boys a year. I hate to recruit. But back then I loved it.

Well, why wouldn't I? It was a way to contribute. I liked to travel, I got to see things. To meet people. Even the first few years as a head coach I didn't mind it. I did it day and night. If there was one thing that got me going as a coach it was recruiting, and you naturally take to things that go well for you.

There are a lot of stories. My first or second year as an Alabama assistant we were after a boy in a military academy in West Virginia. I drove up there in an old Plymouth the coaches used. Took me all day and night, and when I got there he'd already gone home, to another city.

So I followed him there. I'll never forget, his name was Lambert. About 6 P.M. that next night, in his living room, I talked old Lambert into Alabama. And just to be sure, I had him pack his bag and get in the car with me and we headed back. I got so sleepy driving I had to holler to myself to stay awake, and put the window down and let the cold air in, and pinch my legs.

72

We finally rolled into Tuscaloosa about 9 A.M. I got Lambert squared away and was in the office when Coach Thomas came in. He wasn't the early riser I am. He'd usually make it by ten.

Nothing had been said about Lambert and Coach Thomas had other appointments. I was sinking fast. At the exact moment I passed a remark to one of the other coaches that I was going home to get some sleep Coach Thomas walked in.

He said, "What the hell do you mean, sleep?"

He scared me so bad I didn't say anything. I just stayed in the office, fumbling around, going about my work. Late that afternoon Coach Hank told him what happened, that we had successfully delivered Lambert to his door.

"Bry-annt!"

I could hear him yelling from his office.

"Bry-annt, pal," he said. "I didn't know you did this. Nice go-inng, boy. You better go home and get some sleep now."

The rest is an anticlimax. Lambert was not a player who set the world on fire.

We used to hide boys out, what the pros call baby-sitting now and what they did a lot of when they were battling between the two leagues. We'd take a few prospects off someplace, on boats or on hunting trips, or ride them around until we got them won. That's illegal now, but we had somebody do it on us last year. They took a kid off and not even his parents knew where he was.

It wasn't that difficult. You'd simply tell a kid from Birmingham he was going fishing at a camp in Boligee, and then you'd bring him in on signing day to register. At Kentucky I had Ace Dawson's boat down on a big lake and I took six or seven of our top prospects down there for three days just before school. There was no letter of intent, you just had to get 'em registered to claim them. One story had it that we took a group on a boat and threatened to make them swim home if they didn't sign, which was ridiculous because there was no signing. You couldn't register them at sea.

But if I wanted a kid bad enough I used every trick I could think of. Frank Leahy used to tell everybody that when I was at Kentucky I dressed our manager, Jim Murphy, in a priest's outfit to recruit Gene Donaldson away from Notre Dame. Maybe Jim Murphy did

73

tell Donaldson he was a priest. Shucks, I'd have told him Murphy was Pope Pius if I'd thought we would get Donaldson that way.

Murphy *was* a Catholic, so we weren't far off. And I believe his brother was a priest. The better story about Murphy was that he had come to Kentucky as a tryout. We could do that then, bring them in by the busload if we wanted, put the pads on and have a look, and in his tryout scrimmage Murphy broke his leg and never played. But I liked him, and we went ahead and sent him through school and he became a kind of unofficial scout. After he got out he went to work for Reynolds Aluminum, and sonofagun, he married my secretary.

At Kentucky, more than anywhere else, we offered luxury hideouts. Doug Parrish had a mansion about eight miles out of Lexington, and Bull Hancock let us use Claiborne Stud Farm. The entertainment was pretty good. The rules now, of course, are at the opposite extreme. Not only can't you hide a boy out, but my son Paul, when he was in school, couldn't even invite Steve Sloan or Paul Crane of our 1965 National Championship team down to our lake house to visit, and they were his close friends. Ridiculous.

Usually there are no tricks to recruiting, just a matter of seeing a boy and seeing him again, and you keep seeing him until you win him. When you get down to it it's wrong, because the boy ought to go where he pleases, and he shouldn't have a bunch of slick-talking salesmen influencing his life or selling him on something he doesn't want. If a boy wants to go to Auburn he should go there. If he wants to go to Alabama, the same thing.

One of our quarterbacks now is Richard Todd. I had a tooth extracted last year and was on pain pills when I went on television for my weekly show, and in the course of my little talk I let it slip that Todd was the best quarterback we'd had since Namath, and might even be better because he had two good knees. I said it and I meant it, because Richard is a tremendous athlete. Six-three, 210 pounds, he can fly, and as a passer he has that same quick release Namath had. He hasn't reached Namath's level yet, but he has a chance.

And you wouldn't believe how we got him. I tell it all as an example of the way you *ought* to beat another school out of a prospect. This is really his story, not mine. He told an Alabama writer that I called him right after he made up his mind to go to Auburn. This was in December 1971 and we were trying to finish off an unbeaten

74

season and get ready for the Orange Bowl and I was behind in contacting our top prospects. Todd was just finishing a great career at Davidson High in Mobile. The Auburn recruiter must have done a good job because Richard said he would go there.

When I finally called he told me he'd decided on Auburn. All I said — according to him — was, "Richard, I really wanted you to come to Alabama, but if you've decided on Auburn then go ahead. Good luck, and if you ever get up this way drop by and see us."

I don't know what he heard in that to change his mind, but Todd didn't sign that day. He decided instead to drop by, and when he did Bob Tyler, one of my assistants, talked him into staying and I'm tickled that he did.

You take a boy and wine him and dine him and make a big fuss over him and he has to be pretty solid to stand it. Then he gets to college and finds out he's just another guy. The Columbia Broadcasting System did a big network special a few years ago on the recruiting of two outstanding high school players. If nothing else — I didn't like the show myself — it pointed out how much more attention those boys got than they deserved.

I was involved because I got one of them to come to Alabama, a running back from Florida, and he got hurt in a freak accident — some glass cut him — and he didn't play much for us. He had ability, and he might have been able to come back if we'd been able to get through to him better, but we didn't.

Neither boy lived up to his potential. They got all that attention *before* they played, and when reality hit them it had to be a disillusionment. The other boy, a quarterback, went to a Georgia school and, according to the papers, got into one hassle after another and wound up getting thrown off the team. His daddy got involved in it, too. There was no way that kid could keep his head straight.

A few years ago I had a daddy at scrimmage, and I could see he wasn't very happy. We'd gotten his boy when everybody in the country was after him, and there he was on the fifth team in this scrimmage.

I made it a point to go over and tell the daddy how proud we were to have his boy at Alabama and that he was going to make it, never doubt that, and not to let the boy get discouraged. He must have passed on what I said, because on Monday the boy really perked up.

75

It used to be I wouldn't take the time. I'd say, well, dadgummit, if he doesn't want to play, then take him on home.

What do you do about the cheating? They have a lot of rules now, limits on visitation, and budgeting, that sort of thing. You probably couldn't do what I'd say do — eliminate recruiting entirely, just let a boy choose a school after his junior year and make him stick to it. You can't do it because you'll never curb alumni for long, never stop them from dipping in. And you'll never be able to stop a guy who wants to improve his situation in life from going where something's offered him.

Before the war it wasn't uncommon — it was unethical, but it wasn't uncommon — to raid another campus, drive right in and talk a guy into your car and drive him to your school. Virtually kidnap him. I can't recall the names, but it happened at Alabama. Guys you were counting on were suddenly somewhere else.

Those were the days of the so-called tramp athletes, and I don't think many people yearn for them. Johnny Blood was supposed to have played for four or five schools, by his own account, and some guys were playing pro and college ball at the same time.

I used to get a kick out of listening to Coach Thomas and Harry Mehre and Hunk Anderson and those former Notre Dame players talking about sneaking off to Calumet or someplace to play in pro games on Sunday, the day after they had played for Notre Dame. How they'd be spirited around in cars, with the curtains pulled down. They would peek out trying to figure out where they were going.

One game in particular Coach Thomas always talked about. They had played one of the big Midwest schools on Saturday. He was the Notre Dame quarterback. I don't recall which team, but it had been a dogfight. The next day six or seven of the Notre Dame players got in cars and went to Gary for a pro game. And when they lined up and looked across the field they were facing the same team they'd played the day before.

Raiding was a way of life. We all did it. I drove three boys off the Tennessee campus in Knoxville in the dead of night when I was assistant at Alabama. One of them had called Coach Hank, said he wanted to leave. I was told to go get all three, but if I got caught not to forget to tell them I was doing it on my own. I got up there, after driving most of the night, and piled the three in the car and headed back. They were the eatingest sonsabitches I ever saw. We couldn't drive past a restaurant without them wanting something. I couldn't get them to stop eating.

After the war there was another flurry of activity. A boy named Bell was a prominent case. Vanderbilt had him, and the next day he was at Georgia Tech. Another guy who is a head coach in the NFL right now was with us at Kentucky one day, then in the Detroit Lions camp the next, then back with us again.

Another school came in there and stole two in one night off my Kentucky freshman roster. The raider accidently left the bottom of a $500 check from a company — call it McDonald Bakers, but that's not the name — that happened to be in the school's hometown. The money paved the way for the defection. I called the school's athletic director about it. He confessed. He said they were starting a new program and he was desperate.

He said, "Bear, we just had to have them."

Hell yes he did. They were the two best prospects around that year. I still have the bottom of that check.

The schools that recruited actively in my playing days and early coaching days were Arkansas, Alabama, Tennessee and Georgia Tech. The great majority weren't so gung-ho. Recruiting was mostly done by mail, and was kind of haphazard.

When I first started I'd take a swing up through Pennsylvania, and a couple of coaches would go to Arkansas, and maybe we'd see a prospect one time apiece. After the war the rat race began, and now you might see that same boy 15 times. Besides that, you go watch him play and you have his coach send you films. The real good one who might have had one or two schools interested now has every school in the country after him. It takes a lot of character to cope with that kind of pressure.

Ten

Anyway, recruiting was a challenge to me. It was something new and I got a kick out of it. One boy I helped get that first year, Sandy Sanford, won two games with field goals for Alabama and put us in that 1938 Rose Bowl.

Sanford was over in Russellville, Arkansas, at a junior college, and I went with Coach Drew to try to change his mind about going to the University of Arkansas. We talked and talked, and it was no use. It got to be 10:30 and Coach Drew said he was going back to the hotel.

I wasn't satisfied. I went back to the dorm and up to Sandy's room. He wasn't in, so I waited, and when he didn't show I curled up in his bunk.

About 2 A.M. he finally came in, and by 3:30 we were trying to work some math problems so he could turn in a paper he needed to graduate. I already had him talked into coming to Alabama, but I still had to get him out of there before those Arkansas people showed up, and I didn't know a thing about math. Then I had to take him to tell his mama and daddy in Dona, Arkansas.

This was during the time of the 1937 flood, when there were so many casualties in Ohio and all up and down the Mississippi, and the White River in Arkansas was backed up. It was headlines everywhere. Roads were closed. We were the last car to get through between Little Rock and Memphis on the way to Dona, and going over we hit a place in the road where it was flooded, and the car went dead. We had to push it to get out. It was cold as a welldigger's ass. I said the heck with this and headed back to Russellville, getting there just about the time Coach Drew and another recruit, Alvin (Pig) Davis, were walking out of the dining room after breakfast. They didn't know I had Sanford.

Drew stood there in the lobby and lit up a cigar and said, "No sense hanging around, better be on our way." I just nodded. I was dying to tell him.

They went out to the car and there sat Sanford. Coach Drew almost swallowed his cigar.

Pig Davis is a high school coach now in Columbus, Georgia, and all of his sons have played for him and at Alabama. The fourth, Mike, is on our team now. They've all been kicking specialists. The third son, Bill, was our leading scorer the last three years and set SEC kicking records that will be tough to beat. The Davises are proud, wonderful people.

It wasn't until I went to Vanderbilt that I got to be known as a good recruiter. After four years under Coach Thomas I was anxious to try my wings. Red Sanders had just gotten out of prep school coaching. He was putting a staff together at Vanderbilt, and Fred Russell, the Nashville sports columnist, suggested me. Red called from West Point, Mississippi, where he was interviewing Murray Warmath for the job. Murray had turned him down.

I said, "What are you offering?"

He said, "I want you to be my number 1 assistant."

Boy, that was flattering.

I went home and asked Mary Harmon what she thought about living in Nashville. She gave me about thirty reasons why it was out of the question. I said, "Well, honey, I've already accepted the job."

She just about died. But as always, she stuck by me, and as has been the case almost everywhere we've gone it turned out to be a good experience for both of us. Red Sanders and Fred Russell introduced us to a lot of Vanderbilt people, and we were exposed to some very successful men. We learned a lot.

79

In Nashville you could brew a pot of coffee and bake a cake and entertain anybody. You didn't have to put on the dog. I still have a deep respect for that school, and that city, and I'm proud as I can be that one of my boys, Steve Sloan, is coaching there now. If anybody can bring Vanderbilt football back to the Sanders level, Steve can.

Red was just getting started good then, but you could see his approach to the game was sound. He got better when he went to UCLA. My 1955 Texas A&M team went out there to play him in our first game and he had Ronnie Knox at quarterback and Knox threw three touchdown passes and beat us, 21-0. Red's concepts of offense were superb.

Maybe it was because he was trying to get his own feet on the ground, but Sanders gave me a lot of leeway. I recruited up a storm. There was one boy over at Benton, Arkansas, named J. P. Moore. Great prospect. Six-footer, won the sprints. Red had the boy sold, but he was afraid J. P.'s parents wanted him to stay close to home. I went in there and I practically lived at his house. His mother really took to me, a big old Arkansas country boy, and if the mother's for you not much can be against you. I'd be in the back room eating cake while coaches from other schools were visiting in the living room.

The day J. P. was going to graduate from high school I was standing back in the kitchen eating cake, his stuff packed in my car ready to go, when his mother looked up at J. P. and got that forlorn look on her face and said, "Oh, my baby boy!"

I just about threw up. I could see my whole deal ruined and Red firing me. But when J. P. came down that aisle he walked right out of the auditorium with me, past those other coaches, who stood there agonizing, and took off for Vanderbilt.

The trouble was Red only had 18 or 19 scholarships to work with, and you couldn't be too careless. J. P. Moore's brother, Ken, sold me on a stubby guard that didn't look like much. When Sanders saw him he threw a fit.

"Hell, Bear," he said, "anybody can look at that scrawny little runt and tell he ain't no football player."

And he was right. Red *should* have fired me for that. Instead, he gave me the first chance I had to run a game from the sidelines. As it turned out, he should have fired me for that, too.

I got the job by default. Red had an appendectomy just before Vanderbilt's game with Kentucky, and was laid up in the hospital. They had a telephone hookup to Red's bed and he spoke to the team before the game. They were really keyed up. If I had just turned in the lineup and left town they'd have won.

The night before the game I went out into the country and puked my guts out. My big chance. All I really had to do was go give them that lineup. Instead I coached a 7-0 victory into a 7-7 tie. Kentucky didn't have a great team. We struggled along and finally went ahead in the first half when an Irish kid named Flannagan, our tailback, passed for a touchdown.

So in the second half I didn't let Flannagan throw any more passes. And Kentucky tied the game in the fourth quarter.

Naturally I thought the officials cheated us somehow, else we'd have won. No young coach is going to believe he lost on his own merit. Preacher Franklin, who has the Coca-Cola distributorship in Birmingham now and is one of my television sponsors, was the Vanderbilt team manager, and he always had my ear. Preacher wanted me to go out there and kill the referee, a distinguished gentleman named Bill McMasters. Preacher had on his white coveralls and he was hopping around egging me on. He was like that. Even today when we lose old Preach thinks we got cheated.

I had made a couple of steps toward McMasters, who was looking at me out of one eye, when Bernie Shively, the Kentucky athletic director, came up from behind and put his big arms around me and pulled me away. If he hadn't I'd have probably got thrown out of football before my time. I didn't get a chance to say a word.

After I cooled off I couldn't have been more ashamed. And lucky, too. Years later when I was at Texas A&M I was invited to St. Petersburg for a speaking engagement. They offered me a pretty good fee so I went. And — the man who met me at the airport was Bill McMasters.

He said, "You're staying with me," and lugged me on home. We had a nice evening, and I enjoyed his family. I figured he had forgotten what had happened at Kentucky. Late that night everybody had gone to bed except the two of us. We were in his den, reminiscing over a nightcap, and he laughed and said, "Say, Bear, you remember that Vanderbilt game when —"

I shook my head and held up my hands and said, "Oh, I hoped you had forgotten."

The thing about recruiting is that you have to learn — and learn fast — that you can't make the chicken salad without the chicken. Sheer volume isn't the answer. You have to have winners, and you have to be able to recognize them. After a while you can almost tell just by sitting across the desk from one. Lee Roy Jordan was like that. Jordan looked me right in the eye and told me he just wanted a chance to play on a winner, and I knew right away I could bet my life on him.

Another kid — well, Clem Gryska, one of my assistants, went with me a couple years ago to see a prospect. We were with him three hours, at dinner and then afterward. When we were coming home on the plane I said to Clem, "We're not going to get him. And I don't want him."

Clem said, "Why, Coach? Why not?"

He was a big, fine-looking kid, too. Smart and inquisitive. Asked a jillion questions, about school and everything else. But as I said to Clem, "Not once did he mention anything about winning. About beating somebody." The boy went to another school and never did play.

There's more talent available to coaches now than ever before. There are more people, for one thing. Eighty million more than there were in 1945, and athletes are bigger and better. Their mamas and papas are bigger, they're born into the world bigger, they eat better and grow bigger. They're faster, stronger, better equipped. There is no comparison.

But percentage-wise you don't find as many who want to sacrifice and be dedicated, because they've got too much. Having a chance to get something that he never had has a lot to do with making a winner. That's why the blacks are doing so well now. They're hungry for recognition, for something better, the way we were when I was in school.

I was a long time reaching the point where I thought I could recognize winners, but I knew you had to have them, and that if I ever got a chance to be a head coach I would make sure right away that I'd have good players with me.

I had tried to get the Arkansas job in 1941. It was coming up vacant, and a friend of Bill Dickey's family introduced me to him. He had influence in Arkansas, there was no doubt about that. He had just gotten home from the World Series, and I called and we talked, and he offered to see Governor Homer Adkins for me. I went over and we both saw him. Bill suggested we see him again. And we went back a couple times more.

On my way back to Vanderbilt I knew the job was mine. That was the indication I had. I was 28 years old and couldn't have been more filled with myself. I wanted to be a head coach, and Arkansas was my home. This was Sunday, December 7. The announcement came over the radio while I was driving into Nashville that Japanese warplanes had bombed Pearl Harbor.

About all I had time to do when I got home was kiss Mary Harmon hello and good-bye. The next day I was in Washington, and shortly after I was in the U.S. Navy.

I was at Norfolk, awaiting assignment, when I got my orders to go overseas. I'd been horsing to get over there, and scared to death they'd send me. The orders said I was to report to "Hedron 14," whatever that was. Mary Harmon and I said our good-byes and she left. She said it was the saddest day of her life. I *know* it was the saddest day of mine.

The next day I poked around and found out that Hedron 14 was in North Africa. They issued me my gear — canteen, helmet, gas mask, camouflage suit, a big old pistol, a big gun that was either a carbine or a machine gun, I'm not sure which, never having fired it. I put it all on and shipped the rest of my clothes by sea trunk, thinking I wouldn't need them until I got to Africa.

That night Jack Curtis, the football coach, and my old Alabama teammate Jimmy Walker went out and brought some 70-cents-a-bottle champagne at the PX and gave me a little going-away party. When I got on the plane I was sleepy from the champagne, and scared. I remember sitting next to an army officer, a full colonel, but I didn't know the insignias and I kept calling him "lieutenant."

The transport was a big old prop that droned along, and I fell right to sleep. I dreamed I was in a big meadow, with only one tree on it. And the Germans were strafing me. I kept running and they kept strafing. I knew I was a goner. I don't know how long they kept it up, but when I woke we were landing. I could see the lights.

If they were enemy lights we were mighty close to the front.

Then I saw a big sign: "Welcome. La Guardia Field."

I wasn't going overseas right away after all. I was being held in New York a couple of days. I didn't have any clothes to change to, so I went downtown in my battle gear. When I got out of the cab at the old New Yorker Hotel people started surrounding me, jumping up and down, slapping me on the back. They thought I was a hero back from the war. Girls kissed me. Kids actually followed me around. I was too embarrassed to tell the truth.

Then, in the lobby of the New Yorker, Ike Winston, an old friend from Alabama, came rushing up and started pumping my hand, telling me how proud he was. I said, "Wait a minute, Ike. I ain't been anywhere yet."

That night I went over to Toots Shor's place, and he closed up early and took me out on the town. I felt like an idiot in those battle clothes, but I still had a good time.

The troopship they eventually put me on was the U.S.S. *Uruguay*, a great big one that just rolled and rolled. I was sick before we got out of the harbor. But I was alert enough to get friendly with an officer and he gave me permission to stay topside with him. Sometimes we'd sit up there all night. I dreaded going down into that hold to sleep. The smell of people sick was bad enough, but I knew a submarine would get us and I'd be the first one in that cold water. I made up my mind if I was going in I wanted to be high so I could be the last. Or maybe even go down with the ship.

Four or five days out we were rammed by another ship in the convoy. Put a hole in the *Uruguay* two hundred sixty feet long. I was playing poker at the time and I grabbed my canteen and my machine gun and ran topside. I got as far up from the water as I could. There were soldiers all around me, praying, and I was leading 'em.

The captain's voice came over the intercom: "Abandon ship." I don't know how many jumped off — altogether more than two hundred were lost after the accident — but I stayed aboard. Then the captain changed his mind. He announced we were going to ride it out. The ship was listing, but it wasn't sinking.

We lay dead in the water about three days. Nobody slept. A German sub could have taken us with a pocket knife. Finally another U.S. ship came along and rescued us, and took us back to Bermuda. Nobody seemed to know I was there. I kept telling them I was available, and they ignored me. Eventually they put me on a tanker for Africa, one that was loaded with ammunition, the last thing I wanted to be on.

I immediately made friends with the gunnery officers and they let me stay topside with them. We made it to North Africa without incident, and they put me to work in the Hedron program. I was really no more than an errand boy for the next year and a half, helping look after the navy planes on patrol.

I never did fight anybody. I was in Commander Tom Hamilton's program for most of my three-and-a-half-year hitch. I had been assigned to Georgia Pre-Flight before going to North Africa. When I got back I was sent to North Carolina Pre-Flight at Chapel Hill to coach there. We were given a good bunch of boys to work with. Men, actually. By the time I was released I had their future and mine lined up.

I had met George Preston Marshall, the owner of the Washington Redskins, a few years before when we went to Washington for Riley Smith's wedding. Mary Harmon was in it. Riley was marrying her former roommate, the daughter of a congressman. I borrowed the money for the trip, and at the stag party the night before I was introduced to Mr. Marshall.

We hit it off immediately. Before the night was over about fifteen of us, including some newspapermen, had moved the party to Marshall's house. The more I got to know George the more I liked him, and when I was walking out that night he said, "You oughta be working for me."

"What I oughta do," I said, "is scout for you."

"All right, scout for me."

That year I sent him reports on some players in our area, Bill Young and Fred Davis of Alabama and some boys from Tennessee, and he wound up signing about seven I recommended. They all made the Washington team. At Christmas I got a check from the Redskins' office for $500. Naturally, I kept scouting. Pro teams were using college assistants as scouts then, and you could pick up three or four hundred bucks a season. I did some traveling for him, too, to Texas and a couple of other places, and he brought me to Washington every now and then to visit. When I was at North Carolina Pre-Flight it was a lot easier to get together.

Late in 1945, when I was trying to speed up my discharge, I went to Chicago for the All-Star Game. The night before the game the *Chicago Tribune* held its annual press party, and I was there with Hutson and Killer Cain and Francis Stann, the Washington sportswriter. Hutson was playing in the game for the Packers. And George Marshall showed up.

It was so noisy inside we went out on the hotel mezzanine to talk. He said he wanted me to come work for him. As an assistant.

I told him I'd already turned down assistant coaching jobs at Alabama and Georgia Tech. Bill Alexander of Tech had told me he knew I was ambitious and would pay me $500 a month and I could quit any time I pleased, but I said no.

Marshall said, "What the hell *do* you want, a head coaching job?"

I said, "Well, yessir."

He said, "Why didn't you say so?"

Marshall left and came back in a few minutes and told me to get up to my room, because there'd be a call for me. I went on over to the Palmer House, and when I walked into my room the phone was ringing and a voice said, "This is Curly Byrd, president of the University of Maryland. Are you interested in being my football coach?"

I said I sure was.

He said, "How soon can you be here?"

This was Thursday night. The All-Star Game was the next night and Hutson was going to play, so I said, "How would Saturday be?"

He said, "Young man, if you want this job be in my office in the morning at eight."

I was there at eight, and air travel wasn't what it is today.

I was thirty-two years old, a child by head coaching standards. I got my discharge five days before Maryland's first game, but I handpicked seventeen players and two managers from my North Carolina Pre-Flight team and took them with me. They were the heart of the squad. We gave each one of them a full scholarship, which actually meant a double scholarship because of the GI bill, and that meant extra money for them. You can't do that today, of course.

There was talk immediately that they would be declared ineligible.

86

I had to nip that right away so I went up to see Curly Byrd — "The Boss," we called him. He said, "Don't you worry about that. I make the rules here."

Curly wasn't kidding. He *was* boss and there weren't any recruiting rules to speak of. Besides that, most institutions were either morally obliged or obligated by law to take any kid who had been in the service. Some of those seventeen were outstanding young men, too, like Harry Bonk and Red Polling, who are big executives now in Maryland. Vic Turyn became a high-ranking official with the FBI.

I took Carney Laslie and Frank Moseley and an All-Conference center from Rice named Ken Whitlow to be my assistants, along with Herman Ball, who was already there. Carney was a senior when I was a freshman at Alabama. He had coached high school football in Arkansas, then was at VMI before joining me at North Carolina Pre-Flight. With the exception of a five-year period working for Earl Blaik at West Point, Carney was with me from then on. You can't buy that kind of loyalty.

When Carney Laslie died it was a sad day for a lot of people, but a tragic one for me. It used to be said that he was one of the few men in Alabama who didn't call me "Coach Bryant." He always called me "Paul," the way Sam Bailey does now. Sam has been with me since 1956. But I'll tell you how I feel about Carney Laslie. I should have called *him* "Coach."

Frank Moseley had been an assistant at Kentucky before the war, and an old friend. We had agreed that whichever one got a head job first would send for the other. He was on an aircraft carrier in San Francisco, the *Lexington*, when I put in the call. Frank is athletic director at VPI now and recently hired one of my favorite players, Jimmy Sharpe, to be *his* football coach. Sharpe had been on my staff for ten years. This kind of thing keeps happening to me. I don't know if it's success or old age. Probably both.

It was 1945, and everything was jammed — houses, hotels, apartments. We lucked into a place George Washington had slept in, and we four coaches moved in. Mary Harmon and the children — Mae Martin was nine and Paul not quite a year — stayed in Birmingham. Right across the street was a Krystal Hamburgers stand. We ate hamburgers breakfast, lunch and dinner.

Maryland had won only one game the year before, but from the beginning our group played like they thought they were competing for the Rose Bowl. We won six out of nine, starting with a 60–6 victory over a little school named Guilford. Carney said the way I fretted and carried on you would have thought we were playing the Russian army. The team itself really lost only one. I blew the VPI game by personally scouting them in a 40–0 loss. I thought we'd win easy, and I didn't have the team ready. When we got behind, 21–13, late in the third quarter I panicked and pulled the first team out. If I had stuck with them longer we would have won.

I take the blame, too, for the tie with West Virginia. A blocked punt did it and it was my fault for setting us up wrong. I allowed a man to go unblocked. I give the entire team and coaching staff credit for the 33–14 loss to William and Mary.

We finished with three straight victories, and the last two were upsets — over Virginia and South Carolina. The Virginia game was the biggest of my life to that point, and for many reasons — good and bad — it is unforgettable.

Virginia had won sixteen in a row, but I could see our boys were ready. The night before the game Mary Harmon arrived by train; Ken and Cotton Whitlow had rented a little house and we went out there for dinner. It was the coldest place I have ever been in. They had a little coal stove in the middle of the living room floor, and we cooked our hot dogs and beans on it, bundled up in our overcoats, our boots, earmuffs and hats. We were more interested in the stove than the food.

Mary Harmon slept there that night, and it must have been near a highway where the big semitrailers had to climb a hill. She said she learned for the first time that night that trucks had four gears. She would lie there, unable to sleep because of the cold, and count the gears, waiting for the pause as the drivers shifted into fourth.

Vic Turyn, our best back, was hurt for the game, but we still played like champions. We made about twenty first downs to Virginia's five. We also stumbled around enough to be behind 13–12 late in the fourth quarter. We were on our last drive, and got penalized, and it came up fourth and 28.

And I called a dumb play. A reverse pass. It's dumb because in that situation the defense normally will let you reverse all you want. They will just lay back and cover your receivers.

But Red Polling came around on the reverse, cocked his arm, and threw the ball as high and far as he could. Donnie Gleason raced down the middle of the field, somehow got under the ball, caught it, and fell backward into the end zone. We had won.

After the game so many crazy things happened I still have to shake my head. Our players had been complaining about getting bitten in the pile-ups, and I hadn't paid much attention. When they undressed they showed me the toothmarks. George Marshall came in, wearing a big bearskin coat. This was in old Griffith Stadium, and the guard at the locker room door stopped him and said, "Who are you and what do you want?"

"I own the goddamn place," Marshall said, and brushed him aside.

Then Dr. Byrd came in and announced that there would be a big celebration, a banquet that night at the Statler. He said Sam Rayburn, the congressman, would be master of ceremonies. Sure enough, we did have a banquet, and Rayburn was the M.C. Curly came in all decked out, wearing a good-looking girl about twenty-two on his sleeve. He was a widower and famous for squiring around good-looking girls.

Right in the middle of everything Curly got up and said, "Is Bump Watkins here?" Bump was a big building contractor and Maryland alumnus.

He said, "Bump, I want you and Mary Harmon to get together *tonight*, and I want you to build the Bryants the finest home in Maryland. Over by the chemistry building."

I didn't know where the chemistry building was, but it sounded like a great spot to me.

He said, "I mean the *finest*, because Bear's got a lifetime contract."

After the banquet we went over to Don and Eleanore Adams's place. Don was another alumnus, a big hotel and restaurant supplier, and he'd invited us to spend the night. It was a new house, the first I'd ever seen with wall-to-wall carpeting. It felt so good I took my shoes off and just wallowed around the floor. We didn't leave until four the next afternoon, the only Sunday I can ever remember not working. It was just too good to leave.

Clear the decks for reality. I didn't have any lifetime contract, at least not in writing. And never got one.

89

Two nights before the Virginia game the campus police told me one of my tackles, a real big guy who was also a star lacrosse player, had been seen the night before in a beer joint. We only had three tackles on the squad, but I fired this one the next day.

Well, we won those last two, and right after the season I found us a house to rent and went to Birmingham for Christmas. And when I got back to get things settled so the family could come to College Park, two things happened that blew everything up.

The president, Dr. Byrd, had fired my assistant Herman Ball. Straight out fired him without telling me a thing. And when I went over to the office I saw this big tackle I had fired going up the dormitory stairs. I asked why he was still there.

"Well, the boss just took him back." Carney told me. The boy's daddy, he said, was a politician.

I knew then I had to quit. It broke my heart. I picked up a bunch of telegrams that had accumulated on my desk and went over to my new house nobody even knew I had and sat down and cried like a baby. I thought the world of Curly Byrd, but he had been a coach himself and he ran things at Maryland, no doubt about that.

He was a big, impressive-looking man. Very polished and poised, with a dominating personality. And powerful politically at the time. Dr. H. C. Byrd. Curly Byrd. The name meant something. When he walked into a room you knew he was there. The only other person I've been closely associated with who was like that was our former president at Alabama, Dr. Frank Rose. They both had a way, too, of rubbing people wrong, staff or faculty members or somebody. There was always someone mad at Curly.

He had coached at Maryland for twenty-three years, from 1912, and he thought he knew as much football as the coaches he hired. He hired some good ones, too. Clark Shaughnessy followed me, and then Jim Tatum, who got him a National Championship in 1953. I'm sure Curly Byrd knew more about football than I did then, but I didn't think so. I also knew if he was going to pull things like this I couldn't coach for him. I was glad then I didn't have a contract.

Finally I went through those telegrams, and there was one four days old: IF YOU WANT TO BE HEAD COACH AT KENTUCKY CALL ME COLLECT. DR. HERMAN DONOVAN, PRESIDENT.

I read it five times, then put in a call to Don Adams, who was president of the Maryland Alumni Association. Don had played on one of Curly's teams. I asked him if I ought to talk to Maryland first. He said, hell, no, get the job. So I called Dr. Donovan.

Kentucky was going to announce it on Tuesday night, but I wanted to tell my players first. I'd brought these boys in there, and I felt a strong obligation. So I called a team meeting for four o'clock, and about two I went up to see the boss.

Curly said he wouldn't let me leave. We stayed in there and stayed in there, and he crooked that neck and made me talk, and I kept saying, "I'm going." I didn't get out of his office until after dark, and the boys had already gone.

Next morning I got to the campus about ten, and there was this big crowd of students — must have been three thousand of them — yelling and holding up newspapers with the headline: STUDENTS STRIKE OVER COACH LEAVING. And, mercy, it hit me. Somebody must have heard us arguing and carrying on in the boss's office and told the press. The team blamed the president and raised so much hell the kids decided to strike.

The reasons weren't hard to find. One, we had suddenly brought football to life again at Maryland, and football has always been a campus rallying point. Two, Curly Byrd wasn't the most popular president around. And, three, those seventeen service veterans made a pretty strong caucus.

I got through the crowd to the administration building, and Dr. Byrd came out and I put my arm around him, and you talk about begging and pleading to get them back to class. We finally got them dispersed, but in the afternoon they started up again, and we got them to reassemble in the gym, where we made another appeal. I told them it was my decision to go. Finally I got in my car and headed for Kentucky, thinking all along the people there weren't going to like having a rabble-rouser for a coach.

When I got to Lexington, lo and behold, it was another crowd, and I thought, oh, Lord, they're not going to let me in.

Then I saw this big sign: Welcome Bear.

Well, I was the luckiest son of a gun. What had happened was that everybody had been on the Kentucky people for not hiring a name coach. Nobody had ever heard of me until that strike shook things up at Maryland. Brother, I had a name now.

Eleven

Carney Laslie, Ken Whitlow and Frank Moseley, who had all been at Maryland, went with me, and we found at Kentucky what I have found almost everywhere I've gone. They had good material coming in every year, big fine-looking boys who wallowed around and wouldn't play. Kentucky had more stars than you could count, but they didn't beat anybody.

There are a lot of temptations at Kentucky. It's a good-time place, and I loved it. But every Kentucky coach had been fired for something other than coaching, and I made up my mind if I got fired it was going to be for one reason only. For losing.

We ran off a few and worked some of them extra hard, and they quit, too, and I probably made more mistakes and mishandled more people than anyone ever has. But we got the rest of them motivated, and they started winning that first year. They won seven out of ten, upsetting Mississippi and losing only to Georgia, Alabama and Tennessee.

I was determined I was going to outwork everybody, and I worked day and night, talking with people, sitting home hours by myself working on things, going on so many recruiting trips.

If the other coaches were due at 5:30, I got there at 5. If they were due at 4:30, I was there at 4. Everything I did or said had a reason. I have to say I was a helluva coach in those days, and no small part of it was because I could do the things I wanted done.

I was fired up so much I couldn't resist getting into the trenches with them. Charley McClendon used to say I made him my human guinea pig because I was always demonstrating on him, showing how a defensive lineman should explode on an offensive lineman or something. I knew my limits, though. One day I began to sense old Charley Mac was getting his back up, and when I got down eyeball-to-eyeball with him I knew I had picked a wrong time.

I straightened up and said, "Anyway, Charley, we get the idea."

On that first team there were players back from the service who were older than I was, and I suppose I got to be so close to all of them it was hard to tell us apart. We were having our pregame dinner in Knoxville before the Tennessee game that year and the waiter refused to serve me coffee. He said I had to drink milk or tea just like the players.

I said, "Never mind that, bring me some coffee."

He said, "I'll have to check with the coach."

One of those grizzly war veterans sitting near me said, "It's all right, waiter. Give the boy some coffee."

We brought players in from all over the country for tryouts, and the school gave us three old buildings to house them in. I think at one point we had 150 boys in there, and my coaches who stayed with them said it wasn't the crowding they minded as much as they did the rats. I was so intense I didn't notice because I was over there myself, being with them, preaching my sermons. There could have been lions and tigers in there and I wouldn't have noticed.

I still had that fear of failing, of going back to the wagon with Mama, and it colored everything I did. I know now I neglected my family. Every young coach who ever lived does it, and it's not right, but if he has succeeded you'll find his family sacrificed a lot.

I must have thought I was a one-man show, trainer and everything, because I was everywhere. Got about four hours sleep a night, and that usually wasn't very restful. I always had trouble sleeping until recently. I can sleep fine now with a couple of mild sleeping pills. I don't have to take them unless I want to sleep.

My coaches never got home before one or two in the morning. Pat

James used to talk about one meeting that lasted till 4 A.M. his first year as a full-time assistant. We looked at every film we had taken from spring practice on, and the two games we had already played, and lost. We made five personnel changes the next day, and didn't lose another game the rest of the year. Against Villanova, Gene Fillipski returned a punt for a touchdown on us, and the following Monday we worked an hour and a half just covering punts.

I don't do that anymore with my coaches, and don't recommend it. Now when we're having two-a-day workouts I ask my coaches to take a nap in between. But then I was so intense and my coaches were the same, or ashamed not to be. What dedicated people they were. Their wives must have hated the sight of me, as much as I demanded of their time. The only one who ever said anything was Jim Owens's wife, Martha, after Jim came to work for me later. Every time we got together at a party or something, and she got to feeling sassy, she would chew my ears off.

Jim went on to become the head coach at Washington and was on the job about three months when I got a letter from Martha. Evidently she'd made a few discoveries. She said, "Papa, you were right."

As much as I asked, though, I never had to fire a coach for not performing. The only coach I ever had to fire was one who couldn't handle his liquor. Over the years I've learned a lot about coaching staffs, and the one piece of advice I would pass on to a young head coach — or a corporation executive or even a bank president — is this: Don't make them in your image. Don't even try. My assistants don't look alike, think alike or have the same personalities. And I sure don't want them all thinking like I do.

You don't strive for sameness, you strive for balance. Kids are different, and you want different personalities around them. They can't all relate to one type. On the coaching end, there are blackboard coaches and there are field coaches, and a rare few who are both. With some it's not how much they know but how much they can teach. Hank Crisp wasn't worth a darn on a blackboard, but when he got on that field he could make things happen. I was that way, a field coach. I've never been brilliant with xs and os.

My shortcomings at Kentucky those first few years were usually shown in my reaction to mistakes. If something displeased me, I'd

94

take it out on the players and ruin practice, which was stupid. George Blanda used to say he never worked as hard in his life as he did at Kentucky. Out of fear, partly. He said in a book he wrote that "playing for Bryant was like going to war. You may come out intact, but you'll never forget the experience."

I had made one of my dumbest moves with George. That first year we were using the old Notre Dame box and I made him a blocking back. In the box or the single-wing offense that position is called quarterback, but it is no more than a guard lined up in the backfield. He's a blocker, period. And George didn't like it. And I don't blame him. He could pass, run, and kick, and his talents were being wasted.

So he moped around, and I got mad and demoted him to the B team. As a linebacker. Did he react? You're damn right he reacted. He went wild. We had a scrimmage and he tackled everybody in sight and if I had let him go on he'd probably have maimed somebody, or himself. He told me later he got kicked in the face by one of my varsity halfbacks that day and he didn't even notice. He didn't remain a linebacker long, I can tell you that.

Blanda's an old guy like me now, and he says he learned discipline, respect and dedication at Kentucky. But it nearly killed him. He said he was usually so tired after practice he could barely move, and then we would make him run to the locker room "because when you played for Bryant you ran every place," which was right. "If he caught you walking, he'd tell you to turn in your uniform," which was right, too.

Then he wrote something else. He wrote, "Thank you, Bear, for that miserable, instructive background. I think it might have something to do with the fact that I'm still playing today."

You'll laugh at this, but I honestly did have a hard time getting to work without getting sick. I'll never forget one night, we went over to Bull Hancock's place at Claiborne Farm to have a steak, and I got so sick I darn near died. What it was, I hadn't eaten in two days.

My new coaches now, like Mal Moore and Bill Oliver, hear all those stories and see me relaxing around, and they probably think, well gol-lee, what's this business about hard work? But I guarantee you I used to be at that dorm every night, stopping by this room or that, preaching my sermon. If I hadn't gone to Babe Parilli's room every night he would have thought something was wrong. He sat around waiting for me. We had this little game we played. We were quarterbacks, and we had another quarterback to referee and tell us how much we gained or lost on a given play against a given defense.

I was busy all the time, trying to find ways to get more done, to get some enthusiasm going for our program. Monday was military day at Kentucky and ordinarily the teams didn't practice, so I ordered night practices for Mondays. Bob Hope and Jane Russell came to town for some kind of weekend show, and through Governor Happy Chandler I tried to get them to come out and be cocoaches at one of our games. I figured if they were there we'd fill the stadium, and they could make some money, too.

I was foolish, of course. A few extra dollars wouldn't impress Hope much, and we couldn't get hold of him anyway. I had a secret mad on about it. The night he was to perform at the show I was sitting in my office pouting when the door opened without a knock and this guy walks in and said, "Hello, Bear, I'm Bob Hope."

He still couldn't make the game, but I appreciated that. I needed a few morale boosters, all the blank walls I was running into. One of my boys, a very dedicated player, had been ruled ineligible that day because he had flunked a certain course. Our guy in charge of academics — we called him our brain coach — said the professor failed him despite the fact he'd attended every class. That sounded unreasonable to me.

I said, "I'll fix that professor."

Two weeks later my brain coach came in and said, "You sure fixed him good. The university made him head of the department yesterday."

I used to tell our players we were the black sheep of the family, playing second fiddle to basketball. That we didn't have the prospects the opposition had, or the facilities, and we probably wouldn't be able to outsmart them, that we would just have to outwork them. When we played over at Mississippi State one year, and they had their best team with Jackie Parker and that bunch, I took the entire squad around to where they had built six new fraternity houses, and I said this was the kind of plush life we could lead if we were winners. Beating Mississippi State, I said, would be a good start, which they then did.

All we had, of course, were those old houses side by side that we used for dorms, and that I found out later were rat-infested. They built a nice fieldhouse after I left, where the players could live. I've always believed in keeping a team together, where I know I can find them, where we can mingle and talk. Some coaches like John McKay at USC don't think it's necessary. They'd just as soon their players live the way the rest of the students live. It's apples vs. walnuts, and for McKay it seems to work all right. I tell ours that they are special and deserve to have their own place.

When I first went to Kentucky I told President Donovan that I had myself on a five-year plan, that we'd win by the fifth year. If I had been more mature I'd have gotten better results before that. We had some very talented players. Blanda for one. And Dopey Phelps. Dopey was one of the boys I had fired for missing classes or some-thing and then took back. He was from Danville, a terrific prospect everybody had tried to get. His daddy couldn't handle him, and I didn't do a very good job, either. If I had we'd have had windfall profits because he could run. He scored four touchdowns against Michigan State one year. The only problem Dopey had on the field was remembering the plays.

Happy Chandler had told us about how good he was and Happy's son Dan knew him. Dan had come home from school one day and said, "I had a class with Dopey Phelps today, and his name is really well founded."

Bob Gain and Steve Meilinger were two more I should have handled better, and I'll get to them later. Walt Yaworski was an-other. He arrived on campus in a zoot suit and was supposed to have said, "All right, where's the Bear?" We always had Walt running punishment laps for something. Dude Hennessey, who's on my staff now and played on those teams as a 5-foot-8-inch end, remembers Yaworski out there running those laps, and each time he'd pass Freshman Coach Bill McCubbin he'd say, "I'll be here when you're gone, McCubbin." He was, too.

I had absolutely no patience then for any fooling around. When we went up to play Marquette in 1948 I left the entire starting backfield home, Phelps included, just because they weren't try-ing hard enough. I knew we'd win eventually, our plan would win, but I was hearing those boos I was telling you about and it was rough. The team looked terrible. We'd won seven games in 1946, and eight in '47, and here everybody was expecting great things and we were one and three.

When we got to Milwaukee Don Hutson and George Marshall took me to dinner at Buckets Goldenberg's restaurant. Buckets played with Hutson for the Packers. Hutson could see I was worried, and he couldn't understand it.

"This isn't an SEC team," he said. "How can you be worried about Marquette?"

"Well, I'm worried all right."

And Mr. Marshall said, "Listen, Bear. Forget Kentucky. Come coach the Redskins."

I said, "I'm not interested in being an assistant coach in the pros."

"Who said assistant? I'm talking about taking over. Running the club."

I said, "Mr. Marshall, if I did that I would have to admit I'd failed here. I haven't won enough to satisfy them, or me." We had won more in two years than they had in ten, but it wasn't enough. It never is.

Hutson said, "He's right, Mr. Marshall. He oughta prove something first."

If nothing else, we proved something to Marquette. I wasn't the only one keyed up. Al Bruno was an end on that team, and when we went out to practice after arriving in Milwaukee he woke up late for the bus and was so scared I'd fire him he ran all the way to the practice field. I don't know how many miles it was. He played, too. I started him at safety and he intercepted two passes and we won, 25–0.

We switched from the box to the T formation that year, with Blanda as my first T quarterback. If we had done it sooner, and if I had been more experienced, Blanda would have made All-America. Bobby Dodd came up from Georgia Tech to show it to us that spring. He and Alice stayed at our house and visited for about a week, and when he left he gave me his playbook. As far as I was concerned that book was written for Babe Parilli.

Parilli was the best fake-and-throw passer I have ever seen, so quick and strong with his hands he could pump three times before he threw. We adjusted to Babe, not him to us. We built around him. College coaches do that all the time, in case you hadn't noticed. Find the talent and relate to it. It's not like the pros, who draft players to fit a system. That's why the college game is never stereotyped, and never will be. Every four years there's a complete turnover in personnel.

Parilli set all kinds of passing records at Kentucky, including 54 touchdowns in three years. You talk about winners. In our opening game in 1950 he took a terrific shot to the groin against North Texas State, and he had to be operated on to relieve the pressure from internal bleeding. The next week we were to play LSU, and I counted him out.

He said he'd play.

But instead of improving he got worse. He wasn't eating and he wasn't getting any rest because of all the well-wishers at the hospital and at the dorm. He got weaker instead of stronger.

So Mary Harmon went over and got him and brought him home to live with us. By Thursday he looked a little better, and Friday I got the coaches together and we put in a spread formation, similar to what they called the shotgun later on. We set him 10 yards on a direct snap from center so he wouldn't have to run back, and that allowed him to go back 5 yards more before he threw.

Game day was a hot one in Lexington. LSU was a big rugged team, and before the kickoff Pat James, a starting guard on our team, told the offensive linemen if "you let anyone lay a hand on Babe I'll personally kill you."

The first time we had the ball we ran seventeen plays — every one a pass. Parilli was still hurting and he wasn't as sharp as he had been, but he kept hitting on third and fourth downs and we moved the length of the field. By the time the drive was over LSU's big old burly linemen were worn out trying to reach him. It was 15 yards plus just to get in his vicinity, and they had our blockers to contend with (Pat James had them in a frenzy), and there was the heat and they just flat wore out. In the second half we went back to some of our regular stuff and wound up a 14–0 winner.

Twelve

The fifth year of my five-year plan at Kentucky was 1950. We went to the Orange Bowl after the 1949 season, but we lost to Santa Clara there, and as far as I was concerned we still hadn't won a big game. For one thing, we hadn't beaten Tennessee. And we didn't in 1950, either.

We won ten in a row, including the first four by shutouts. We scored 380 points, or 38 a game, which was more than anybody, and we had the second leading defense in the country.

There were so many fine players — Parilli, Bill Leskovar, Wilbur Jamerson, Ben Zaranka, Bob Gain, Yaworski, Jim Mackenzie, Pat James, Doug Moseley, Charley McClendon, Harry and Larry Jones, Al Bruno, Bill Wannamaker, Gene Donaldson, John Ignarski. Too many to name without listing the entire roster.

But it came up snowing in Knoxville, a freak storm. Parilli was virtually grounded and we got shut out, 7–0. In more ways than one.

To this day I would tell General Neyland or anybody in the state of Tennessee that the officials took that one. I'm trying to be more humble and all now, but they took it from us. We had a tackle eligible play, a favorite of mine until the rules committee outlawed it in the late sixties, and I had alerted the officials beforehand. We ran it three times and made a mile, and instead of giving it to us they brought it back and penalized us every time. If it had been in Birmingham or Tuscaloosa I'd have gone out and sat on the ball, but this was General Neyland's territory, and I'd have just got penalized more.

The Sugar Bowl had already chosen Oklahoma, and everybody in Kentucky thought we were set as the opposing team. But we weren't. We had nothing. I thought we were going to win the National Championship, and I had been holding the bowls off, thinking we'd have pickin's and maybe go to the Rose Bowl. Nobody knew that but me.

It was still snowing in Knoxville when I put the team on the plane to fly home. Bernie Shively, our athletic director, and Bernie Moore, the SEC commissioner, went back to the hotel with me to see if we could salvage a bowl. Charlie Zatarain of the Sugar Bowl was there, but not looking too happy.

Charlie wanted us, but his people in New Orleans were dickering around. Wyoming was undefeated that year, and Miami, and although Oklahoma and Kentucky wound up ranked 1–2 they were making me sweat. And I was sweating, too. They had a conference call set up, and Charlie was arguing for us.

Finally he said, "Here, Bear, you talk to 'em."

And I got on knowing I had to come up with something. If I went back to Lexington without a bowl bid for those success-starved Kentucky fans I was going to get lynched.

I made them a proposition. I said, "If you give us the bid, I will guarantee you we will beat Oklahoma's ass. I will guarantee it."

Charlie Zatarain got back on and spoke a while longer, then he turned to Bernie and me and said, "Will you accept the Sugar Bowl bid?"

Well, as I said, I had been coaching all this time and I still didn't feel that I'd won a big game. If I could live up to my bragging, Oklahoma would be it. Bud Wilkinson had great players that year — Billy Vessels, Buck McPhail, Eddie Crowder, Leon Heath — and they had won thirty-one straight, including the last two Sugar Bowls.

The game was sold out weeks in advance. I remember Red Herd coming by every day, trying to luck into some more tickets, and complaining about the scalpers.

We sure didn't have to do any selling, so right after the season, and before we called the teams back to begin practice for the game, Bud Wilkinson and I went on a speaking tour in Texas. We have always been close, and talk pretty plain to each other. I was curious about his new split-T, and he was picking me about our defense. That year we had stopped the opposition nineteen times inside our 3-yard line, and he wanted to know how we did it.

I said, "Bud, all we do is make 'em pass."

And I explained how we lined up and tried to effect as close to an eleven-man line as possible. It's the toughest place to throw, anyway, because there isn't much room and it's a high-pressure area.

"Yeah, but what if they *do* pass?" he said.

"They're liable to drop it, for one. Or somebody's liable to shoot 'em from the stands. Or they're just liable to screw up. They're going to score anyway if you don't make them pass, so we try to make 'em pass."

We traveled together for about a week and a half, making speeches and having a little vacation. All the time he was picking me and I was trying to decide on a defense for his split-T and coming up empty. And you won't believe this, but I had a dream. Carney Laslie knew about it because I told him the next day. I dreamed we had a four-tackle scheme with certain keys, and beat Oklahoma.

The next day the more I thought about it the more I liked it. And that's what we did — played four tackles, Yaworski, John Ignarski, Bob Gain and Jim Mackenzie. Yaworski took the place of an end, Ignarski a middle guard.

The idea was to intimidate the Oklahoma forwards with all that size and talent. We were keying, too, which nobody knew, and we played the corners up tight and made virtually a nine-man line. Bud was used to playing against those children in the Big Eight (it's a lot tougher conference now), and I wanted him to see some men.

We took the Kentucky team down to Mobile to practice, and they darn near killed one another. I've never seen a team so fired up. I had overprepared for the Orange Bowl the year before, so I packed them up and took them home. We gave them a couple days off, then headed for Baton Rouge. And it was just as wild there. Lloyd

Wooddell, our best linebacker, got his head banged so bad the doctor said he couldn't play. It might kill him, he said.

I said, "Call our team doctor." I didn't want to lose Wooddell.

The next day the doctor arrived from Lexington, checked Wooddell over, and said, "Shoot, Bear, there's nothing wrong with him. Play him and I'll be responsible." Which we did, and he was.

Three days before the game we held our last scrimmage. It was so rough we had to stop it. They were going to kill one another for sure.

I had the governor's suite at the hotel in Baton Rouge, sharing it with Carney Laslie. We always roomed together until he started snoring so bad. That night I didn't know what to do. I said, "Damn, Carney, we've screwed up again. We've spent ourselves."

He said he didn't think so.

The next day I got what is called in the trade "a feeler" from Southern Cal. Nobody knows this, but the one place I always wanted to coach was at USC. I had fallen in love with the area as a player, all that glamour and the screen test and all, and I knew you could win there if you were sound. John McKay can't be pried out of that job now. He has had more money offered him than a crooked judge, but he stays.

I might have been susceptible if they had called a couple of weeks before. I had turned down every available job in America that year, but USC was one I'd have had to consider. But not the week of the Sugar Bowl. I said no, and they got somebody else.

Well, our four-tackle defense surprised Oklahoma a little. And Dom Fucci was kicking the ball nine miles high. And Parilli completed thirteen out of fifteen passes in the first half, two for touchdowns to Shorty Jamerson and Al Bruno. He threw another one to Benny Zaranka on a little out pattern into the end zone, and his feet were so clearly inbounds you could see it in the movies, but they ruled it out. That would have made it 20–0 and a lock, because the defense was terrific.

Early in the game Charley McClendon came off the field with the side of his face torn off. When I turned to call the trainer and looked around he was already going back on the field with the defense. His tackling caused three fumbles that day.

103

Yaworski was voted the player of the game. He wouldn't have started if it hadn't been for the four-tackle defense. And when Oklahoma did get down on our goal line in the third quarter, we went into that pass-or-else defense. Wilkinson called a pass — and Frankie Anderson, his best receiver, was wide open and dropped the ball. Yaworski then threw the quarterback for losses twice in a row and Oklahoma wound up on the 10-yard line.

In the second half I lost my guts. I wouldn't let Parilli pass. Midway in the fourth quarter Billy Vessels threw a running pass and caught us in a mix-up and Oklahoma scored, and it was 13–7. Bless their hearts, the offense bailed us out. They kept the ball the next seven and a half minutes on the loveliest nonscoring drive I ever saw. I must have looked at the clock a jillion times. It's a curious-looking thing, anyway, and it never did move very fast.

By the time Oklahoma got another chance it was too late. We forced an interception and the game was over.

And Bud Wilkinson taught me something that day. He showed me the class I wish I had. He came into our dressing room afterward and shook hands with me and as many of the players as he could reach. I had never done that before, or seen it done. But I've done it since.

Hutson and his wife Temp were there, and after the team party that night in New Orleans he and I went to a friend's gambling boat to shoot craps. I won at that, too. There was no way for me to lose. I don't know what time we got in, but that afternoon we were going duck-hunting, and at 4:30 I got up and went across the street to a little restaurant. Charlie Mac and his pretty wife were in there, and my cousin Dale Kilgore, and they looked as numb as I was. Happiness can do that to you.

I went and got on the boat to go into the bayous to hunt, and they let me off on the best stand they had. I couldn't imagine so many good things happening at once. They left me and went away. And all at once I woke up to what sounded like a war. I'd fallen asleep in the blind, and there were ducks everywhere, and shotguns blazing all around, and I was so confused I didn't get a shot off.

It was almost dark then, and it was so eerie I had a sudden foreboding that it was all a dream. That none of it happened. I couldn't wait to get back to check the newspapers.

When I finally returned to Lexington I found sixty-four Sugar Bowl tickets in my desk, tickets I had bought and paid for, and forgotten.

The next year, with Bud Wilkinson's help, I put in the split-T. It was Parilli's last season, his prelude to sixteen years in the pros, but I knew then as I do now that you can't keep winning by just passing all the time. The split-T gave us another dimension, a way to win when we didn't have a passer of his ability. And the year after that, my last at Kentucky, we finally beat Tennessee.

My trouble coaching against Tennessee — specifically, against General Neyland — was that every time we played I went out there like a wild man and changed everything around. One year we painted all the dummies orange, then took the team out to a horse farm, and brought the clergy in, and had everybody so tight they could barely move. Next day we lost 6–0. We had a lot of gimmicks, and I threw out all the things we could do, the good plays, and put in something new. For Neyland.

Robert Reese Neyland was his full name. He had been schooled at West Point, and had won the Distinguished Service Medal as an aide to General MacArthur. As a football coach he was a model of consistency. He always did the same thing, and he always won. He was more of Coach Thomas's era than mine, but he was a giant and the respect (or dread) Coach Thomas had for him carried over to me. Neyland stuck with the single wing all his football life. People called his offense "the covered wagon," but like Hank Crisp used to say, "Try and stop it."

They used to kid me around the office that anytime Tennessee was mentioned during a coffee break I had to excuse myself and be sick. They weren't far wrong. I lost my breakfast regularly before the Tennessee game. Everybody thought Neyland had a jinx on us. It was no jinx. He was a better coach, and he had better football players — and I couldn't stand it. We managed a couple of ties against him, but I never beat him. He retired after the 1952 season.

In 1953 I made up my mind I'd had enough of this Tennessee foolishness. I had five simple plays that were sound and proven. This time I threw everything else out. Just three running plays — an option, a fullback off-tackle and a counter — and two passes. Our boys knew those good. I would have bet my life we were going to win.

Then, on Friday, when we usually began tensing up, I called a halt to practice and said, "Let's have a kicking contest. I'll kick left-footed."

What they didn't know was that Hutson and I used to fool around kicking left-footed when we were players. I bet them ice cream cones, and they loved it, even though I won the contest. It loosened them right up. First time I'd seen a smile before a Tennessee game in eight years.

I still almost blew it. Everything went according to form. We were better than they were, and we were whipping them good, and then I made a change at quarterback just before the half and we fumbled. Tennessee recovered on our 20. I ordered a goal-line defense. Our goal-line defense wasn't worth a nickel. They scored.

And damn if we don't go into the fourth quarter trailing. We're twice as good as they are, and we're behind, 21–20. We had it on the 40-yard line with time running out, and Bob Hardy, our quarterback, stumbled coming back to make a handoff. He turned it into one of the greatest plays I ever saw. Somehow he got the ball to the fullback, Ralph Paolone, and Paolone broke through the line, reversed his field, and an official got in the way of three Tennessee players. They went down in a pile and Paolone went all the way. We won 27–21.

It had been that kind of year. Against LSU Dick Shafto made a fourth-and-6 play that got us a 6–6 tie, and I didn't realize what down it was. If I had known I'd have punted. After the game I chewed the team out good for losing. I was back at the hotel making a tape with our radio announcer, J. B. Faulconer, when he mentioned "the tie." I jumped about four feet. I called Gaynell Tinsley, the LSU coach, and asked him what the score was. He said, "You drunk this quick?"

After the Tennessee game Martha Owens, Jim's wife, came over to the house to help Mary Harmon and me entertain the press. If beating Tennessee didn't bring them I knew Martha would. If she's coming, they're coming, she's that good-looking. There were so many people there that night you couldn't move. Press and guests and former players. Mostly looking at Martha and Mary Harmon.

We were all going over to the Campbell House for dinner afterward, but everybody was having a helluva time and it got late. Finally they filed out. And when I looked on my bed somebody had left his hat. A good brown one, with a soft brim, the kind of hat a big executive would wear. I wore it for ten years after that.

The Bryant family, of Moro Bottom, Arkansas, c. 1915. The barefoot mama's boy on the far left is me.

The Fordyce High Red Bugs were Arkansas State Champions in 1930, despite the fact that the starting left tackle was better known as a bear wrestler. I was not a great player, but I loved the game and was proud to wear the uniform.

JAMES A. PATTILLO, FORDYCE, ARKANSAS

The starting line against Stanford in the 1935 Rose Bowl had the great Don Hutson on one end (*right*) and me on the other, with (*left to right*) Captain Bill Lee, Bob Ed Morrow, Kay Francis, Charlie Marr, and Ben Baswell in between.

As a young coach at Maryland, Kentucky, and Texas A&M, I was brash enough to get a few words in with officials. I don't say I was always right.

The surprise welcome I got in Kentucky in 1946 was more than an unheralded coach deserved.

With winners like D[ ]
Moseley (*left*) and B[ ]
Parilli (*right*), we w[ ]
soon treating Kentu[ ]
fans to Bowl trips. [ ]
biggest win was the 1[ ]
Sugar Bowl upset of B[ ]
Wilkinson's numb[ ]
one–ranked Oklaho[ ]
team.

I probably would still be coaching at Kentucky had I not felt boxed out by the presence of basketball coach Adolph Rupp.

At Texas A&M we plowed [ ]
long row in a short time w[ ]
All-American Charlie Krueg[ ]
(*left*) and John David Cro[ ]

1961 we won our first ational Championship, and ere were more leaders on e team than you could unt, including (*left to right*) ommy Brooker, Pat Tramell, Darwin Holt, and Billy Neighbors.

On press day at Lake Martin, I always enjoyed taking charge of the barbecue.

ank Howard of Clemn didn't believe we uld win with such lite boys and doubted our ogram weight. We let m check the scales himself.

Xs and Os make for impressive-looking blackboards, but the joy of coaching for me has always been on the field, where I could be in the middle of things, getting my message over.

In the heat of a game, the chairman of the board has the last say, but I have always had good assistance to lean on, including Bebes Stallings at my right, Clem Gryska behind me.

In the 1963 Florida game when it was fourth down for Florida and the officials said third, I risked going onto the field to protest. I won the point, but could have been penalized. When you measure the breadth of victory, a penalty can beat you.

──── Thirteen ────

So we won at Kentucky, and I don't think I would ever have left if I hadn't gotten pigheaded. It was probably the most stupid thing I ever did. I could have had about anything I wanted, and Mary Harmon loved it. We had a social position coaches seldom have — good friends with Governor Wetherby and all — and we lived right there near the Idle Hour Country Club. Guy Huguelet got us an honorary membership and that's a club that some people wait years to get into.

Mr. Huguelet is dead now, but when he was alive he was the one I'd go to. He had made a lot of money with Southeastern Greyhound and was chairman of the Board of Trustees and chairman of the Athletic Committee at Kentucky. He practically adopted us. Mary Harmon said he was like a father, son and boyfriend all in one. He just loved her.

There's another tipoff for you, the kind of people you tie to. Whatever I wanted I could go to Mr. Huguelet. If I asked for money he'd have given me a sackful. Ace Dawson, a big contractor, was another person like that. And Lawrence Wetherby, who became governor — we called him "X-1" — and kept a room in the mansion vacant for me. And I used it, too. And Doug Parrish, who let me use his airplane to make trips. And the late Bull Hancock of Claiborne Stud. And Dr. Ralph Angelucci. We used to play bridge with Governor Happy Chandler and his wife, Mildred.

But Mr. Huguelet was my number 1 guy, and I think I won him the first day. We were talking contract and I said, "Just pay me so much for a win and so much for a bowl game and I'll be satisfied." They hadn't had any coaches who talked that way, and the idea must have appealed to him because I did get some incentive clauses in my contract.

I believe in performance clauses and incentives. If I had it to do over, when I went to Alabama I'd have had them buy me a twenty-year annuity, say for half a million dollars, and if I stayed the twenty years it would be mine. I suggested that recently to a coach who was being hired by a friend of mine. There's a certain respectability to an insurance deal, and if you've been on a job ten or twelve years and the cash value of the policy has gotten up there pretty good you'll think twice before you leave. If I had done that at Alabama I'd be eligible for a half-million-dollar payoff in a couple of years, and I'd have that protection, too. And it would be tax-free.

Nevertheless, we had sunk roots in Kentucky. We had built a new house, and I was on the verge of making some real money. I had turned down half a dozen good jobs. Arkansas tried to abolish the athletic directorship to sign me in 1952 when I said I wanted the football program to be autonomous. The Arkansas legislature approved it. A member of the board at LSU said to me, "Dammit, everybody has a price, Bear. What's yours?"

And I put it up there pretty good for those days — something like $25,000, a home, a TV program, everything I could think of.

His name was Morris Gottlieb. He said, "Bear, you know no college athletic department can do that."

I said, "Nosir."

"Well then, how about if the contract is written with my bank?"

"I guess so."

"OK, it's a deal."

I said, "Hold on. I've got to think about it." And when I thought about it I backed out.

Alabama people came to see me and I wouldn't even talk to them because at the time Red Drew was the head coach, and he had been *my* coach and I wouldn't be a party to his being replaced. And Texas A&M and a couple others approached me.

Governor Wetherby made statements later that he believed I would have stayed if we had been able to get Paul Hornung. Hornung was the biggest thing to come out of Louisville until Cassius Clay, and when he was at Flaget High in 1953 I did try hard to get him. And X-1 helped me. He made several trips to the Hornung house. I wasn't a stranger there, either. But Paul's mother wanted him to go to Notre Dame, and it turned out to be a good move. He won the Heisman Trophy and was a star for the Green Bay Packers.

But I've missed on a lot of great players. Losing one more isn't going to make me throw in.

When I try to put my finger on it I can't say exactly why I left Kentucky, but one thing I want to make clear. I never tried to get the late Bernie Shively's job as athletic director, and the athletic directorship had nothing to do with what you could call a clash of objectives between me and Adolph Rupp. I guess, to be perfectly honest about it, that was the crux of the matter, me and Coach Rupp.

If Rupp had retired as basketball coach when they said he was going to, I would probably still be at Kentucky. The trouble was we were too much alike, and he wanted basketball number 1 and I wanted football number 1. In an environment like that one or the other has to go.

Rupp and I never had a cross word, actually. I just got tired of seeing the papers full of basketball. There has to be two sides to it. I probably went there for more money than he was making. I was at $8,500, then $9,000, then they raised me to $12,000 when Alabama offered me a job after the first year. Basketball made money at Kentucky, though, and everywhere I went trying to sell the football program it was "basketball and Rupp, basketball and Rupp," and I was jealous.

I was recruiting in Harrodsburg, Kentucky, my first year, before we played a game. I had driven all the way from East Chicago to sign this boy. I could have sent anybody because he was definitely coming, but they wanted me because "there'll be a big crowd and it's good publicity."

When I got there the crowd was twenty people, and when the guy introduced me he said, "I'm sorry we couldn't give Coach Bryant the key to the city, but we have given one to Coach Rupp for all the championships he's had. We'll save one for when Coach Bryant wins as many games."

I got up burning. And I shouldn't have but I said, "I don't want a key to the city. When I win as many games as Coach Rupp I'll be able to buy the damn city and never miss the money." And sat down.

You either liked Rupp or you hated him. There didn't seem to be a middle ground. Some of my friends who were high in the university administration didn't like him, and I probably let them know how jealous I was. He had that abrasive way of talking and dealing with people, and if you didn't like it you didn't like him.

Our offices were right next to each other in the old athletic building for a while, and I could hear him interviewing players. Funniest thing in the world. He called the door to his office the "pearly gates," and he would announce to a kid in that Kansas twang, "By gad, you just walked into the pearly gates of basketball!" And he'd give them the darnedest talks you ever heard, all about how good he and his program were. All the truth, too.

A friend of mine who's in the movies now was a basketball player Rupp talked to, Forest Tucker. I heard Rupp give him that spiel, then he said, "Only trouble is, son, you're just too damned short. I don't think we'll be able to use you around here. But here's a dollar. Take this and get yourself something to eat and go get the bus home."

Like him or not, you had to be impressed the way he took the bull by the horns. One year they had a faculty group investigating the Kentucky athletic department. They talked to me about finances and budgets and things, and to the other coaches, and when they got to Rupp he was ready for them. I could hear it plain as day.

He said, "By gad come on in here! I been waiting for you bastards! I wanta know what the hell happened to my basketball player over there in your English class," and he named a player.

"By gad you expect me to take these pine knots and make All-Americas out of them and I send you a B student and he's making a goddamn D!"

He just ate their fannies, and they haven't sat down yet. They haven't even opened their mouths. They're in there trying to investigate athletics and he's attacking academics. They got out of there in a hurry. After we moved to the Coliseum I got an office as far away as I could, at the other end of the hall, away from Rupp and all that traffic.

I didn't appreciate Adolph until I left. I can now, and I can see my own position a little more clearly. When I hired C. M. Newton to be the Alabama basketball coach I know he must have felt the way I did long ago. He must have thought he was facing impossible odds, which he has certainly overcome. I don't know if he resented football or not, but I wouldn't blame him if he did. He sure made it tough for people to ignore basketball anymore, and I'm for him.

If I had it to do over I would have gone in there and asked Rupp to do something for me. He'd have liked that and he'd have done it, and he'd have been my friend.

I have this picture in my den of Bud Wilkinson laughing at a banquet over a story I told about that time we won the SEC championship at Kentucky, the only time a Kentucky football team ever has. Rupp had won it in basketball for the umpteenth time and they gave him a great big blue Cadillac with whitewall tires, and I said at this banquet, "And here's what I got."

And I held up this little old cigarette lighter.

Well, when the thing came to a head I remembered that cigarette lighter, and I knew I was too far behind to ever catch up.

Adolph and I are real close now, and I honestly think a lot of him. Last year I sent a plane for him to come to the Alabama-Kentucky game. I heard they had scratched his name off the list the time before, and I didn't want that to happen again. I still like to listen to him, all that talk of his, and down inside he was just like I am. He was just going to win, see. I know we respected each other as coaches. I think he was the best there was in basketball.

I know he did something I'll never forget. I went to A&M and lost nine games that first year, the only losing season I ever had, and we were doing a clinic together in Utah. There were newspapermen there, and Adolph got up and with that Kansas twang of his said:

"I want to tell you gentlemen something. Paul Bryant over there was at Kentucky, and he left us for a lot of money [which I didn't]. You think he's down a little bit now, but I'll tell you, he will win. *He will win*. And you gentlemen in Texas who are playing him, he will run you right out of business. Five, ten years from now he will be the top man, make no mistake about it, and don't forget Uncle Adolph told you."

He sure didn't have to say that, but, boy, I appreciated it. Practically every paper in Texas picked it up, and a whole lot of eyebrows were raised.

I had tried to resign in 1952, both because of the basketball scandal at Kentucky and to take the Arkansas job. They had caught some of the boys shaving points for gamblers, fixing games. The trial was coming up and I thought the bad publicity was hurting my program. I was trying to recruit at the time and I thought, "Why the hell do I have to go through this, as tough as it is to recruit in Kentucky."

But every time I went to Dr. Donovan about it he bulldogged me into staying. The first time was in 1946. Coach Thomas had been calling me, saying he was sick and going to retire, and after we played Alabama at Montgomery that year, and lost, 21–7, we talked again and I agreed to take the job. I said I'd come down after the season was over.

Dr. Donovan got wind of it and said he forbade me to leave the campus. I said, "I'm going, sir."

He said, "You've got a contract here. You're not going anywhere. Besides that we're going to raise you to $12,000 and give you a ten-year contract."

I already had a five. He just wasn't giving me a choice, period. I called Coach Thomas and told him I couldn't leave and signed the new contract.

When Alabama approached me again Coach Drew was there and I wouldn't listen. That was the same time I had the LSU offer and was approached by Minnesota. For a while there I was catching them faster than I could string them. The Arkansas job was the one I really wanted then, and I'd go into Dr. Donovan's office, and we'd talk. Mr. Huguelet was there. He'd lie down on the couch and fall asleep while we were talking.

Governor Wetherby — old X-1 — was in my corner. He drove me to Memphis where the Arkansas people picked me up in a little old one-engine private plane and flew me to Little Rock. I met the governor and the university president, and they offered me all the goodies they could, and Pete Ranay and Jack Stevens offered me stock in their oil company, Arkansas-Louisiana Gas. A chance to get in on the ground floor. If I had taken it I'd be worth 40 million now.

I should have. I should have just said the hell with it and left, which is what I eventually did. Some people in Arkansas thought I was using them to make a better deal, but that's not true. Dr. Donovan wouldn't give me my release and I wanted it to be proper.

After that I felt like a different person, like an outsider looking in. I knew eventually I'd have to go. I hated the way they had handled that basketball thing. Not Coach Rupp, the people close to the program.

Eventually Dr. Donovan led me to believe Rupp was going to resign, and that he thought that would clear the air. He said after that next season Rupp would never coach another basketball game at Kentucky. A year later Bernie Shively and I were going down to the conference meeting at Birmingham, and when we changed planes in Louisville I picked up a paper, and there it was. Rupp was not retiring at all, he had signed another contract, and Dr. Donovan was saying how pleased he was.

That did it. I made up my mind to go. I had been led to believe Adolph was going to retire, and I'm glad now he didn't because he has meant so much to basketball.

I anticipated Dr. Donovan's refusal so I went to Governor Wetherby to have him intercede. X-1 said, "I know why you're here, and I don't blame you."

He really kind of threatened them into letting me go. He said, "If this boy's not released by five o'clock today" — it was February 4, 1954, and I had ten years left on my contract — "you all will come by me."

This is what going off half-cocked will do for you. My timing was bad. It was during the semester break and my boys weren't there. If they were they wouldn't have let me go, because I'd have told them the reason and there would have been hell to pay. Besides that, I'd dealt myself into a corner. The only offer I had left, the only one still open, was Texas A&M. I had to take it.

I went off and left Kentucky with the second best squad I had there. Howard Schnellenberger was on that team, and Bob Hardy, and Blanton Collier came in as coach and had a winner right away. Kentucky won eight games in 1954, while we were winning one at Texas A&M. You don't think I regretted that?

Plus that I had borrowed money at 3 percent interest from Dr. Angelucci and built that big house across from the Idle Hour, and we had the first air-conditioning unit in Lexington. We had it in the window of our bedroom, and Bull Hancock came over, and Louis Haggin, and we sat on the bed and drank whiskey and had a helluva time with that air conditioner. Even today I'm a nut for air-conditioning.

The Kentucky program petered out after that, and I don't mean that as a reflection on Blanton Collier. He's more a pro-style coach anyway, and it takes a special kind of guy to win at Kentucky. In the first place there aren't enough high schools to draw from, so you have to recruit like crazy out of state. Secondly, you have to be a mean sonofagun and not mind stepping on toes because there are a lot of people who will get in your way.

When I was there the deans were tough on the program, but I think I won them over. The president helped, and Mr. Huguelet. Deans can make it tough for you unconsciously by being a little harder on football players, or going against your borderline cases. You get that everywhere. We have it at Alabama, and we had it when I was playing. I had a professor who was a track man and an A Club member, but he announced when I came into the class, "Any football players in here? If there are you better get out, because you'll never pass this course."

I got out, too.

Leaving Kentucky broke Mary Harmon's heart. Worse than that, when she got off the plane at College Station, Texas, she turned white.

Fourteen

At first glance, Texas A&M looked like a penitentiary. No girls. No glamour. A lifeless community. A&M is a great educational institution, but at the time it was the toughest place in the world to recruit because nobody wanted to go there.

Don Meredith, for example. I wanted him in the worst way, and he'd tell you even now that he wanted to go to Bud Wilkinson or Bear Bryant when he died. But he did *not* want to go to Texas A&M. I'll never forget how he charmed Mary Harmon. Meredith was Mr. Personality even then. Still just a kid, and she fell in love with him. He walked into my little house and back where she was washing dishes, and he just picked up a rag and started drying.

I knew he respected me, and he said he wanted to play for me. I didn't send a child to get him. When it came down to the nut-cutting it was a matter of selling him on A&M, and I couldn't do it. I flew up to Mount Vernon and he drove me to his house, and the tears came to his eyes. When I saw those tears I knew I'd lost him.

He said, "Coach, if you were anywhere in the world except A&M — anywhere in the *world* . . ."

A&M didn't lack for football tradition. Homer Norton is in the

Hall of Fame and won a National Championship there in 1939 with an All-America fullback named John Kimbrough.

And those doggone wonderful Aggies are unbelievable. Aggie Exes, they call them. They make the worst enemies there are. You get two of them together and you get big talking. Just the sweetest, most obnoxious guys.

They aren't country clubbers. They belong to the International Club or the Cibango Club or something, and they would always be popping off what we were going to do, how badly we were going to beat Texas, or how SMU was "horseshit." You could never sneak up on anybody because they bragged too much. There's no way to stop them. They're ex-students, whether they went to A&M or not, and they'll be ex-students the rest of their lives.

The thing is, they are proud of that school. I've got two nephews, one played football at A&M and graduated and one who went there and didn't play anything and didn't graduate. The latter is a bigger ex-Aggie than the former. He goes whole hog for everything. He's the epitome of what is known in Texas as "the Aggie joke."

To a Longhorn an Aggie is inept, dimwitted and not very good at sex. They tell those corny jokes. A Longhorn asks: "How could you break an arm and a leg raking leaves?" The Aggie answers: "I fell out of the tree." None are any funnier than that, but the Longhorns love them. I don't tell them because I'm an Aggie myself now. Just don't ask me to go back there to live.

They used to call it Sing Sing on the Brazos, being out there in the sticks and all. It was founded in 1876, in east central Texas, where there are wolves and deer. Texas people like to say its specific location is the middle of nowhere. Actually it is northwest of Houston on Highway 6, along very pretty, very rich farmland, with beautiful walnut and live oak trees.

But a boy had to want to play football awful bad to go there. At the time it was the only school in the Southwest Conference without coeds, and they had to wear those uniforms and put up with all that military discipline. The Cadet Corps was the spirit of the school, what they call the "Twelfth Man." They stand and cheer throughout every game. They just hadn't had much to cheer about.

I was like Mary Harmon. I nearly died when I saw what I was getting into. I remember what Dr. Thom Harrington, the chancellor, told me. He said, "Paul, this place will grow on you," and he was right. Mary Harmon cried her eyes out that first night. And when we left, she cried all over again.

As soon as I made up my mind to leave Kentucky I called Jack Finney, who was on the A&M athletic board, and told him to get his pencil sharpened. I said, "I'll meet you in Dallas tonight."

They had the drapes pulled in the little room at the airport when I got there, making it out to be a real hush-hush deal.

I said, "If we could offer a boy the same scholarship deal Texas does, and there were twenty good prospects, how many would we sign?"

Jack said, "Ten."

"You mean we could get half?"

"At least."

That impressed me because I knew I could win with that. But I didn't know the Aggies then like I know them now. Old Jack was exaggerating. You couldn't get ten. You would be lucky to get one. The chances were you wouldn't get any. Not then.

I agreed to a six-year contract, which was five more than any coach had at A&M since Homer Norton was paid off by the alumni in 1947. I was to be head coach, succeeding Ray George, and athletic director, succeeding Barlow Irwin.

Finally it got down to money. That should always be the last consideration because if you can't win the money's no good anyway.

I said, "What do the heads of your departments make? I want to make the same, no more, no less."

They gave me the figure: $15,000.

I said, "Of course, you know I can't come for that."

And W. T. (Doc) Doherty spoke up. He said, "We'll put you on my company payroll," which was the Welsh Foundation.

He meant I'd be getting a check from them, too. For another $10,000. I accepted. When I quit years later Doherty was more bitter than anybody and I guess that was the reason. But I couldn't feel too bad about it. If I had guaranteed them the conference championship they'd have given me ten times that.

I was at a conference meeting in Cincinnati when the word got out. While I was there I went on a radio debate show with some faculty guy who objected to the idea that a coach could get a contract and he couldn't.

I asked him, "Sir, how many people watch you give a final exam? Fifty thousand people watch me give one." I have never felt for a minute that football is the reason an institution exists, or that it is the most important reason. But I don't doubt its importance as a rallying point. It's pretty tough to rally around a math class.

I was due in College Station at 4:00 P.M. on February 8, at the little Easterwood Airport there. You could throw a rock from the airport to Kyle Field, where the Aggies played. The flight out of Cincinnati was full, however, and Bob Rule, the sports editor of the *Houston Press*, which has since gone out of business, had a seat and I didn't.

I tried to talk him out of it. He said, "You don't think I'm going to stay in Cincinnati and let all the other Texas writers greet you in College Station, do you?"

So I was bumped to a later flight and got in around eight. There must have been three thousand Cadets there, and half of them escorted me to the Memorial Student Center where they had hotel rooms. I was trying to register, and they were crowding around, and I made several false starts with the pen. The "address" part threw me.

Finally I put down, "Paul W. Bryant, Texas A&M, College Station, Texas." The Aggies loved it.

They took me over to the Grove outdoor theater where they have their Twelfth Man yell sessions. Jones Ramsey, the publicity director, coached me on what to do when I faced those Aggies, five thousand of them, all suited up and screaming.

I took off my coat and stomped on it.

Then I took off my tie and stomped on it.

Then as I was walking up to the mike I rolled up my sleeves.

It was like voodoo. Those Aggies went crazy. I was awed, I'll tell you. Ten Aggies can yell louder than a hundred of anybody else.

I brought in Phil Cutchin, Jerry Claiborne, Jim Owens, Elmer Smith and Pat James as assistant coaches, and Smokey Harper, who had been with me at Kentucky, as my trainer, and interviewed everybody who was already on the payroll, keeping them or firing them on the strength of the interview. I kept one coach, Willie

Zapalac, who was young and, as the saying goes, didn't have a petition out with the players. Willie was eager to learn, and he was obviously going somewhere. He's Darrell Royal's offensive coordinator at Texas now.

I asked Babe Parilli to come help teach our quarterbacks the split-T in the spring. Babe stayed with Smokey Harper. Smokey was about as lonesome as he could be. He didn't have a driver's license and he was always calling Jones Ramsey to come get him.

I was staying at the student center, too, waiting for Mary Harmon to move our belongings from Kentucky, but I didn't have time to get lonely. At spring practice we were even having trouble getting the ball from center. Our quarterbacks kept fumbling it, and I finally went over to Mississippi State and asked Royal, who was an assistant there at the time but had been Bud Wilkinson's quarterback at Oklahoma, to give me some help. I spent three days with him on it.

After about ten days of practice even my staff was moping around, feeling sorry for what they'd gotten into. We had 115 players on scholarship, and not many of them impressed anybody. I tried to list the players I thought were as good as some of my Kentucky All-Americans, but that didn't cheer anybody up. If you can't even snap the ball from center you're in pretty sad shape.

Ramsey came into my office. By now I was lonely, and upset, too, because I'd just gotten word that a friend's son had died in Kentucky. Jones said he'd handle the condolences for me, and he kind of hemmed and hawed around, standing on one foot and then the other.

Finally I said, "Dammit, Jones, if you're trying to invite me to dinner, I accept."

We went to his house and polished off a bottle of bourbon. I'm a Scotch drinker myself, but Jones couldn't beg any in the neighborhood, and he came up with the bourbon. I made believe I didn't know the difference. We drowned our sorrows pretty good, and I think I converted old Jones that night. We talked about four hours. Years later, before he went to Texas to be Darrell's PR man, he named his last son after me.

Well, I'll get into tough football and hard work — what some coaches call "brutality" — in more detail later, but I tell you that first year was brutal. We could hardly get anybody to come to A&M,

and I know some of our alumni went out and paid a few boys. We did get hundreds of high school coaches in there to watch our practices and to sell prospects on our program. That was important, because a good high school coach does more real coaching and recruiting than anybody.

Now they've got an athletic dormitory with a swimming pool and everything, but then life was really Spartan. If you got a boy into A&M and kept him there, you could get more out of him, because there was nothing to do except study and play football and maybe go to some little old Mexican joint across the street for a bowl of chili.

If we couldn't do anything else, we could work. You could set your watch by my schedule, beginning with six o'clock breakfast at the Twelfth Man Inn at the North Gate. I never had a staff that recruited so hard with such discouraging results. I sent Elmer Smith to Alabama late that summer, trying to find out who was signed and who wasn't. He called from an all-star game, and he was low.

I said, "Are there *any* that aren't signed, any who can play?"

"Yeah, there's one."

"Then sign him."

"Well, coach, there is one thing. He's only got one arm."

I said, "Damn, the pickin's *are* slim." Elmer signed him anyway. He was Murray Trimble, and he made All-Conference guard his sophomore year and his brother Wayne later played for us at Alabama.

It was a short summer. I knew we had a lot to do, and the way those Aggie Exes and various hangers-on were coming around putting their two cents in, I knew I had to get us away from College Station. Willie Zapalac suggested Junction. I had never heard of it, but it won the Southwest Conference championship for us two years later.

Junction is a flyspeck on the map out in the hill country near Kerrville. It housed the summer training program for the A&M physics and geology majors. A perfect spot for a boot camp. We were there for ten days, living in those old Quonset huts, which were no more than cement floors, wooden walls four feet high, then screening and tenting on top. The facilities were so sorry that just looking at the place would discourage you.

The players who were with us took pride in how tough it was. A lot of them — Jack Pardee, Charlie Krueger, Bebes Stallings, John Crow — sit around now, laughing and lying and telling big stories. And to tell the truth if I had a kid now I would like him to go through what they did, that's how strongly I believe in it. The twenty-seven who stuck it out will be more proud of that than anything they do in their entire lives.

The only thing we had at Junction that you could call first class was the food. There was plenty of that. We practiced early in the morning, at 5 A.M., and late in the afternoon, to beat the heat, and there was a little swimming hole they could go to, but there wasn't any entertainment outside of having Mickey Herskowitz there.

Mickey was on his first big assignment for the *Houston Post* and he and Jones had a room that was really just a division at the back of the Quonset hut where the coaches met. Our coaches' meetings were pretty lively. I let them yell at one another, and I'd referee, and Mickey and Jones would eavesdrop. The afternoon after our first practice we were meeting and Mickey was dictating his story to Houston on the phone. There wasn't any Western Union.

I could hear him through the partition. He was saying, "Jack, they had a full-scale scrimmage, the very first thing, and guys were throwing up all over the place, and the trainer was working his butt off . . ." And then he started dictating the story.

I hushed up the coaches and listened, then went outside and around the little rock path to Mickey and Jones's room, walked in, and sat there while he finished up. I could see he wasn't too pleased to see me.

He hung up and I said, "Now, Mickey, you know that story's going to upset a lot of mamas and papas when they read it."

"Yessir."

"And it's so unnecessary. That was no full-scale scrimmage. That was no more than a dummy scrimmage. Don't you think you ought to call your paper and tell them what really happened?"

Mickey had a hard time convincing his office to change his lead, but he got it changed.

Part of the reason the upperclassmen left Junction was the very fact that it was a new regime. A change is going to disrupt anybody, and a radical change is going to discourage a lot of people. We were

130

a change, and I told them it made sense to quit if they couldn't adapt.

We took two full busloads to Junction that September, and came back with less than half a load. Twenty-nine boys.

When the press tour finally got out there — Junction wasn't exactly on the beaten track, and those writers came in there with flat tires and sand in their throats and half hung over — they couldn't understand what had happened to all of us. Every day Jones had been calling Dallas to announce the latest defections, and every night we were counting heads to see who sneaked out, and the day the writers got there we were eight fewer than we had been the night before.

Jones cut a stencil of the roster sideways on an 8½ x 11 piece of paper. Blackie Sherrod, the Dallas writer, said it was the only roster in America you could do that with.

Well, when you're teaching a boy to work for the first time in his life and teaching him to sacrifice and suck up his guts when he's behind, which are lessons he has to learn sooner or later, you are going to find boys who are not willing to pay the price. Those sophomores who went with us to Junction must have been impressed with something because five of the eight are coaching now.

When I finally got us training table privileges I put it on a merit basis. I remember, our first game that year Texas Tech beat the devil out of us, and on Monday I only had five boys on training table. One of them was Bebes Stallings, who became the head coach at A&M after being my assistant at Alabama for seven years. Bebes is with the Cowboys now. It was just like the time Coach Hank Crisp got up and bragged on me and got me to play when I had a broken bone in my leg.

I said, "Gentlemen" — Bebes talks about this all the time — "we're just going to have people at that table who will go all out and be proud of that uniform and make us proud he's wearing it, and this little old skinny boy here" — I pointed to Stallings — "is going to be one of them."

After you get to know your material you are pretty sure who is going to quit and who isn't — I mean quit on the field, where it matters — and you have to be prepared for it. A lot of times I have been wrong. Most of the boys who quit the squad usually do it at the beginning of fall practice, when it's hot, or as soon as they see they're not going to play. Many of them have the guts to tell you, "It just doesn't mean enough to me anymore," and some come back — or try to — within a week.

I've dealt with them in a lot of ways. When a kid looked like he might not be good enough to play I used to order my coaches to push him harder, to see if he'd improve or throw in, to conserve time. We've gone the opposite way lately. Work the better boys harder and give the lesser ones a chance to mature. That way you don't get as much discouragement, and you keep more.

But there's one thing about quitters you have to guard against, they are contagious. If one boy goes, the chances are he'll take somebody with him, and you don't want that. So when they would start acting that way I used to pack them up and get them out, or embarrass them, or do something to turn them around.

It's always sad, really, because if a kid quits I've got to feel I've failed — not him or his daddy or anybody else, but me. I've failed by selecting him in the first place, or by not handling him right.

We were losing all those boys at Junction that year, and I had been trying to embarrass this big old center into becoming something besides deadweight. He had made All-Conference the year before, but we graded the films and he didn't grade higher than 37 percent in any of them.

I'd told Jones Ramsey to be prepared. We had graded those films, wore 'em out grading 'em, and the sight of the center wallowing around made me mad. We were across the street from the campus, at the White Way Cafe, having some turnip greens and chicken-fried steak. It was a beer joint, really, but the little Greek guy who ran it could make good cornbread and homemade gravy and we used to go over there and eat a whole loaf of bread and that gravy in one sitting.

Ramsey had come in, and I said, "Jones, if So-and-So makes All-Conference again this fall, your ass is fired." I didn't want that fat-ass center getting any unnecessary publicity.

Jones said, "Yessir."

The thing was the boy could have been a good football player, and I was after him. And right in the middle of practice he started walking off the field. I didn't know what to do. Never had had that happen, because most boys quit where they won't be noticed.

I said, "Young man, where you going?"

No answer.

"You better think about it now."

He didn't say a word, just kept walking.

Well, when we got back to the place that night and lined up to eat he was first in line. Big sonofagun, and I was scared of him, too.

I said, "Young fella, you must be making a mistake. A&M football players eat here."

"You mean I can't eat here?"

"I mean exactly that. You can't ever eat here again."

He turned and left, and about ten o'clock Benny Sinclair, our captain, came and asked me to take him back.

I think I won Benny right there. I said, "Benny, I'm not going to take him back. He's quit before, hasn't he?"

He said, "Yessir, lots of times."

I said, "This is the last time. We want players we can count on. We've got a long way to go, and we don't want anybody laying down once we get started."

The next day the headlines are this big. We'd fired an All-Conference center. And about five o'clock that morning I looked up and here come five more of them, all centers, a delegation of them, which means I won't have a center left.

I didn't give them a chance to say anything, just walked up and said, "Good morning, gentlemen," and shook their hands right down the line. "Good-bye, good-bye, bless your hearts, good-bye."

So we called a squad meeting. I said, "Fellows, there ain't many of us left. We're not faint-hearted, but we're in a helluva fix. It's not worrying me, because I know the kinda folks I got left. We'll do all right, but we gotta have somebody to snap the ball back. Anybody ever play center?"

No, sir.

I said, "Well, does anybody want to play center?"

And I'll never forget it. Lloyd Hale, a little old sophomore guard, stood up and said, "I will *play* center," and outside of Paul Crane he was the best offensive center I ever had.

Lloyd's legs weren't any longer than a midget's, which is good because you want a long-bodied center with short legs, and he was quick as a cat. And smart — he's making his fortune with a big oil company now. And Lloyd played every minute of every game and as a senior made All-Conference unanimously.

Fifteen

Dennis Goehring was one of those we took to Junction and hoped wouldn't stay. He was just a little bitty guard, and Smokey Harper was afraid he'd get killed. Smokey wasn't the type of trainer who cried over spilt blood. He was always saying, "Take a hot shower, you'll be all right," when somebody had a complaint. But he was a fine trainer, as Jimmy Goosetree is for us now, and he knew a boy's capacity.

Smokey advised Goehring to give it up, and Dennis doesn't know this but Smokey came and told me his reply. Smokey was grinning. He said Dennis looked him right in the eye and said he wouldn't quit. He said, "I'll be here when you and Bryant are *both* gone." And he is. He's president of the A&M Bank at College Station right now, and I've got stock in it.

There's a sequel to the story that has to be told, because it involves one of my all-time favorite players. Charlie Krueger was in that group. He had come out of Caldwell, Texas, where he lived on a sharecropper's farm that belonged to one of my rich friends, Marvin Porter. All the windows in Charlie's house were covered with croaker sacks, that's how poor he was.

I'll never forget the first day I saw him. Marvin came to a baseball game we were having and I saw this big old skinny-legged blond boy with him and I immediately made room in the stands. He was so humble and so eager. He only had one scholarship offer, from Houston. I was willing to give him a one-year deal and take our chances. Marvin said Houston had offered him four years. He said Charlie's daddy didn't have enough to make it if anything went wrong.

I said all right, four years. And we shook hands.

Krueger was 6–6, and skinny. But when we started feeding him he filled out nice, and by his sophomore year he looked like a million dollars. So a coach from another school came in there and stole him from us. I was mad enough to spit in his eye. I told Elmer Smith, "If that's the way he's going to be, let him go."

And Elmer Smith, a very wise man, said, "Coach, when I was his age in his kinda fix, I'd have gone, too."

This was on a weekend. That afternoon Dennis Goehring and Dee Powell came to my house. Dennis had the guts of a burgler. He said, "Let me go after him." The next day they drove up with Charlie.

He was ashamed, and so honest explaining why he did it. They had offered him an automobile and this that and the other, and the guarantee he would play regularly. He apologized and I let him come back, and all he did was make All-America for us and all-pro for the San Francisco 49ers, who thought enough of him to retire his number. He and Bob Gain were the best tackles I ever had. Every time I see him now he blushes and laughs as if it all happened yesterday.

We took those twenty-seven little boys to Athens to play Georgia the third game that first year. Old Lloyd Hale wasn't much for long snapbacks, so we had our manager suited up to center the ball for fourth-down punts. Harry Mehre and Ed Danforth of the Atlanta papers didn't believe what they saw.

"You mean this is all the players you got?"

I said, "No, these are the ones that want to play."

And damned if they didn't beat Georgia 6–0, the only game we won all year.

I'll tell you how we did it, because Wally Butts never did forgive me. Butts and I had become friends when I was at Kentucky. When we'd take a team to Athens he had Winnie fix me black-eyed peas and corn bread, and when he came to Lexington all I could find was some bananas and milk, and we'd lay on the floor and pick each other's brains and eat those bananas. One year he was about a 20-point favorite and we beat Georgia, 25-0. He blamed it on the food.

Anyway, Georgia had us outmanned. We didn't have any players. But we did have an exchange film of the Georgia team. Elmer Smith must have looked at it five thousand times.

In the middle of one showing Elmer snapped his fingers. "Hey, I got something."

He said by watching the Georgia quarterback's feet he could call every play except one, the draw play. If the quarterback's feet were parallel to the line he was going to hand off. If one was behind the other it was a pass, and the foot to the rear would be the direction he was going. We watched, and Elmer was right.

I had Jack Pardee calling defensive signals. Jack watched the quarterback's feet, and called out our defenses accordingly. It worked almost every time. Georgia made a lot of yards but they didn't score. And in the middle of the third quarter we hit Pardee with a little pass and he ran for a touchdown, and that was all there was to it. Smokey Harper and I danced a jig in the dressing room after the game.

Later I went around and told Wally about his quarterback's feet, but he didn't appreciate it. On Monday I called him and told him again. He gave me a quick brushoff. He wasn't happy at all about being the only team our little boys had whipped, so I said the hell with it, let him find his own mistakes.

I know that for a losing coach I stepped on a lot of toes that year, and did it deliberately. The first chance I had to speak to an alumni group I stuck my chin out at those Aggies and said, "Up to now, we've had too many chiefs and not enough Indians around here. From now on I'm the chief and you're the Indians. I know how to coach football. You may think you do, but I *know* I do. So I don't need your advice."

That caused a stir, but I was just warming up.

I'd been there only a couple of weeks when a man in a big black Cadillac drove up and got out, together with five boys he had in the car. He said he was from Palestine, in East Texas, and he had brought me some prospects. Elmer Smith had just gotten back from a recruiting trip to Palestine and the coach there told him there were no prospects in the area.

I figured this guy was looking for something.

I said, "Well, if thin shoulders and a skinny tail will get the job done you got five All-Americans," and turned and walked away. The man never came back.

The only team that beat us badly was Texas Tech, 41–9, in that opener when we fumbled ten times. Nobody can win that way. But we kept hanging in there, and the well-wishers kept deserting us. So one Sunday I called in Jones Ramsey and said I wanted him to send out a release.

I said, "Tell them when I started last spring I got a lot of nice alumni coming around asking me 'How's our team doing, Coach?' They still come around, but now they say, 'How's your team, Coach?' Well, I want them to know I accept this team. It's mine now, and I'm proud of every player on it. And if I catch any one of them not giving 100 percent they will be disassociated immediately from the outfit."

Jones said, "Gol-lee, Coach, that's great. How did you ever think of that?"

I said, "I didn't. Frank Howard said that years ago at Clemson. I was borrowing it."

I don't know how my assistants stood it, as touchy as I was. Elmer Smith said I made a nervous wreck out of Pat James.

This is Elmer's story, not mine:

One morning we discussed moving a guard named Patterson to tackle. That afternoon when the coaches were dressing for practice I came in and dressed without a word, which, according to Elmer, was my usual way. Just as I was going out the door I turned and said, "I moved Patterson."

And Pat James said in a kinda flip way, "I'll buy that."

I reopened the door and stuck my nose in and said, "I don't give a goddamn if you buy it or not," and slammed it again.

Elmer said Pat got up, opened the door, looked down the hall to see if I'd gone, then closed and locked it, and got down in a lineman's stance and said, "One of these days I'm going home and lock myself in the closet and cuss hell out of that sonofabitch!"

You say, but what kind of coaching is that when you create all that animosity, and wind up with 27 boys out of 115 and a lot of damaged egos?

For one thing, I have to believe I wouldn't lose that many today, because I'm not the driver I was and I probably don't demand as much, but let me tell you that was the beginning of a change in attitude at A&M.

It was never easy, though. The press was on me from the start, and some of the stuff that came out of Fort Worth and other cities was brutal. One columnist quoted me as boasting I could "win any reporter with a bottle of booze and a steak." Well, I didn't win him until the day he died, and didn't try because he was on my butt all the time. I had unintentionally snubbed him once when I was at Kentucky and he came up for a Texas A&M game. Mary Harmon and I were going to dinner with Governor Weatherby and I invited Bill Rives, the Dallas writer, and didn't invite the writer from Fort Worth. Whether he held it against me or not I'll never know, but he made it plain in miles of print that he disliked me.

But I have to give him credit. After we beat TCU down there one year, he said, "I don't like the sonofabitch, but he can coach."

Being at A&M is double rough because not only is everybody against you, thinking you deserve to be on the bottom, being an Aggie, but you don't have a big newspaper to defend you. No big city daily like the *Dallas News* or the *Houston Post*. You're stuck out there, and you're fair game.

The thing I resented most was that every time something came up, usually at recruiting time or before a big game, a rumor would start about us going on probation, or after we were on probation, about staying there. Or silly stuff, like "Bryant's going to move the press box from the east side to the west." Anything to foul us up.

After that one year at Junction the conference put in a rule against off-campus training sites. You don't think that was harassment? The week of the Texas game in 1956, when we were undefeated, I said to the team in private, "If we win the conference championship, which I know you're going to do, I have arranged for a game with the University of Hawaii in Honolulu." Which I had. "If they don't want us to go to a bowl, we'll have a bowl, our own bowl."

Two days later the headlines in the paper were a foot tall:

SOUTHWEST CONFERENCE SAYS A&M CAN'T GO TO HONOLULU. Boy, I tell you it was brutal. I wound up with a mad on for every coach in the league. They were out to get me, and I thought there was a lot of hypocritical stuff going on. I hated all of them. I hated Jess Neely of Rice more, but I got over it and later we invested in some land together.

I made up my mind early I was going to beat them or kill myself trying. Looking back, and knowing how much we made them swallow — the idea of losing to A&M — I have to admit I would probably have done the same thing in their position.

We'd put them to work, no doubt about that. Our first recruiting year we got two star players from outside Texas, a rarity at A&M, and some of the better backs *in* Texas, and the freshman team won the SWC freshman title. That winter we outrecruited everybody in the state. There was no way for that to go down easy. Somebody wrote, "Bryant has been brazenly, insultingly successful." They couldn't stand it.

A couple years later even *Life* came out and did a big spread on us, the way we'd shook up the Southwest Conference. I told them my system was based on the "ant plan," that I'd gotten the idea watching a colony of ants in Africa during the war. A whole bunch of ants working toward a common goal.

I know now we should have been put on probation. I know, too, I was not just trying to justify it in my mind when I said that if we were paying players, then other schools were doing it twice as bad, which some were. I'm not going to go soft on that point.

I'm not sure how many of our boys got something; I guess about four or five did. I didn't know what they got, and I didn't want to know, but they got something because they had other offers and I told my alumni to meet the competition.

Bob Manning, a quarterback, and Tom Sestak, a lineman, signed affidavits that they got $200 to sign and $50 a month over tuition. They said they didn't want to go to A&M anymore. Coaches from Baylor and Texas helped them file. One of the coaches was J. T. King, who later came to work for me. Sestak wound up at Baylor, and I don't know what he got to go there. He made a good pro lineman. Ten years later, Charley Waller, who as an assistant at Texas had gotten Manning to sign the affidavit, told me, "Bear, you must hate my guts, but I had to do what I did. I'm ashamed of it now, but I had to do it."

One boy said he was promised a job for his brother when he got out of the service. One said he had been promised a down payment on a car, and help if he couldn't make the payments. One said he was promised an apartment if he got married, rent-free. I'm not suggesting they were lying, because I don't know exactly what they got or were offered, and I'm not going to hem and haw as if I weren't responsible. It was my program, so I'm responsible.

I have never thought you could have a bunch of hired football players. Maybe you can have two or three or four getting something extra. I've had them, but you can usually tell one of them a block away, the way he goes about things, the way he puts out. If an alumnus working such and such a place finds he's losing a boy he might give him something, but he'll usually tell you, too, because he wants you to know what he thinks he's doing for you.

It's mighty hard to turn something down if you've never had anything. I can understand that, and it's hard for the parents, too. Back when I played it was nickel and dime stuff, and there were no rules. No NCAA investigations, anyway. It was all kind of loose and unrestrained. Bobby Dodd and Ray Graves used to joke about Tennessee's "pay scale," the first team getting so much, the second so much, and there was supposed to be a guy at the bank handling it.

At Alabama the only one I know who got anything to speak of was Dixie Howell. One summer he wanted a suit of clothes, and he said if he didn't get it he wasn't coming back. That sonofagun wouldn't have, either. The rest of us more or less depended on Coach Hank's roll of ones.

After the war it was no longer a laughing matter. You were faced with it all the time — I told you about that $500 checkstub I found after I got robbed of those two boys at Kentucky — and there had to be some legislation.

But by today's standards it was piddling. It's worse than ever now.

A coach recently told me of a certain institution that gave a boy $15,000, or the equivalent of it, and still lost him to another school. I know the name of another that offered a boy $48,000 over a four-year period, and lost him. He must have gone pretty high. The athletic departments aren't doing it, of course, because that would be suicide. They couldn't afford it anyway. They let the alumni do it.

The commissioner's office told me of a boy with seven brothers and sisters, the family on relief. He suddenly showed up driving a new LTD. The investigator checked it out and found a cash payment of $1,400, and $110 monthly installments being made. It doesn't take a Philadelphia lawyer to figure that one out.

I have personally had boys tell me what they were getting, and I wouldn't touch them with a ten-foot pole. A lot of it is big talking, of course. I'm not a freshman on the subject. I know a kid likes to big-dog himself, tell everybody how much he's getting, and about half of what they say is right. But half is still a lot.

I don't know why the cheating has gotten so bad again, unless it's a product of all we read about on the front page, or inflation. But it has. And it's not just the young coaches trying to make their mark, it's the older ones, too. Frank Broyles told me it was the worst he'd ever seen, and Joe Paterno is quoted saying the same. Darrell Royal says it. I say it. The NCAA has heard about it. The SEC commissioner knows about it.

Can anything be done about it? Sure. Do a net worth on every kid and his parents when he's in the eleventh grade — I'm talking about the kid who is a skilled athlete, the one schools are going to be after — and then do another net worth on them when he's a junior in college and see what they have earned in the meantime. That includes clothes, automobiles, everything. You would either end the gossip or find some interesting things.

Can the NCAA do such a thing? Hell, yes, if they want to. And if they get a boy or a school who won't tell where the goodies came from, or if they turn out to be crooks, ban the boy for life and ban the coach, too. Make 'em both ineligible. A kid knows. A parent knows. An alumnus knows when he gives something. But nothing happens to them.

It's stupid to punish the school. Some people who cheat want to win, period. They don't care if they're on probation, they just want to beat somebody's tail. Ban that kid for life, and kick the coach out of the conference, and you won't have to ban anymore. You'll put the fear of God in them.

Sixteen

At A&M I don't know whether we would have won or not without paying players, but I'll say this, most of the kids didn't play like they got something.

After we got put on probation I told our people — our alumni, *everybody* — if there was any doubt in my mind about a boy getting something, we weren't going to play him. I'll never forget a boy we signed right after that. There was a question in my mind about him, because my wife got close to the family and the mother confided in her what another school had offered.

I called the alumnus in that area and told him, "Don't lie to me, don't put me on the spot. If that boy's getting something I want to know it."

He swore he wasn't.

Well, the day I left A&M he was driving me out to the airport.

He said, "Bear, remember the time you questioned me about that boy, and I told you I didn't give him anything?"

I said, "Yeah."

He said, "Well, I told you a damned lie."

When I came to Alabama in 1958 I told the people here we wouldn't cheat, that we wouldn't violate the rules or let anybody else do it, and we'd adhere to the spirit of the rules, which we have and our kids know it. I inherited one boy who some alumni were paying and I put a stop to it. The boy grumbled around that he was going to quit if he didn't get paid. He didn't say anything to me because he didn't know I knew.

I waited till all the boys were in the dressing room, and then I walked over to this one and said, "Ray" — that's not his name — "Ray, I understand you're going to quit if you don't get your money."

I said, "You're not going to get your money. Nobody's going to get any money. If you're unhappy about it I'll help you pack right now and you can be out of here in no time."

He nearly fainted. He stuttered anyway, and he couldn't get a word out. But I'll tell you something. He stayed, and was a fine athlete, and turned out to be a fine young man. He's coaching now, and one of these days he may be working for me.

Lately, when we play certain teams and they have boys who wanted to come to Alabama, I tell my kids the only reason they aren't with us is that they're getting something, but that I believe the game means more to our boys than it does to theirs.

I always try to point out to the good ones that the money, or the automobile, or whatever it is that jeopardized their chances won't be anything later on to compare with an education. And winning. This may sound ironic but Joe Namath helped us get a boy one year who was being offered things. Joe told him that that $4,000 automobile was nothing to what playing and going to school at Alabama could do for him later on.

I had another prospect, a quarterback whose parents were Alabama graduates, tell me he'd wanted to play here all his life. He said, "All my life that's been my ambition." Two days later he went somewhere else, so what am I supposed to think? That his lifetime ambition died in two days? We beat him three years in a row, too.

I don't mean to make Alabama sound like some kind of sanctuary or something. I'm sure if I said, the way I used to, "I need this boy," we'd get him — our alumni would — with whatever it took. I've had some of my people beg to buy players who were being offered something somewhere else, and if I were a young coach starting out I might give in, but I'm not going to now.

I don't have to, and I wouldn't, and it's not worth it. The ones who do it for you eventually want something in return, and I came to the conclusion about 1953 or 1954 that I could do without that. I don't think I've done too badly since then. You get a little older, you recognize the fact you may be a little sounder, you might be able to outcoach somebody. If we have one who's getting so much as a penny now I'll eat your tie, but we're beating teams I *know* are paying.

We were at Houston in May 1955 for the league meeting when the affidavits came to my desk. Jim Owens was with me, and the night before the story broke we had our meeting of athletic directors. I wanted to talk about this thing, but all those guys wanted to do was play poker.

We were at the Rice Hotel in Houston, playing quarter limit, and I hated that because you play all night with a quarter limit. I can still see old D. X. Bible, deliberating over whether to throw in a quarter or not. I kept agitating to discuss the affidavits I'd seen.

Howard Grubbs of the SWC, who's a good fellow and does a good job but then was just on the wrong side, said, "We can't discuss any business here tonight."

I said, "Well, I *want* to."

And he said, "We can't, period."

So we played cards all night long — D. X. Bible, Matty Bell, Dutch Meyer, Jess Neely and John Barnhill. George Sauer played awhile, but he was scared the Baptists would catch him and he quit.

At 8 A.M. we broke up, and John Barnhill of Arkansas and I went down to breakfast to have some cereal. Barney always had to have that cereal. He leaned over and said, "Bear, you know we do what we want to at Arkansas —" I knew, all right, because I'd seen the books when they were after me to coach there. "— but they got you. They're going to cut your guts out. It's been going on for years, but they got you now and they're going to stick it to you and you just gotta face it."

So I went up to my room with Owens, and it was already on the radio and TV and everything: A&M is going on a two-year probation for recruiting violations. The league had already had its meeting and decided it, and the athletic directors knew it even before we sat down to play cards. Our athletic committeeman hadn't told me; he had just gone on home.

I doubt any team that lost nine out of ten games ever got put on probation before. They canceled our letters of intent and denied us the use of the letters during the probation, and they barred us from postseason participation in all sports, which meant, as it turned out, we never got to the Cotton Bowl while I was there, though we won the conference championship.

They reprimanded Pat Jones, too, and one of our alumni got blackballed. The ruling said if any boy got caught talking to him the boy would be ineligible. The alumnus was one who had made the payoffs to Manning and Sestak, and when the decision first came out he denied it and I tried to get him to sue the conference. He said, "Well, Bear, I got a family . . ." I knew then he had lied.

Well, Jim drove and I cried all the way back to A&M. At six o'clock I had to make a banquet speech, and I got up and said something about when the going is tough the tough get going, and I was tough and a going sonofagun, and I started crying again, and the Aggies went wild.

That night I had my weekly television show. The Aggies paid for it because I couldn't sell it to anybody. Lloyd Gregory, the old sports editor of the *Houston Post*, was my co-host, and he had guts coming out of his ears.

He said, "I want to talk to you Texas and Rice people. I've been in this league thirty-five years and everything you're accusing this boy of doing you've done ten to one."

He even named some names of the players he had bought for Rice.

He said, "Imagine some of you sons——, some of you gentlemen trying to crucify this boy! You've been doing it, and I know because I've been a part of it."

After the show Jess Neely called him to complain, and Lloyd chewed Neely out, too.

They talked a lot to those boys who quit in the next few weeks, and that made the whole program look bad. But when they invalidated those letters of intent they left us wide open for a wholesale walkout — and not one more left us. Every one of them wired or called or came in and said, "I'm staying," and "I'll be there in the fall." Nobody bothered to talk to them. I guess it's true that it's not news if you *don't* rob a bank. The quitters got the headlines.

146

But I wish they'd asked Crow or Krueger or Bebes Stallings if it was worth it. Not just then but afterward, when they had to go out and scratch for something.

The A&M administration came to my defense and Lorin Mc-Mullen of the *Fort Worth Star Telegram* really took after us.

He said it was "regrettable that a few A&M people cling to the belief that they are responsible for and honor bound to support this professional from the scandalized Kentucky campus who had distorted their aims, mocked their spirit and severed their unity."

Well, the only spirit we disturbed was the peace of mind of the rest of these coaches, because we challenged them and they couldn't stand it. I don't deny we dumped over private apple carts. We attacked geographical spheres of influence. We darned near ruined their recruiting programs. It was a personal vendetta they had waged against me, in the press and by rival coaches, and I made up my mind I'd take it out of their hides.

It wasn't all war, of course. Some of it was even funny. Morris Frank, the Houston columnist and master of ceremonies, came to our defense whenever he had the chance. He'd say, "Look at that poor old John David Crow, having to drive around in that little old Oldsmobile. You know there's nothing crooked about him. As good as he is he could have a Cadillac." And that's right.

Elmer Smith had recruited Crow for us. Out of Louisiana. Crow's brother had played for Elmer in high school and loved him. When Elmer said, "I'll get Crow," I didn't realize he could.

John David was anybody's type of kid. His son Johnny is on my squad now and reminds me a lot of him. When Elmer brought me films of John David in high school it was like watching a grown man play with children.

One side of his face was paralyzed from the time he was four, but he never let anybody feel uncomfortable about it. He was still a big, fine-looking, blond-haired boy. He had married his high school sweetheart, which didn't hurt him any. Mary Harmon and I practically adopted him and Carolyn. I told him they could have a key to my house, a key to my pool, and Mother would give them a key to her Cadillac.

Crow had so much pride. He would never let you have a bad practice. When we were wallowing around doing nothing I'd make some sarcastic remark to him or Charlie Krueger and they'd get everybody riled up and make things happen. That's pride.

Despite everything that had happened, I knew with players like Crow and Krueger and Stallings we would win even the next year. Even after UCLA beat us 21–0 in that first game. UCLA was the defending national champion, and Red Sanders had one of his best teams, so it was no disgrace.

I now had what they called my "bottle babies," the good ones I had recruited that first winter, and they were maturing fast. That week LSU beat the Kentucky team I'd left behind, and the next Saturday night in Dallas we played LSU.

I don't ordinarily do much pep-talking on game day, but I did that night. I said, "I want every one of you gentlemen to come by me on your way out, and shake hands and look in that mirror, because when you come back in here tonight you're going to look in it again. You'll have to decide then if you gave your best. And every morning you shave from now on you're going to think about giving your best, because I'm going to make you. I'm going to be reminding you."

I wasn't interested in "not being disgraced" anymore. We were one and ten. I wanted to beat somebody.

It wasn't all that pretty, but we beat LSU, 28–0. We ran a trap play and both guards pulled and ran head-on into one another. Somehow Crow busted through the mess and ran 81 yards for a touchdown. He must have shook off fifteen tackles, the greatest single run I ever saw.

And when he came back to the bench he patted everybody on the back. "Great blocking, boys. Great blocking." Ain't nobody blocked anybody, but he was giving them the credit.

I knew then we were on our way. We didn't lose another game until the last one, against Texas. And we tied Arkansas, the defending conference champion.

With Crow mainly responsible, we beat Arkansas two in a row after that. I'll never forget the last one because I thought I'd finally come to gettin' day.

We were staying in Fort Smith the night before, because there are no good hotels in Fayetteville, and about 1 A.M. I woke up wringing wet, with pains in my chest. I knew I was having a heart attack.

I called Dr. Harrison, the team physician, and he came to the room and examined me.

"I don't think you've had any heart attack," he said. He gave me something to make me sleep. I took it but I couldn't sleep. I was scared I'd die. I got up and put on my britches and walked the streets the rest of the night.

The next morning I felt better, and we got on the plane for the fifteen-minute flight to Fayetteville. I was sitting with Roddy Osborne, my quarterback. And we couldn't land. We were in a holding pattern. Fayetteville isn't exactly O'Hare Field, but traffic control wasn't as sophisticated as it is now. We kept flying around and passed over the stadium, and I could see it was already full. I went up and asked the pilot what was going on and he said, "There's nothing we can do. We gotta wait our turn."

We were still up there when Arkansas came out to warm up. When we finally landed I made the bus driver drive as fast as he could on the wrong side of the street. He was a nice old gentleman, but he didn't like that too much. I told him if he got stopped just to refer the police to me, that I'd take full responsibility.

We made it three minutes before the kickoff. All we had time to do was jump up and down a few times. I had forgotten my heart attack, and I didn't have time to worry about it during the game. It was a heart-stopper, anyway. With less than a minute to play we were ahead, 7–0, and had the ball on the Arkansas 35. I sent in a run-the-clock-out play, actually an option pass, where we send one guy out and everybody else is supposed to block while the quarterback runs around using up time.

Roddy Osborne sprinted out and raised his arm, making believe he was going to throw to Crow, who was clear. There were only twenty-eight seconds left, and he wasn't going to throw it. He hesitated, then it looked so tempting he decided he'd kinda shot-put it to Crow. When he did an Arkansas defensive back named Moody, who was a sprinter, intercepted it and was immediately in the open field running wide open.

Osborne, who was no sprinter, ran him down from behind near our 20-yard line.

Then Crow made two of the greatest plays I've ever seen to save the game. Arkansas had the ball on our 14, after completing a pass to the side where they put out two receivers. Crow had made the tackle. He almost took the guy's head off.

Arkansas called time.

With five seconds left, they came back with the same play, which was smart. Crow was laying back there just coiled. The quarterback threw to the short man and Crow came up and tore the receiver loose from the ball, knocking it up in the air, and while he was twisted around he caught it himself in the end zone.

The next day Herman Heep, the president of Heep Oil Company and a dear friend, arranged to fly me to Houston to have my heart checked. They put me through every test known to man, and I barely got out of there in time to make my television show. I had those nitroglycerin pills and every time I'd get a flutter I'd pop one in my mouth.

That night Mary Harmon and I were at Johnny Mitchell's house — another friend who made a fortune in Texas, and lost a couple, too — for dinner and the doctor came and told me there wasn't a thing wrong with my heart. He said I was just a big fat hypochondriac, that's all, which I already knew. I know, too, if my heart was bad, I'da been dead before then, all I'd been through.

The next morning Bobby Dodd called from Georgia Tech. He had read about the game, and he said he couldn't understand it.

He said, "How in the world could a slow guy like Osborne catch a speed demon like that Moody."

I said, "The difference was that Moody was running for a touchdown. Osborne was running for his life."

—— Seventeen ——

As I said, they'd have given me a million dollars, those A&M people, if I could have guaranteed a Southwest Conference championship, so whatever I finally made in Texas — which wasn't a million by a long shot — they got their money's worth in 1956.

By that time the Texas Christian University game had taken on extra meaning for me because of the bad press I was getting in Fort Worth. They called me every kind of dirty name, and I'll never know why. Maybe because TCU had the best team in the conference during that period and we were challenging.

I didn't help us any when I went somewhere to have a couple drinks and got to sounding like those Aggies, telling people how we would beat TCU like a drum. Jim Shofner, who heads the TCU staff now and played on those teams, told me later if I had kept my mouth shut they wouldn't have been so mad to beat us.

The first year they had us 21–0 at the half, but had to hang on to win, 21–20. We had the ball when the game was over.

The next year TCU won the league, but we beat them, 19–13. I was prepared. I had a defense setup where Crow was going to guard Swink one-on-one. If Swink went to the bathroom Crow was going to be right next to him. And darned if on the third play of the game one of their guys hit Crow on the leg and injured him. He couldn't even get up, and there went my defense for Swink. So much for preparation.

In our championship year, 1956, we played them at College Station, but TCU was favored. It was a sellout, a beautiful sunny day, until just before the kickoff a tornado hit. The wind was actually blowing the rain horizontally, upwards of 50 miles an hour. The tornado struck at a nearby airport and damaged 150 private planes. The light poles were waving in the wind.

My captain was so fired up he didn't know where he was. TCU won the toss, elected to receive, and my captain chose the wrong goal. We not only had to kick off, we had to kick off into that wind. The ball wound up on the 50-yard line, and they didn't even have to touch it.

While the wind was blowing TCU got a touchdown, missed the point, and almost got another one. We stopped them less than a foot from the goal. There was a big fuss about it later. The TCU people claimed that the movies showed Swink had scored.

Midway the fourth quarter it suddenly quit blowing and raining, and the sun came out again. Just like before. Donny Watson intercepted a TCU pass in our end zone and we drove 80 yards for the touchdown that won the game, 7–6. The only pass we threw all day was Crow's little halfback floater to Watson for the touchdown.

When the game was over, Cliff Shaw, who was one of the top referees in the SWC and has retired now to his dairy in Little Rock, called Abe Martin and me to the center of the field and said, "Gentlemen, in all my years of officiating college football that was the hardest fought, cleanest game I've ever seen, and I want to congratulate you both."

We went unbeaten that year, though we were tied by Houston, and we polished it off with A&M's only victory ever over Texas at Memorial Stadium in Austin. There is a little sociology worth telling about that game, so bear with me.

The game was played on Thanksgiving, traditionally, and the A&M teams always went into Austin the night before with their suits of armor on, all charged up. Then after one look at those Texas coeds they'd go wild. They knew they were going to stay the night after the game, and they got inspired for the wrong reasons.

I said, unh-unh. No romancing this time. We'll just play and get out.

At game time the custom at Memorial Stadium was for the Texas band to blast you with "The Eyes of Texas Are Upon You" as you ran onto the field. The students raise hell, you hear that band, and you wet your pants six times before the kickoff.

I said, unh-unh. I don't want any eyes of Texas on *me*. If they insist on playing it we will wait till they finish before we go out.

I didn't take any chances. When we were dressed and ready, we waited. They sent a man in to get us.

I said, "I ain't heard 'The Eyes of Texas' yet. We ain't coming out till we hear it."

He left. And we waited.

They came and called us again.

I said, "As soon as they play that damn song and the Texas team is out there, we'll come."

They had to delay the kickoff, but we made them play it, and Texas was already on the field when we came out. They still looked eight feet tall to me, compared with our little boys. But I mean to tell you we ate 'em alive.

We had a 21–0 lead just before the half, and I took out my first team, which was stupid. Texas scored. But Jack Pardee ran the second-half kickoff back for a touchdown to cancel out my error.

Those darn Longhorns never did give up. Every time I tried to rest our first team they'd rally, and we were still battling at the finish, when it was 34–21.

Smokey Harper made the comment of the day. We always had a little silent prayer in the dressing room before a game, and right in the middle of it he raised up and said, "I hope you gentlemen pray you got some guts out there so we don't screw this thing up again, because we're better'n they are." We were, too.

After the game I told 'em we wouldn't go home that night after all. They could chase those girls as much as they wanted. They threw me in the shower and by the time I got out my ride had left and I had to walk three miles to town, dripping wet.

Mary Harmon wasn't there because she had pneumonia and had

stayed in College Station. She didn't know it but a delegation of Alabama alumni had come to see me at the hotel the night before, wanting me to come home to coach. When I got to the hotel those Aggies were crawling all over the place, and I was so happy I knew I couldn't leave. The next day Herman Heep took me hunting, and I promised him I wouldn't go to Alabama. Not then.

I tell you, there were a lot of wonderful people who stuck with us during that time, men who deserved to have a championship team to fluff their feathers over. Mr. Heep and Mr. Pat Zachry, a very wealthy alumnus, let me use their private planes, and Mr. Heep cut me in on an oil deal that I'll be getting checks from for years to come — not much money but a thoughtful gesture.

Mr. Heep was my best friend there. He's dead now but his wife Minnie Bell still lives on the big ranch twelve miles outside of Austin that got to be like another home to me. Mr. Heep had it all — big swimming pool, guest house, barber shop — on that ranch.

I'll never forget the first day I met him. He had never been active as an Aggie alumnus, and we wanted him to be. We were down in his guest house and he was telling me all about football, which is a typical Aggie.

Finally I said, "Mr. Heep, I didn't come way out here to ask you about football. That's something I know something about. I came out here to find out if you're with me."

He was a short little Dutchman, and he laughed and clapped and said, "Dammit, that's what I wanted to hear." And he stuck out his hand. "I'm with you." And he was.

He was always doing something. He called one time and said, "I'd like Mary Harmon to go with Minnie Bell to Acapulco. I think she's going to have a nervous breakdown if she doesn't get away, and she wants Mary Harmon to go with her."

The next day Minnie Bell called me and said, "Herman says you want me to take Mary Harmon to Acapulco. That she's about to have a nervous breakdown and has to get away."

I didn't let on. After we put them on the plane I went out to his ranch and we had some steaks and drank some whiskey, and at eleven o'clock he said, "How about going into business together?"

I said, "What kinda business?" I didn't have any money.

"Drill some oil wells."

I nearly puked. I had been that route and made nothing. But I wanted to humor him. I got my briefcase and got out a check. "How much is this going to cost?"

He said, "You dumb bastard, put that away. We're going to let the government pay for them."

So we went into business, on the spot, and ate our steaks, and about midnight the phone rang.

He said into the phone, "Well, isn't that great. Just great. I'll tell you, that is so great. Coach is going to be glad to hear that, too."

He hung up and said, "You got to be the luckiest sonofabitch that ever lived!"

I said, "How's that, Ludlow?" I always called him "Ludlow." His name was Herman Ludlow Heep and he didn't like that middle name much.

He said, "Those damn oil wells you just bought into done come in, and they're *dual*."

"What's that mean?"

"They're gas *and* oil."

It was a setup, of course, and I'll be getting those $25 and $35 monthly checks as long as I live.

It was the only money I ever made in Texas. I lost on some apartment houses I built, and I made some poor investments, two or three stock deals. Johnny Mitchell and I were together in a few things, and still are. Johnny had more money than a showdog could jump over. He once hit 151 straight wells, missed one, and hit 18 more. But he could lose it as fast as he made it.

If it weren't for Mr. Heep I would have been a washout in Texas. I went away owing him around $15,000. I said, "Ludlow, I can't pay you now, but I'll pay you in three months."

He said, "You should, to clear the books." He had loaned it to me interest-free.

I made the last payment two weeks before he died. He was in Honolulu and sick with hepatitis, and when he got back he got sicker and sicker. When he died Minnie Bell sold his plane to Lyndon Johnson. I was at the funeral. She told me one of the last things he said was "to make sure you get Paul to come out here and be president of my company."

She told him, "But, Herman, Paul doesn't know anything about the oil business."

And he said, "That's all right. He knows about people."

After we won the championship they wanted to give me a bonus. I said, no, just buy my house, which they did for about a $10,000 profit to me, with long-term capital gains tax. The Texas legislature made a big fuss over it after I left. Somebody claimed I received too much on the sale. It was a scrawny little old house, too. So they sent an internal revenue man to see me, and I wound up making another $800.

One more thing. They put in my contract that I would get a percentage of the gate — a little over 1 percent — for our 1957 home games. Worked out to about $5,000. I don't think any coach ever got that kind of deal before or since.

We would have won the National Championship in 1957 if it hadn't leaked out that I was going to Alabama. We started the season with a 21–13 victory over Jim Tatum's Maryland team, the defending champion, on national television in Dallas, and we knew we had something pretty good. If we could hold that Maryland team to 13 points nobody else would get many.

We won eight in a row, and we were number 1 in all the polls by a bushel of votes. Then, with Rice and Texas to play, word got out. Dr. Frank Rose, the Alabama president, began talking about "getting the greatest coach in America," and the Houston papers — Jack Gallagher of the *Post*, actually — put two and two together, and the day before the Rice game the story broke in big headlines: BEAR GOES TO BAMA.

The leak fouled up everything. We lost to Rice, 7–6, and then to Darrell Royal's first Texas team, 9–7, and instead of the National Championship and the Cotton Bowl we had to settle for a bid to play Tennessee in the Gator Bowl.

I had already told the athletic board of my decision to go. No, first I told Mr. Heep and he *helped* me tell them. We were going down to play Texas and I asked him to meet me at the airport. I told him what I planned to do.

He said, "What do you want, what will it take to make you stay?"

I said, "Ludlow, I don't want anything. I've just got to go. And I want you to help me." I had eight years left on my contract and I knew they would try to hold me to it.

He said, "I will." If he hadn't I don't think I would have got out of there alive. He was by far the most powerful man on the board, and he made them listen.

He said, "I'm convinced Paul is telling the truth. He's got to go, and you've got to let him go."

I was sitting right there. It was pretty damn sticky, I'll tell you.

Doc Doherty was probably more upset than anybody when I left. He was a fine man and was probably most responsible for my being there. He had me on his company payroll, and we were really close. When I told him I was leaving he couldn't understand it. "What do you want? What do you want?"

I said it wasn't the money. No one seemed to understand that, that there were things money couldn't buy.

Mr. Doherty just couldn't imagine me not wanting to be an Aggie anymore. I heard he got real bitter after that and made statements that the way I left was absurd, that I didn't treat them right. I wrote him a letter thanking him for all he had done and trying to explain how I felt, but I never received an answer.

The worst thing of all was going in there to tell my boys. I hadn't had to do that at Kentucky because they were away on vacation. I called them together in our meeting room beside the dining hall, and I tried to tell them but I never did.

I would start a sentence and then I'd choke up. They knew. They knew what I wanted to say, but I couldn't say it. I got to crying, and it got to be like a Holy Roller meeting, everybody crying, old John Crow and everybody.

Crow, Osborne, Krueger — they were upsetting enough, but they were seniors. The ones I was more concerned about were Charlie Milstead and some of those who had come there because of me. I was leaving them without the coach they had tied to. Charlie's daddy used to send me khaki britches, with the baggy seats built in, and I truly hated leaving him. He was just a sophomore, but he and Meredith were the best quarterbacks in the conference that year.

Charlie had tried to get me to say I was never going to leave A&M when I signed him, but I didn't. I had told some boys I'd never leave Kentucky and when I did I was ashamed and I made up my mind that would not happen again. Charlie did all right, though. The last time I saw him he was vice-president of some big Texas outfit.

We still had Tennessee to play in the Gator Bowl, but we were like a pack of whipped puppies. It didn't take a genius to see nobody had any heart for the game. Coaches and players were confused, not knowing what was in store, and the workouts were lousy. All those Aggie Exes were around being sore at me. In that situation I couldn't reach the players.

I told the staff we had to do something. "If we don't get their attention we're going to get killed. We're not ready to play Tennessee."

That afternoon at the team meeting I waited till all the players were in and seated, and when I came in I must have paced up and down for five minutes, nobody saying anything.

Bum Phillips, who was on my staff then, remembers this. Having Bum was like having a hidden camera, the way he could remember things.

Finally I wheeled around and said, "You know what they're saying about you, Crow?"

Crow looked up, startled, like he'd been jabbed. "They're saying you don't care anything about this game. They're saying you just want to make sure you don't get hurt so you can sign a big pro contract."

I turned to Charley Krueger.

"And Krueger. You know what they're saying about you? They're saying you don't give a damn about this game. All you're worrying about is which all-star game you're going to and how much money you'll make."

I was moving from player to player, picking on the best ones.

"And Osborne, you're not thinking about this game. You're thinking about the banquet you're going to speak at.

"And Richard Gay. You're not thinking about football. Football can't do anything for you. You're thinking about getting married and falling into a $50,000-a-year job.

"And Tracy. You know what they're saying about you? They're saying you won't even go on the field. You've been hurt all year and you're petting yourself and feeling sorry for yourself and you probably won't even suit up."

I paused and walked back and forth some more, and nobody said a word. Then I turned and faced them all and said, "And do you know what they're saying about the rest of you? Nothing. They don't think you'll play good enough to even mention.

"And do you know who *they* are?" I crooked my thumb at my chest. "Me."

The way Bum tells it, I shocked everybody, including the coaches. I walked out and they were a while deciding whether to follow, but they did, and I want to tell you they came alive that day. The first period was kickoff coverage and nobody had any pads on, just helmets and sweats, and the whistle blew and twenty-two guys came together at midfield in the damnedest wreck you ever saw.

I'd like to tell you how we went out and tore Tennessee apart in the Gator Bowl, but I can't. We lost 3 to 0. But we made a game of it, and if we hadn't come to our senses it would have been 30 to 0.

Well, the truth was I didn't want to go back to Alabama, never intended to. I could have gone back two or three times and I refused. Mary Harmon said it was silly to have fought and bled like I had and now with things opening up for us at last, with a chance to make some money and the program going so well, and even the press coming around, it was foolish to throw it all away.

But the Alabama people kept reminding me what the school had done for me, and how I was the only one who could bring Alabama football back to where it once was, which wasn't true, but it sure got to me. Every day I was getting a sackful of letters, hundreds of them from grade school kids telling me they wanted to play for me if I came back. Some of them did, eventually. Heck, I just couldn't refuse.

Some people said I got $50,000 raised by the alumni as an outright gift to come back, but that's not true. I was offered $250,000 over a five-year period from an alumnus who is a good friend of mine, but I wouldn't accept it.

I put everything I could think of in my contract to help the program, though, and I'm an old hand at writing contracts. Red Drew was quoted as saying, "Bear got the green light on everything. Frank

Thomas never had it that good." That may be, but the only material things I asked for were the same salary the deans were making and permission to make my own television deal. I did get them to get me a house to live in, which the university owned and I paid the taxes on.

On December 3, 1957, at the Shamrock Hotel in Houston, I made the announcement at a press conference. I told them it was the most difficult thing I ever had to do, and I said, "The only reason I'm going back is because my school called me."

On January 30, 1958, Mary Harmon and Paul Junior and I, and a crippled old dachshund named Doc, drove into Tuscaloosa in a white air-conditioned Cadillac.

They had a sign on one of the billboards: "Welcome Home Bear and Mary Harmon." And I'll never forget the look on Mary Harmon's face. She was in hog's heaven.

She said, "All my life, *all* my life I've wanted to come back here to live."

I wished then I'd gone back ten years sooner.

Eighteen

I had no doubt we would win at Alabama. I just didn't know how long it would take.

The team I inherited in 1958 was a fat, raggedy bunch. The best players, the ones with ability, quit us, and recruiting was actually over, so we weren't going to get much for the following year except the boys Coach Hank Crisp and Jerry Claiborne got busy and signed when I was still in Texas coming to terms and getting my A&M team ready for the Gator Bowl.

Coach Hank had a list of prospects that he brought over to Houston the day of the announcement, and when the press and everybody had left the Shamrock we went up to my room and went through it.

I wasn't able to talk with each one in person before they signed, so Jerry and Coach Hank lined it up so I could visit most of them by phone. I remember I talked to Pat Trammell, the quarterback who turned out to be the best leader I ever had, from New York when I was at a banquet. Sometimes I talked to five or six of them in a row, long distance.

They were probably the best freshman group I ever had, too, in terms of character and dedication. I take none of the credit. They were hand-delivered by Jerry Claiborne and Hank Crisp.

Coach Hank was the last reason I had to resist coming back. He was the Alabama athletic director then, and there was no man in my football life I was closer to. As a player I worshiped him, and for years afterward he was the man I went to. I knew I had to have both jobs — head football coach and athletic director — to make my program work, but I sure didn't want him hurt. So I hesitated.

And just as he did in 1931 when he drove to Arkansas in that old Ford to fetch me back when I tried to quit the Alabama team, Coach Hank came to Texas and set me straight.

He said, "Paul, I want you to take it. I'm tired and want out, anyhow. They're going to make me head of the intramural department."

I checked with a member of the athletic board and he confirmed it. Boy, was that a load off my mind.

On New Year's Eve, Mary Harmon and I checked into the Stafford Hotel, then took a drive out to the Tuscaloosa Country Club for a dinner dance. I didn't do much more than shake a few hands before we made our exit. My stomach was churning. I couldn't wait to get to work.

I was up before dawn and went over and opened up the office, and sat there doing what I always do at a time like that — worrying.

But from that first day on, from the very beginning, you could tell this was a great bunch of kids, kids who were there with a purpose. I never had a group like that in my life.

I talked to each one of them individually, sat down and asked how they were doing and talked about their brothers and sisters, and visited. Other places, Kentucky and Texas A&M, I just went in there and laid it on the line — we're going to do this and this, and either you're with me or you're gone. I had that sign at Kentucky: Be Good or Be Gone. I told that alumni group at A&M there was only one chief and the rest were Indians, that I wouldn't be needing their advice.

I never had to do that at Alabama, and I don't know which is the best way, because we've won both ways. But I'll never forget that first meeting at Alabama.

I had come back from New York, after attending the Coaches

All-America banquet, and ordered the full squad to assemble at Friedman Hall. I didn't even mention football. I talked to them about their lives, what they had to do to be successful.

I told them how I wanted them to conduct themselves, how to look and act. Little things, like writing home to their mamas and papas, and smiling, and recognizing the contributions of others on the campus. Fred Sington, who was All-America tackle at Alabama in the '30s, had two sons on that team, Fred Junior and David. He came to me later and told me how much his boys had been impressed that day.

In the fall, in that same room, I met with just the freshmen. It was to be a regular thing from then on, those noon meetings, but that first one set the tone.

I could just sense they were something special. I told them what football should mean to them, and what the program would be. Then I challenged them.

I said, "What are you doing here?" And I waited. It was so quiet in there you could hear a pin drop.

I said, "What are you doing here? Tell me why you're here. If you're not here to win the National Championship you're in the wrong place."

Then I told them what I thought it would take to do it, and they believed me. They believed every word.

They believed it then, and they believed it all the way through school — Pat Trammell, Lee Roy Jordan, Jimmy Sharpe, Billy Rice, Richard Williamson, Bill Oliver, Charlie Pell. Just special people. Trammell and Gary Phillips and Tim Davis became doctors. Billy Neighbors was great in the pros. Tommy Brooker, Billy Battle, Butch Wilson. Every one of them winners. They were eight and ten years old when Alabama had last been on top, and they remembered.

When I walked out that day I knew we were going to win the National Championship with that group. Before that I had just talked about it, thought about it, and dreamed about it. This time I was sure. And every time I saw them after that I felt that way. The pride they had. They had a goal and they never lost sight of it.

Well, I'm not going to tell you word for word what else I said because that's my blood, that's what I live on, and I might have to think of something to say next year. But one other thing had to be a strong factor. The tradition these kids had been raised on in Alabama, and were proud of, which made winning a whole lot easier than it had been for me before. Billy Neighbors was born and raised in Tuscaloosa and he said he didn't know there was another college.

Mary Harmon, Paul Junior and I lived at the Stafford for the next few months while she found us the house on Lakeshore Drive, a big, solid brick one with the look of permanence about it. J. B. (Ears) Whitworth, my predecessor, hadn't gotten around to buying a house. He had rented. I wanted them to know I wasn't thinking about going anywhere.

The university paid $57,000 for the house. It would cost three times that now. It had eight rooms plus a big game room where we entertained as many as three hundred people, and was surrounded by oak trees and big pines. Naturally, I had it air-conditioned.

In the meantime Julian Lackey and Young Boozer, two old friends, raised more than $50,000 in private donations to air condition the dorm the boys lived in, Friedman Hall. Did it that summer. It didn't cost the university a dime, either. And to keep the kids we had signed eligible we instituted a study program, with tutors.

We tore up the football offices on the first floor of the men's gymnasium, and though it's nothing to compare with what we have now, these plush quarters we're living in at the new Coliseum, it was pretty grand by previous standards. We made six rooms where there had been eight, and arranged to have a large reception area, with a nice-looking little brunette to receive callers. Ears hadn't had one of those either.

We chucked out the wooden furniture and put in some modern stuff made of metal tubes and light fabric, and we changed the cream-colored walls to a light green. We tore out the parquet wood floors and put down inlaid tile, and installed fluorescent lighting.

And I put up my sign: Winning Isn't Everything, But It Beats Anything That Comes In Second.

Then I ordered some more air conditioners. I put in nine, two of my own I'd brought from College Station, and out of pocket I bought seven, six for my assistants and one for the coaches' dressing room.

You say, boy, Bryant sure was a nut for that air conditioning, and

I was, ever since that night in Kentucky when we entertained the Bull Hancocks and Louis Hagans and Charlie Mitchell in our bedroom in front of that little old window unit.

I'll never forget Jim Tatum. After the war they started holding coaches' clinics overseas. My first trip was to Europe with Herman Hickman, Fritz Crisler and Biggie Munn. The Europeans thought Americans were richer if they were fatter, and Herman got a lot of attention. Folks actually followed him around Paris. And then Tatum, Duffy Daugherty and I went to the Far East, to a hotel in Japan owned by the government.

Tatum had this air-conditioned room, and one night he called Duffy Daugherty and me to tell us he was dying. We went up there and he looked like he was having a stroke. We were drying Tatum's face off with towels, trying to keep him calm, when the doctor came in and made the diagnosis. He said the air conditioning had gone off and Tatum got so hot he almost smothered.

With recruiting over, we went to work on the high school coaches in the state, trying to get them on our side. That's important because, as I said, high school coaches do more real coaching than anybody, and they can help you if you have their confidence. We held a big coaches' clinic, had them come in there free, and invited them to spring practice. I had heard the majority of the high school people had been leaning toward Auburn and the other state schools. The record shows we ironed out that problem.

Well, we didn't pussyfoot trying to find out who could play and who couldn't among the holdovers, the ones we'd have to go with that first season. We started right in with about as hard a series of spring practices as I could dream up.

I initiated a One Hundred Percent Club, which helped spirit a little. Membership was based entirely on effort, not on a player's ability. And we didn't slack up in the fall, either. My plan was to bleed 'em and gut 'em, because I didn't want any well-wishers hanging around.

The first year doesn't count when you're on a five-year plan because you're playing with someone else's material, but the ones who stayed got the idea, all right. I had one boy saying he was going to quit, and I wanted to nip that in the bud so I went to his locker and took all his things out and threw them into the street. I wouldn't do that now. I would try to save him. But then I felt I had to set some examples. I didn't want quitting to be too honorable.

We worked some of them awfully hard, though, and lost them. Upperclassmen who didn't appreciate what we were trying to do, and I can't blame them for that. It's mighty tough getting used to another way when you've been living easier. The boys who stayed were like those who went with us down to Junction and gutted it out. They were proud just to have lasted, and that had to be double good because they hadn't had anything to be proud of before. Alabama had won four games in the last thirty-six.

That season, out of necessity, we played what I call garbage football. Getting-by football. A lot of quick-kicking and crazy plays that were really as conservative as could be. They just *looked* flashy. If you don't have the talent to win with talent alone, you have to compensate.

Two who stayed were our center, Jimmy Blevins, a real leader, and our quarterback that year, Bobby Jackson. I wish I'd had him longer because he was a good one. He was a senior who had been hurt, a knee injury, and he decided to ride it out with us and see what happened.

We built our offense around Jackson, for what it was worth. He could pass, but he didn't have much protection. He could run, too, so we ran the option or some kind of keeper play most of the time. We lined up in every offensive set known to man and then let Jackson keep it. Or we'd quick-kick. We had a fine quick-kicker in Gary O'Steen. Jackson and O'Steen were our offense.

There is no doubt we were a conservative team that year. I don't believe you play football like it was poker. Get wild and woolly when you don't have ability and instead of losing 6 to 0, with a chance to luck one out, it'll be 60 to 0. I told Jackson to run every time if he could make 5 yards, because somebody might shoot his receiver from the stands, and that's what Jackson did.

We won one out of our first four games. We got a scoreless tie with Vanderbilt, and beat Furman pretty good, and played LSU and Tennessee tough before losing 13–3 and 14–7. LSU won the National Championship that year. Teams without a lot of talent at the skilled positions can make up for it to an extent by being tenacious on defense, which we were. Pride has a lot to do with it.

Then in the fourth game we went up to Starkeville to play one of Mississippi State's better teams, picked by some to win the SEC, and we got our first bonus.

This is mainly Red Blount's story, or at least from his viewpoint. Red has been on the Alabama athletic board for a long time, and had a big hand in bringing me back. He had done a lot of bragging on me. He was a football expert because he had been a big star in high school.

Red's up there holding court with the Alabama people in his choice seat as we kick off. Mississippi State drives all the way to about our 6-yard line, and we stop 'em, and Red tells everybody what a fine coach I am. We take the ball, and Gary O'Steen quick-kicks 70 yards. On first down.

Red says, "What's going on?"

State comes right back with it and gets down to about our 15, and we stop them again. We run one play for 9 yards, and Red's up there leading his group in a lot of clapping. On second down we quick-kick. The ball rolls all the way down to about their 20.

Red's flabbergasted. He says, "How you gonna win kicking all the time?"

But it's still no score. State drives back down to our 12, eating up a lot of time. Our guys are scratching for every yard, playing like their lives depend on it. Scooter Dyess got hit and when he came off he kind of fell into my arms — he only weighed about 140 pounds and I could pick him up like a child — and I looked into his eyes and they were crossed.

We stop them there again, and on first down we make almost 10 yards. They actually have to measure. Red's up there telling everybody how much better he feels, and on second down Gary O'Steen quick-kicks. Red leaps right out of his seat.

He says, "Hell's bells! We done hired ourselves an idiot!"

This time the ball rolls all the way to the Mississippi State 4. And they screw around with it, and we wind up blocking a punt for a safety. It's 2 to 0, our favor.

State finally scores, though, and we go into the fourth quarter trailing, 7–2. State has gained about 500 yards. We have the ball on our 24, and Jackson runs twice and gets 9 yards. And for the fifth time that day Gary O'Steen quick-kicks. This time it rolls all the way to the State 2.

Red Blount is a little more subdued. He says, "I dunno. That old boy may know what he's doing after all."

State messes around and finally gets out to the 10, and on fourth down we partially block a punt and get the ball on their 14.

And then Bobby Jackson pulls a play we don't even have in our game plan. He rolls out and hits Norbie Ronsonet on a little cross pass for a touchdown, and we win the game, 9–7.

Now, you have to appreciate Red Blount was not born yesterday. He was postmaster general of the United States at one time, and he knows his way around. He called me up that very night.

He said, "Bear, I just want you to know that I don't understand what you're doing, but whatever it is I'm for it."

Well, you say that's a helluva way to win a football game, but it happens to be the only way when you're in the fix we were in.

The next week we beat Georgia 12–0 and it was practically a rerun. Georgia was so good that year, and so physical. They had a guy from Texas, a big linebacker, who was so tough people would walk on the other side of the street when they saw him coming. Fran Tarkenton was on that club, sharing the quarterbacking with Charlie Britt.

Georgia gained over 500 yards on us, but we intercepted four passes and three of them were behind our goal. Every time they'd get down there Wally Butts would take Tarkenton out and put Britt in and Britt would throw an interception.

Gary O'Steen quick-kicked four times for a 78-yard average. We might have been the best quick-kicking team in history that year. But a little old skinny-legged guard named Wayne Sims finally won it for us.

We had been holding them off with O'Steen's kicks, but with about ten minutes to go Georgia got it down to our 7, and we were worn out. If they had scored, we would have lost, because we'd have collapsed for sure then.

Then on second down Sims slanted in and somehow ran around the interference and threw the Georgia runner for a 12-yard loss. On the next play we intercepted.

Then the biggest fight I ever saw broke out on the field. I don't know how or why it started, but both benches emptied and were out there in an instant flailing away. I hate that because it shows a lack of class. Neither team showed any that day.

Pat Dye says I was on the field in three jumps, grabbing people. The first one I grabbed, according to Pat, was the biggest, toughest guy on our team, a 245-pounder named Carl Valletto, and I tried to shake his head off.

I said, "You haven't fought all day! You want to fight somebody, come on in the dressing room and I'll take you on one at a time!" I was so mad and ashamed I was shaking.

We finally got them quieted down, and after the game Wally congratulated me and said, "Paul, you just beat a damn good football team." We didn't, really, we just outlucked them.

After we had dressed and everybody was gone, I was walking across campus to where my car was parked when President Rose fell in step beside me. He always liked to let me know how much he knew about football, and I used to enjoy kidding him about how smart he was for a third-string guard.

When we got between the Alpha Gamma Delta and Kappa Delta houses he started laughing.

I said, "What the hell's wrong with you?"

He said, "Aw, that show you put on today, that big fight. Georgia wasn't worth a hoot, and you know it, and you shoulda beat 'em by four touchdowns."

I said, "I'll tell you one thing, Dr. Rose. I respect you in every way possible. But never again will I think you know a damn thing about football."

─── Nineteen ───

We wound up 5–4–1 that first year, including a 17–8 upset of Georgia Tech in Atlanta, Tech's homecoming game. We were two-touchdown underdogs and had 17 points in the first quarter before they woke up, and we hung on. Tech was a far superior team. We probably won the alumni *and* Red Blount that day. Alabama hadn't beaten Georgia Tech in five years, and hadn't had a winning season during that period.

I won't say it was that much easier for us to win at Alabama than it had been at A&M or Kentucky, because in some respects it was harder. So much was expected so soon. But it didn't take a detective to recognize the signs. I had to marvel the way those boys wanted to play. We had a reserve quarterback named Carlton Rankin a couple years later, and in a scrimmage he came off the field with blood pouring onto his jersey from a cleat slash on his upper lip. I never saw so much blood. In the dressing room the doctor said he'd have to take six or eight stitches just to stop it, and the doctor told me later that Carlton was like a wild man.

"You can't do that, doc!" he said. "I might lose my place! Can't you just put a clamp on it?"

Carlton Rankin never won a game for us, was never a regular for us, but his kind of attitude was what *did* win games.

In 1959 we began to play the real tough defense that characterized those early teams. Billy Neighbors was short for a tackle, but he was great, and wound up All-America. I never had another one like Lee Roy Jordan. He was a center/linebacker, going both ways at 190 pounds, playing against guys like Jackie Burkett of Auburn, who was 6-3, 235 pounds.

I still remember the day Lee Roy came into my office that first time, the way he looked me in the eye. He was from Excel, Alabama, population 350. He said there wasn't enough money in the entire town to pay for his schoolbooks at Alabama. Football meant a lot to Lee Roy.

It's a wonder I didn't foul him up, because I tried him at two, three different positions as a sophomore, including offensive tackle, before he became a linebacker — the best linebacker in college football, bar none. He would have made every tackle on every play if they had stayed in bounds.

Had he done well at offensive tackle I might have left him there and messed up his whole career. I can remember nothing bad about Lee Roy: first on the field, full speed every play, no way to get him to take it easy. I can't ever recall him missing a practice. Or being hurt, for that matter.

We beat Auburn for the first time since 1953 that year. We moved Scooter Dyess, our gigantic 140-pound halfback, to split end and passed to him automatically whenever they didn't double cover. Auburn couldn't be right on it. When they did double cover him we were able to run the ball better. In the third quarter Dyess got open on a 35-yard touchdown pass and Tommy Brooker kicked a clutch field goal and we won 10-0.

The funniest thing was Billy Neighbors that day. We had made "bingo" our signal for an interception. Auburn has since copied it and we may go to something else, but the idea was to yell "bingo" when you intercepted a pass so your teammates would know they better block somebody because you're coming.

Late in the game Auburn was trying to get something going, but Gary Phillips put a terrific rush on Dick Wood, the Auburn quarterback. Neighbors had been temporarily blocked on the play, but at the last second he rose up and Wood's pass hit him right in the belly. Neighbors started jumping up and down, and yelling, "Can't think of the word! Can't think of the word!"

After the Georgia game — Tarkenton got even, 17–3 — no team scored more than a touchdown on us, and we wound up 7–1–2 and accepted an invitation to the Liberty Bowl, where Penn State wore us out, 7–0. We've gone to bowls every year since. And we beat Georgia Tech in the rain that year on Scooter Dyess's touchdown and a field goal by Fred Sington's son Fred Junior, 9–7.

But the 1960 Tech game was the one I'll never forget. Not if I live three lifetimes. If it wasn't the greatest comeback I have ever seen it was certainly the greatest one I've been involved in.

We were down, 15–0, at the half. We hadn't even made a first down until the last play of the second quarter. When we came in I didn't know what to do or to say. You have to have a plan, but I was fresh out. If we were down 6–0 I was going to really get after them, make them look me in the eye, but I wasn't prepared for this. I knew they expected me to blow up, rant and rave and chew some tails. But if I did I was afraid we'd lose by 50.

So I went the other way. The first thing I said was, "Where are the Cokes?"

And I walked around, patting 'em on the back and clapping my hands. I said, "Damn, this is great. Now they'll see what kind of mamas and papas we've got. They'll see what we've got in us."

My coaches nearly fainted. Bebes Stallings still talks about it. I got up on the blackboard and threw out a couple of things and told them if I had done as good a job as they had we wouldn't be in the fix we were in. I said it was all right, anyway, because we were still going to win. That I had screwed up a few times, but if they'd help me get things straightened out we would win in the fourth quarter.

I didn't believe it, but they did.

We go back out there, and so many things are happening. I'm dodging liquor bottles from the Tech stands, for one thing. And we're playing a lot better, but still go into the fourth quarter behind, 15–0, with fourth and 12 on our own 6-yard line.

I figured this was no time to be faint-hearted, so I sent Norbie Ronsonet in with a play, a hook pass that was designed to get us 15 yards. But Bobby Skelton, who with Trammell quarterbacked that

'60 team, missed the signal. He called a 6-yard hook pass. Even if we make it we lose the ball.

He threw it right into a Tech tackle's belly.

I yanked Skelton out of the game and got him over on the side-lines. I was so mad I could have bitten his helmet. I have a rule for myself that you never say you're *never* going to do anything, because as sure as you do it gets turned on you.

But I knelt over Skelton and very warmly said, "You little —" and I had a few words for him. I said, "You'll never play another minute for Alabama as long as you live."

He hadn't done what I told him, see.

Meanwhile Tech didn't score, which was a miracle, and we got the ball back. I sent Pat Trammell in and right away he completed about a 30-yard pass. Then on the next play he got hurt.

Now what am I going to do? I had just told Bobby Skelton he'd never play for me again. I had just drummed him out of the corps. Now I have no choice. He's the only quarterback I got. I called him over and put my arm around him, making it look like I was patting him. I was actually squeezing him pretty good.

I said, "I'm going to give you one more chance."

Well, you've never seen anybody perform the way Bobby Skelton did those last six minutes. He had fourth down plays four times on that first drive, and took us in for the touchdown.

At 15–7, we pulled an onside kick and got the ball, and quick as that we're in for another touchdown to make it 15–13. This time we try a 2-point conversion, and don't make it. Time is now down to nothing. We have got to have the ball right now.

Everybody in Grant Field — the sober ones, anyway — knew we had to try an onside kick.

Which we didn't do. We kicked it out of the end zone. Tech took over on the 20. We had four time-outs left, and every time they ran a play we called time. They were able to use up only a few seconds before they had to punt. With the return we put the ball in play on their 45-yard line.

Skelton called a sideline pass to Butch Wilson, our right halfback. Running his pattern at about the Tech 35, Wilson got knocked out of bounds by a defensive back. That would make him an ineligible receiver. But nobody saw it. Not the officials, not the coaches, nobody. He came back in and caught the pass and took it to the 12-yard line, right in front of the goal posts.

And we called our last time-out.

Simple enough now, you'd think. All we have to do is kick a little field goal. But our field goal kicker, Tommy Brooker, is hurt. He can't even walk.

And we had a kid named Richard (Digger) O'Dell, a big end from Lincoln, Alabama, who had been with us two years and never even tried a field goal.

I patted him on the britches and said, "Get on out there, Digger, and kick one." Like he'd done it a thousand times.

What old Digger O'Dell kicked into the air that afternoon looked like a knuckleball. It went this way and that way. But it went through the goal posts and barely over the bar. It might have even grazed the bar. The game was over and we had won, 16–15.

Talk about a lot of stunned folks. The Tech people couldn't believe it. Neither could Bobby Dodd. And neither could I.

A few days after that Bobby and I were talking about ending the series. He was giving me his reasons, which I'll get into, and then suddenly he had a change of thought.

He said, "There's something else I wanta tell you. We've been friends a long time, and you really embarrassed me over there coming from 15–0 to win that game, but damn it, that Wilson was knocked out of bounds on that pass. He came back in to catch the ball. We saw it in the movies."

I said, "Yeah, Bobby, I saw it, too. What's wrong with that?"

And I had to laugh.

In 1961 we had the best team in college football. Not the biggest, but the best. We certainly weren't very big, and we got a lot of attention for that over the next few years. We did not deliberately go out looking for smaller players in those days, but we demanded quickness and it usually came in smaller packages. Bigness is in the heart, anyway.

We didn't have great numbers, either. We had sixteen or seventeen players, the nut of the team (college football still hadn't gone back to two-platoon in 1961), and all sixteen or seventeen were leaders. I was so afraid of getting them hurt I went seven weeks at one point without letting them put the pads on in practice.

Pat Trammell and Billy Neighbors came in a couple of times and tried to get me to order a scrimmage. "Let's get the pads on," Pat said. "The guys need it." I declined because I wanted to save them for Saturdays. But that's the way they were.

I said that year that defense wins, and that's right. We weren't just a good defensive team, we were a *great* defensive team. We led the nation in almost every category. Only three teams scored touchdowns on us. We shut out the last five in a row, and despite a flu epidemic in Biloxi where we practiced, we had enough left to beat Arkansas 10–3 in the Sugar Bowl.

I could name so many "favorite players" on that team. Mike Fracchia ran like an All-American, and would have been one — and a great pro back as well — had he not hurt his knee the next year. Neighbors, Trammell and Jordan did make All-America. Jimmy Sharpe, Billy Williamson, Billy Richardson. Ray Abbruzzese, Billy Rice, Bill Battle, Charley Pell, Darwin Holt, Tommy Brooker, Cotton Clark — they played like it was a sin to give up a point.

Eleven teams got a grand total of 25 on us; no one scored more than 7. We were beating Auburn 34–0 when they reached about our 2-yard line with a first and goal late in the game. Four plays later they were on the 9.

But the bell cow of the whole outfit was Pat Trammell. You'll have to forgive me here for getting sentimental, but Pat Trammell was the favorite person of my entire life and I'm going to tell you as much as I can about him.

As a quarterback he had no ability. He couldn't do anything but win. He was not a great runner, but he scored touchdowns. He didn't pass with great style, but he completed them. He had been an all-star high school basketball and football player from Scottsboro, Alabama, and at 6–2, 205 pounds, he was about as big as any man we had on that 1961 team. As a leader, I have never had another like him.

The Alabama players rallied around him like little puppies. He could make them jump out a window to win. We didn't have any bad practices when he was there because he wouldn't let it happen.

I'd say, "Boy, if we only had some leadership, somebody to take this thing," and he'd take over. He would call 'em back into the huddle and cuss every one of 'em out, and make 'em play.

We had a fine system set up for players and coaches who cussed on the field, but I relaxed it for Pat because he could get pretty salty. He never hesitated to speak his mind. I'll never forget against Auburn that first championship year. We were leading 38–0 in the fourth quarter, with the ball at midfield, and I looked up, and lo and behold Pat was quick-kicking. When he came off the field I said, "What's going on, Pat?"

He said, "Those ———" and he had a few choice words for the first team. "They aren't blocking anybody, so I thought we might as well see if they could play defense."

Pat's daddy was a doctor, and the whole family was highly intelligent and very religious, always doing good things for people. His daddy was like he was, real strong-minded, and he loved Pat to pieces. Pat was never really hurt the whole time he played, but the week of the Mississippi State game that year he had a banged-up leg. Pat's daddy called him. He said, "You gonna play?" (Pat told me all about it later.)

"I don't think so. Coach Bryant says not."

"Then, hell, I ain't coming. I'll stay home and make some money."

I always take a walk with the quarterbacks the morning of the game, and that Saturday in Mississippi I caught a glimpse of Pat's daddy, jumping in the bathroom of a filling station when we were approaching. After we passed I looked back and his daddy was peeping out to see how Pat was walking. He'd come over anyway. Pat threw two touchdown passes to Bill Battle that afternoon.

Pat was a good-looking kid, and he had a girl who was as cute as a speckled pup, the daughter of one of my warm friends when I was in school. They eventually married. Pat studied history with my son Paul. Both wanted to be historians, and they'd get together and talk about the Civil War and the Roman Empire and always go past bedtime. They decided they would wind up starving to death on that route, however, so Paul went into business school and Pat into medicine.

He had a lot of labs, and never seemed to know when he had them. He was always early for practice. Most of the time he came by my office first, like Lee Roy and John Crow and Babe Parilli did. Just come by to talk. I loved that.

With Pat quarterbacking every game that year Alabama was

176

undefeated for the first time since 1945. Against North Carolina State he gained more ground than the entire State team, including Roman Gabriel. But I'm not going to go into all the things he did for us because that would take another book. It's enough to say we wouldn't have done it without him.

So Pat went on to medical school and graduated, and began his practice in Birmingham. The week of the Auburn game in 1968 he called me from his office.

He said, "Coach, I want to tell you before somebody else does. I've got a tumor." He kept talking about it matter-of-factly, using big medical terms, and I didn't realize what he was saying.

I finally said, "Pat, what the hell are you talking about?"

He said, "Dammit, Coach, I got cancer."

My stomach turned over. If I had been standing up I'd probably have dropped to my knees.

He said, "They got a hospital in New York that's supposed to be the best in the world for this type of thing. But I ain't going up there and let them goddamn Yankees work on me."

I said, "What's the name of the hospital?"

"The Ewing Clinic."

I knew the name. I had passed it a hundred times on York Avenue. Ewing specializes in "Cancer and Other Dread Diseases."

I said, "I'll go up there with you."

"Will you?"

"Sure."

"Well, dammit, that's what I was calling to ask you."

"Then I accept."

Pat's doctor and his wife, Baye, took him to New York, and I came up right after. While they were getting him ready, making tests and things, Joe Namath and Ray Abbruzzese, who were already with the Jets then, picked me up and we went out to see him. We sat around for three hours, big-talking.

He'd say to Namath, "Nigger, you're blacker than you were when you were in school," and Joe would laugh, and they'd get on me and on each other. Baye said she wished Joe's critics could have seen him during that session.

After Joe and Ray left I stayed. Baye was worn out. The doctor asked me what I was going to do and I said, "I'm staying." He talked Baye into going back to the hotel to rest.

After she left the doctor came back around with a fifth of Jack Daniels Black. He said, "Coach, Pat can't have anything to eat, but he can have some of this. I'm putting it right here on the dresser, and you and Pat can have a little party and he can tell you what he really thinks of you. And it probably won't be what you think he thinks."

And we had our party. Pat was in rare form. I'd start to say something and he would interrupt, "Goddamit, Coach, shut up. I been listening to you for ten years, now you listen to me."

"OK, Pat."

And he'd tell me how to block this or that trap play, or run this or that pass pattern. He was pretty darn sound on everything he said, too. I don't know how late into the night we talked.

The next morning Baye was back, and they cut open Pat's belly. We were there when the doctor got out of the operating room.

He said, "We got all of it."

I was never so relieved.

The next morning I returned to Alabama convinced he was going to be all right.

Pat went back to practicing medicine that winter, and the following fall he brought little Pat down to Tuscaloosa when we opened practice. They stayed three days in the room named after him at Bryant Hall. I thought that was unusual. As though he didn't want to go.

Just before he left, he got me aside and said, "Coach, I wanted you to know I got that damn tumor again."

He said it was unusual. That out of fifteen thousand cancer cases in Alabama his was the only one like it. A testicular sarcoma, he called it. Had to do with the female hormones, beginning in the testicles and making the breasts swell and get very sore. It spreads quickly, he said. He said he thought at first he had hurt himself playing basketball.

The season wore on and, again, the week of the Auburn game I called him and invited him and Pat Junior, who's now a teenager and a fine little athlete, to come sit on our bench at the game. They came to the hotel and rode out on the bus with us. When we won, Mike Hall, our captain, presented Pat with the game ball. He cried like a baby.

That was on Saturday. Several players told me later how bad he looked, and that when he was off in a corner he seemed to be holding himself rigid, with his lips tight. A week later to the day he was back in the hospital, "in very serious condition," the doctor said.

The next day I went to see him. I don't rightly know why because it was a beautiful Sunday in Tuscaloosa and I had planned to play golf. I got in my car and was driving toward the Indian Hills Country Club, but instead of making the turn at that intersection at Route 59 I just kept going and drove all the way to Birmingham, to University Hospital.

Pat's daddy was there, looking grim. And Baye and most of the family. When I came in Pat shooed everybody out but me and his dad. He said he wanted to talk football. He started in by eating me out about recruiting.

"You oughta be out recruiting," he said. "Who are you going to get sitting around here?"

Just before I left he said, "Coach, I have to admit it. I've never been in so much pain. The damn thing's up in my head."

It was 9 P.M. I had been there four hours. Outside I saw his doctor.

He said, "Pat could go any minute." He said the cancer was spreading so fast. It was in his brain and something had to give. He said he'd lapse into a coma soon, and then he'd go.

He went into a coma the next night, and the following morning about eight they called to say Pat Trammell was dead. Mary Harmon and I drove up to Scottsboro to be with his mama and daddy, and they were so heartbroken. Six months later his daddy was dead, too.

Pat's funeral was the most moving I've ever been to. I escorted his mother. Coach Jordan was there, and a lot of the Auburn players as well as ours. President Nixon and Governor Wallace sent telegrams of condolence. Pat Trammell was everything known to man. Everybody loved him. He was twenty-eight years old when he died. I still miss him.

Twenty

ou would naturally think the happiest years of my life were those first six or seven years at Alabama. Our boys won National Championships and SEC championships, went undefeated three times, and played in bowl games every year but the first. Because of them our income is about ten times what it used to be.

We enlarged Denny Stadium a hundred percent, and even with the economy what it is, we play to sellout crowds every week there and in Legion Field in Birmingham. Our overall income is $2½ million. We built a new fieldhouse that cost $4.8 million. We built the athletes' dormitory, and I'm ham enough to be especially proud of that because by special act of the legislature they named it after me — Paul W. Bryant Hall.

But those years weren't the happiest of my life.

I suppose the trouble started a long time ago, and I'm just deluding myself as I get older if I expect people to look at the record and just listen to those who made it, the players themselves. I feel certain if I told Lee Roy Jordan or Steve Meilinger or John David Crow I needed them they would start walking to Alabama.

The logic of it escapes most people. That if you really taught brutality and treated people as badly as people say I did you would never be able to get a good football player on your team. And if you did you wouldn't get anything out of him, and you sure wouldn't win. When we went on probation at Texas A&M that time and all those scholarships were voided, those boys could have gone wherever they pleased. We were stripped naked. But they didn't. They stayed.

Some silly people still believe we really had a big pit down at A&M and used to put two boys in at a time, and the one who crawled out was a starter.

The pit story got a lot of circulation for a while and I'm not sure where it started. I know of a couple of coaches who tried to help it along. The way it got back to me was a kid from Lake Village, Arkansas, whose daddy was a coach, told another coach in the Southwest Conference that we had boys "bleeding in a pit."

We actually were trying to recruit the kid, and almost got him. His mama was a friend of Sam Bailey's. But any coach that used that against A&M in their recruiting pitch had to be dealing with some ignorant folks. I mean, how could you have something like that and people not know it? Stories not be written and pictures taken, and eyewitnesses?

It was stupid, really.

There was a very popular quote attributed to Shug Jordan, the Auburn coach, a few years back. He said it was a helmet-busting, hell-for-leather, gang-tackling game we play in the Southeastern Conference, that since Bear Bryant came to Alabama it's the only game that can win.

Well, I'm not going to challenge Shug on that. What else could he say? All of a sudden those lean little boys at Alabama were beating those big fine-looking boys at Auburn, and somebody had to say something.

It is true I've sometimes worked teams too hard. I'll never deny that. I overworked that team at Kentucky when we went down to play Santa Clara in the 1950 Orange Bowl game. I lost that game three times.

I worked them too hard at Cocoa, in all that heat and with all those sandspurs. Then we took them to Miami and worked them too hard there, and I was too pigheaded to listen to my trainer, who told me they were exhausted. Finally, when we were leading and had the ball on the 2-yard line just before the half, I let Babe Parilli, just a sophomore then, call the play when I should have had sense enough to call one for him.

Parilli had just completed a screen pass to Bill Leskovar and all I had to do was call an out-of-bounds pass to stop the clock, but I didn't. Lloyd McDermott asked me, "Whata you wanta do, Coach?" And I said, "Oh, Babe'll get it over."

He didn't, and the clock ran out. And at the half, when I should have been telling them something constructive, I just fussed and fumed around and really killed our chances. We lost, 21–13. Len Casanova outcoached me, period.

So I have overworked teams, and that's bad, but there's a thin line. I know we put a lot of gravel in the craw of a lot of people because we were able to beat them physically, and if helmet-cracking football is the kind of football we were playing there for a long while, then I'm for it, and I hope we'll do it again.

I ask my boys to hit them as long as they can see them, to gang-tackle, to get up and hit them again, but it had better be legal. Any player who ever played for us will tell you the first rule in the book is I will not tolerate a guy who draws penalties, because he can't win. I benched a boy at Kentucky one game because he did it twice. He came to me later in the game, wanting to get back in. I said, "Sit down. You're not going to get back in."

Three 15-yard penalties in a game will beat you. Two will beat you if it's a close game and, if it's *real* close, one will beat you. One year we went ten games without a holding penalty.

If hard-nosed football, "brutal" football, is getting a boy to discipline himself, to get him in such keen physical condition that he will make fewer mistakes than the guy who isn't, that's what I'm for. If it took a pit to do that, I would have a pit. And I'd get in there with them.

Common sense tells you the other guy will get careless, get sluggish mentally, and you'll beat him in the fourth quarter because you'll be alert for sudden changes, for blocked kicks and fumbles. You go back and check General Neyland's teams and Wallace Wade's and Frank Thomas's, and I think you'll find they were sounder because they were in better condition.

The only thing I can think of that remotely resembled a pit was something I originated at Kentucky that we called the circle drill. Others called it the bull-in-the-ring and got a lot out of it. You put one man in the middle of a circle, and one player or another charges him, either to block him or tackle him or get by him or something. He has to be alert and quick or he'll get run over.

We also had what we called the challenge system, but we haven't used that in a long time because it's too time-consuming. The idea was that a third-teamer could challenge the regular for his job, head-on-head blocking, tackling and so forth. The others gather around to cheer one or the other on, and the coaches yell and everybody gets a big kick out of it.

The best thing about the challenges was what they did for morale, because they weren't really a good test of anything. I remember one stubby little guy at A&M, strong as a bull, always wanting to challenge somebody, no matter what position it was. But he never worked up a sweat in practice.

I finally got wise to him, and when he issued a challenge I'd say, "OK, Joe, but let's wait until after wind sprints."

Then when he was worn out from running I brought him over, and he'd be so tired he wouldn't challenge anybody.

The point is that we stressed conditioning, believing that a better-conditioned athlete can whip a superior athlete who isn't in top shape. If my 75 percent boy plays 15 percent over his ability and your 100 percent boy slogs around and plays 15 percent under his, then we will beat you every time.

I have always taken pride when people said how tough mentally and physically our teams were, how many teams didn't win the next Saturday after playing us. I took pride in that. But you don't win getting penalties, and you only get penalties when you break the rules.

When I was still at A&M, we recruited Darwin Holt out of Gainesville, Texas. We had tried real hard to get his brother before him, but the brother went to Oklahoma. Darwin transferred to Alabama because of me. His senior year, when we won the National Championship, he was terrific and helped win a lot of ball games. He and Lee Roy Jordan gave us great linebacking, which is the guts of your defense. Holt would go in for Pat Trammell when we went on defense. That was about all the substituting I did in 1961.

Well, I know I have said it a jillion times, that you have to out-mean people, and Darwin and Lee Roy certainly fell into the category of contact football players. The worst part about it all was that they took the brunt of what happened, the unfair criticism that was really an excuse to get at me.

There's no doubt Darwin fouled Chick Graning and the officials should have penalized us, which they didn't. But it could have been anybody in the secondary, not just him. I probably would have disciplined him my own way if those Atlanta sportswriters hadn't set out to crucify him. A penalty is one thing, a crucifixion is another. After that I wouldn't have done anything if they had burned the university down.

Bobby Dodd might have made an effort to stop it if he had known how it was going to be blown out of proportion. He told me two or three times before that if we didn't stop beating him he was going to quit playing us, and I can understand that. Losing to us late in the year wasn't very conducive to bowl bids. He already had Georgia and Florida and Auburn as "traditional" games, and they were tough enough. Nobody was going to beat us very often. Tech beat Alabama one out of seven during that period.

Neither one of us realized at the time how much getting off our schedule, and then out of the Southeastern Conference, would hurt Georgia Tech. At the time Atlanta had no pro baseball, no pro basketball, no pro hockey, no pro football. Tech had a lock on the sports fan. Now Atlanta has every kind of pro team, and I don't know how much that hurt Tech's program. I do feel Tech being out of the SEC hurt the conference. Tech now wants back in, and I'm for it and have campaigned for it because I think it would be good for all of us.

But if Bobby and Tech were looking for an out, the Graning incident gave it to them. I think they would tell you so. Maybe they would have had a problem dropping us from the schedule if this hadn't happened, because Georgia Tech–Alabama was a big game.

Let me set it up a little better. Bobby Dodd and I were very close for years, one of the few men in the business I have felt close to, and I'll always be grateful for the way he helped me. I told you when I was at Kentucky Bobby and his wife, Alice, came up to visit

184

us, and he helped me put in the T formation and gave me his playbook.

And one year there, when we beat him pretty bad, he thanked me for taking my first team out in the fourth quarter. When I was at A&M I went over there for his spring training. He sent a couple of his assistants over to our place a couple seasons before he quit to become Tech's athletic director full-time.

Over the years we always felt we could beat Georgia Tech by just going out and putting that shoulder pad and the bonnet on 'em, because I felt we'd be tougher mentally and physically — and because we may have had the kind of jinx on them that people said Tennessee had on us. My view was, regardless of its ability, if a team wallows around all week playing drop the handkerchief and the players don't think tough or live tough, how can they be tough on Saturday? You can get away with it a few times, but you sure can't get away with it every Saturday. Over the long haul we'd beat you in those days. We worked like hell during the week and had our fun on Saturday.

I realize now that I had a one-track mind then, and that there are many ways to skin a cat. Different coaches have different ways, different philosophies. Mine was different from Coach Dodd's, but he will still go down in history as one of our great coaches. I felt Bobby consistently got more out of talented players than I did and could run a game better.

So my way might be different, and I won't say it's better. But I'd welcome any daddy to spend seven days at any school where they lollygag around, and then have him stick with our squad for seven days, and see which one he would like his son to play for. See the way our boys act and talk and dress.

What would you see at our place? I think you would see a lot more supervision, more direction and probably more work, football or academics or whatever, and you wouldn't see them running off in all directions all the time.

The thing about the Graning incident that really disappointed me, though, was that some sportswriters took out after a young man in an effort to ruin me. For Bobby Dodd and me it's ancient history. We're friends again, and I'm glad we're back on Tech's schedule.

We were playing Tech in Birmingham. There were no hard

185

feelings beforehand. I remember Alice Dodd came up to me before the game and we visited. The game itself turned out kind of one-sided. Lee Roy Jordan and Darwin Holt were all over the field making tackles. Tech wound up with a net 30 yards rushing and 66 passing, and no points, and we got 10 on Mike Fracchia's 16-yard run and a Tim Davis field goal of 32 yards.

Anyway, in the fourth quarter Holt was dropping back on a punt. (It could just as easily have been Lee Roy or Butch Wilson.) His assignment was to take the end out. Graning was the end, and when they came together near the sideline Holt blocked Graning. The official had his back on the play and didn't see it. I didn't see it until I looked at the films.

Actually *we* complained on the play, because Billy Richardson was interfered with catching the punt.

Well, it wouldn't happen once in a thousand times, because Graning wasn't hit hard enough, but somehow an elbow got through his face guard and fractured his jaw. It was lucky for him it wasn't one of our big guys like Billy Neighbors. Darwin wasn't any bigger than a minute, except in the heart.

After the game the late Tonto Coleman, who became commissioner of the SEC but was then Dodd's assistant, came over to our dressing room to congratulate our boys, and he said something about Graning being hurt. If he had said it was serious I'd have gone right over to see Graning. But he didn't know, either, at the time.

Well, the next night, after our TV program, I went to New Orleans on Sugar Bowl business with Dr. Rose, Julian Lackey, Bill Sellers and Winston McCall. We were hoping at the time for a Rose Bowl bid, but we had to cover ourselves. I still didn't know Graning was hurt seriously.

We got back on Tuesday and it was in all the papers, and everybody was yelling for my scalp, so I called Bobby. He was saying buddy this and buddy that and, sonofagun, I hung up and the next paper that came out was worse than the first.

Then I did a small thing I wish I hadn't done. I had one of my assistants go down with the game film and show it to the Alabama writers, had him point out all the violations Tech had committed. They made more than we did by a bushel.

Dodd resented this, and I don't blame him. It was a small thing

186

and showed no class. If I had it to do over I wouldn't, but our people thought the Atlanta writers were trying to destroy me. Or were using the player's mistake to get at me.

Well, you talk about irony. What happened then was child's play next to what that big number 88 did to our All-America guard, Wayne Freeman, in our game with Tech two years later. You want to see something vicious, you look at the films of that game. It was the same year Tech's other end resigned from the team after kicking an Auburn boy in the head.

The game is over, we've got it won, 27–11, and after the last play we have the ball and this guy comes running about 10 yards and hits Freeman with an elbow. Freeman is just standing there relaxed, with his helmet off, and I guarantee you I was afraid he had killed him.

My coaches wanted to blast them on it, but I said no. I felt I'd been wrong kindling the other thing, and I didn't want to compound the mistake.

I wrote Dodd a letter and called his attention to it. I told him, "Bobby, the only reason I mention it is because you might have missed it in the film and I knew you would want to know. I think our boy is going to recover. Whether it will be in time for him to play anymore, I don't know, but I know you wouldn't want it to happen again."

A week or so later I got a letter thanking me and saying it really was a flagrant violation, and it wouldn't happen again. That he would discipline the kid. That was the right way to handle it, instead of through the newspapers.

One thing more about that period. After the 1962 Tech game, the one they beat us, 7–6, I did something that was very difficult for me, under the circumstances. There must have been three thousand people around their dressing room. I walked through that crowd, thinking I would probably get my throat cut, and went in there and called their captains out of the showers and shook hands with them. I congratulated Dodd again, and when I was going back through the crowd a woman who had a boy on Tech's team told me how proud she was. I said she had reason to be.

I did all that, and I didn't mean a darn thing I said, either, but I thought it was the class thing to do. Mama and Papa would have been proud of me.

— Twenty-One —

I believe this, that the reputation I had as a driver preceded me to Alabama. I doubt that the Graning incident would ever have reached the proportions it did if I had not had that reputation. Then there probably would never have been that first story in *The Saturday Evening Post* claiming I was an advocate of brutal football. I wouldn't have sued the *Post* over that, and if I hadn't sued the *Post* I doubt that there would have ever been the second story, the filthy, malicious one that said Wally Butts and I fixed a football game.

The whole thing just snowballed but, looking back on it all, if it meant changing my methods, my program, to avoid the heartaches that followed, then I'd just as soon have had the heartaches.

Listen, don't you know if I didn't believe way down inside what I was talking about we never could have gone ahead and won and gone to a bowl with all this stuff going on? As long as you know within yourself — and the guys with you know it — that you have confidence in the plan, you know you are not going to fail. I never had a doubt about that.

The idea of molding men means a lot to me. I don't know if I have molded many, but, I'll tell you, it makes you feel like you've done right when a guy like Pat Trammell stands up and says how much of an impact you had on his life, that you had more influence than anybody except his father.

I'm afraid I have hurt some others, but I never asked anything of my players I wouldn't do myself or hadn't done at one time or another. I always go back to Hank Crisp, flailing away at us with that leather nub on the end of his arm when he was an assistant coach at Alabama.

People ask me if I ever kicked a guy. Yes, I have. And if a boy lets me kick him and slam him around and he doesn't kick back I have said I don't want him. I'd demonstrate on a boy, show him how to block or do this or that and really let him have it, and then say, "Now you show me," and lots of times they bellied up and really dehorned me.

One boy did it at A&M and, realizing what he'd done, started running off, and I had to call to him, "Hey, come back. You're my kind of player."

I wish I could demonstrate now like I used to. I can show them how *not* to do it, but I can't get down with them like I used to, and I miss that.

I think a boy respects you more when you show him you're willing to sacrifice as much as you want him to. I remember back when Pat James was playing for us at Kentucky and we were practicing down there at the Millersburg Military Academy. That was the first of our boot camps. The boys called it Hell Hollow, but it really brought us together.

I had a rule about being late for practice. You can't bend the rules for anybody, and one day Pat showed up late. He had stayed too long at the little swimming hole we used between practices, and he was thirty minutes late. When practice was over, I said, "Wait a minute, Pat. While you were dillydallying getting to work today we had a kangaroo court and decided your punishment would be to go around and cover up all that mess out there."

We were in a cow pasture, and it was a formidable mess, too. He did. The next day the trainer forgot to wake me or something, because I got there twenty minutes late for the morning workout, and when we headed in after practice Pat said, "Uh, just a minute please, Coach Bryant. We had another kangaroo court while you were sleeping this morning. We decided your punishment would be to dig up all that mess, load it up, and cart it off."

I was out there two hours getting it done.

Well, you get older, and you're bound to do some things differently. Back then I probably beat our teams more than the opposition did. I remember how impetuous I was in 1950, how I was still seething after that Santa Clara loss, and we went out to that Orange Bowl banquet at the Indian Creek Country Club in Miami. Len Casanova got up and made a nice generous speech — he'd won, of course — and then I got up and said, "I'm a win man myself. I don't go for place or show," and sat down. That was a stupid thing.

When I took that A&M team out to the Coast to play UCLA in 1955, and they beat us, 21–0, I snapped at a writer on the Los Angeles paper after the game. He asked me if I had thought we could win, and I said, "You silly so-and-so, what do you think we came here for?"

Those things turn around on you. Jim Murray came over and saw us play and made a fuss over our being considered for the Rose Bowl when we won the National Championship in 1961. He wrote about segregation and the Alabama Ku Klux Klan and every unrelated scandalous thing he could think of, and we didn't get the invitation.

The thing is, if I had some of those teams I overworked now I might be able to get more out of them, or do it with a lot less punishment. I know one thing, we have changed almost completely. It used to be I'd give that third- or fourth-team boy a whole lot of work, yell at him and tell him he'd been on the gravy train three years and it was time he gave the university a return on its investment — you know, make him suck up his guts and do something.

My idea in recent years, as I said, has been to encourage that kid to stay around, not work him as much, because he's not going to play this year anyway, and if he doesn't get discouraged he might mature and wind up being a good player in a couple of years.

Certainly after twenty-nine years of coaching you should know a little more about pace. But you're never sure. Some of those boys we've got now don't know what it's like to be behind, to have to win in the fourth quarter when it's tough. And if you let them graduate without learning that you've done them an injustice, because they're sure going to run into it in life.

I have tried to impress on our young people the value of hard work, the effort involved in winning, not just theirs but all those who have contributed in their lives. Their parents, to begin with. The church, their teachers and high school coaches, the alumni. The secretaries and the custodians. And how stupid it is to do all that work, and accept all that effort on their behalf, and then not be willing to give completely of themselves for that brief amount of time that the game on Saturday represents.

It's not sixty minutes at all, see. It's a matter of a very few minutes, five or six at the most. Don't believe it? Last year we played Tennessee in a game where 63 points were scored. The actual live ball time was 13 minutes, 41.1 seconds.

There were 100 rushing plays that totaled 8 minutes, 44 seconds, or 8.04 seconds per play. There were 28 passes that took 2.17, or 4.89 seconds per pass. The extra points averaged 3.3 seconds, the one field goal 5.4 seconds. There were nine punts, totaling 1.45 and averaging 11.68 seconds per punt and return.

In the game there were a total of 158 plays, and they averaged 5.22 seconds a play. Take away Robin Cary's long punt return, which took 20.9 seconds, and Wilbur Jackson's 80-yard touchdown run, which took 8.9 seconds, and you cut the average time per play to less than five seconds.

Now, if you played the entire game on offense, which you wouldn't do in a modern game with as much substituting as we do, and the offense ran 70 plays, what do you wind up with? Five seconds per play times 70 plays — less than 6 minutes.

If a player goes out there after doing all that preparing, and having accepted all that help, and then wallows around for those vital 5 minutes plus, he has to be stupid or some kind of dog.

So I have asked kids to live tough, to go the extra mile, knowing what was in store. I feel this way. They promised when they came to Alabama to give their best. We feed them, house them, educate them, and provide them with a whole lot more than the average student gets. So they have an obligation, too.

It used to be we had what we called a "fourth quarter" period at practice, a time at the end when they were asked to suck up their guts and put the ball behind the goal. A time when they were to imagine they were behind, and had to show if they were made of anything.

We haven't been in that position lately, where we were losing to a far superior team that was hammering hell out of us, the way Penn State did in the Liberty Bowl so many years ago. Mississippi did it to my Kentucky team in 1948. Gave us the worst physical beating I ever saw. They got stronger as we got weaker. The same thing happened to us several times in 1968, 1969, and 1970.

So what do you do when it gets like that? You can't throw in.

Coming from behind is still one of the greatest lessons, and the ability to do it is the mark of a great team. I told you about that Tech game, when we were down 15-0 at the half and won, 16-15. At Texas A&M in 1955 Rice had us 12-0 with three minutes and twenty-seven seconds to play. And *they had the ball.*

With a minute and seven seconds to play, we had them 20-12, and *we* had the ball on their 4-yard line. That's what I call sucking up your guts.

We were favored that day, but we hadn't played like favorites. And I had done some pretty sorry coaching. We had a play we named after Bobby Joe Conrad, based on the knowledge that Rice was using man-to-man coverage on pass receivers. The only time we pulled the Conrad Special Conrad was on the bench. I had screwed up my substitutions. We didn't even have the first team in.

Nevertheless Lloyd Taylor on first down ran 58 yards for a touchdown to make it 12-7. We pulled an onsides kick and Bebes Stallings got it, and on the first play Jimmy Wright called the Conrad, with Conrad on the bench, and passed to Taylor for another touchdown. Taylor kicked the point, and it was 14-12. Rice got the ball and Jack Pardee intercepted and ran to the 3, and we scored again to make it 20-12. We had intercepted another pass and were back down inside their 10 when the game ended.

And Loyd Taylor, who had made every one of those first 14 points, did something afterward I'll never forget. He said he wanted to say something to the team. He got up on a bench in the dressing room and hollered for quiet.

"Boys," he said, "we pray every time before a game, and do all this stuff. But afterward we don't do anything. What happened today we didn't do. We got some help from upstairs. Let's pray."

It impressed me, I'll tell you. Ever since then we do our praying *after* a game. We don't ask for anything, we go out and do it and then give thanks for whatever happens, win or lose.

After that Rice game Dr. Harrington, the A&M chancellor, walked with me from Rice Stadium to the Shamrock Hotel where we were staying in Houston. When I got there my mailbox was crammed with telegrams, almost every one of them giving me hell for screwing up and losing the game. They had been sent before the game was over.

It's been a long time since I called a team out of the showers and back onto the field, like I did that time with John Crow when I said, "OK, let's do it right." For a while there, too, before we went to the wishbone, we did a lot of passing, with quarterbacks like Namath, and Sloan, Stabler and Scott Hunter, and that meant a lot of backing off and rubbing bellies, trying to pass-protect, which isn't the same as really knocking them out of there like you do with a ball-control team.

I take that back. We did have a little of the old style after we lost to Georgia in the first game in 1965. The following week we weren't getting anything done, so I called a scrimmage. It was still no good, so I said, "That's all, gentlemen," and when they started to leave added, "but be on the field at six o'clock tomorrow morning, because we're going to get this thing done."

I said, "You're here to go to school, to get an education, but you're also here to play football. It works both ways. You promised to give your best. Now, if you don't like this, go on home. Tomorrow morning you're going to give your best or you're going to quit."

I didn't even tell the coaches whether there would be a meeting or not, but I knew I must have shook them up, too, because Dude Hennessey slept the whole night in the coaches' office, curled up on the carpet.

We came out there in the morning at six o'clock and, boy, I was praying we'd do well and nobody would get hurt. I flipped that ball out there, and they liked to knock the ends out of the stadium. Weren't out there more than fifteen minutes.

And I said, "Well, wasn't that fun?" and they agreed.

"Wasn't it ridiculous yesterday? You got to know how stupid it was to come out here and wallow around when you can do it like this and have people compliment you. You can have some fun, and then we can win."

If we had gotten somebody hurt I'd have died, but we didn't. We didn't lose another game all year and beat Nebraska in the Orange Bowl 39–28 for the National Championship.

That's the situation with a team. Individually it's a whole lot different, and you have to learn what makes this or that Sammy run. For one it's a pat on the back, for another it's eating him out, for still another it's a fatherly talk, or something else. You're a fool if you think, as I did as a young coach, that you can treat them all alike.

I know I've sure missed on a lot of them. Ken Hall down at Texas A&M, for example. A 200-pound halfback, ran the 100 in 9.7, probably the most sought-after player in the history of football, a hundred schools after him. He never did start a game for us, and he finally wound up leaving.

Well, it's easy to say he did this or that, but what about me? My job was to get him to play, and I didn't. So there's no doubt in my mind that I failed. I know this, if we had had Ken Hall in 1957 we would have won the National Championship. We were 166 points ahead in the poll with two games to go, and we lost those, 7–6 to Rice and 9–7 to Texas. You don't think Hall was worth three points to us?

I don't know whether Hall got anything, because he signed before we came to A&M, but if he did, whatever it was, he was worth more. He scored 395 points one year in high school — 49 in one game.

I'll never forget how he quit. We had played Baylor in the bloodiest football game I'd ever seen, and Jack Pardee had been hurt. We started Richard Gay for Pardee, a great fullback. Then we put Hall in there, and he broke out and came close to running for a touchdown. He did some things well and had me sold, and that night sitting around the hotel in Waco I told my coaches that nobody was going to beat us now because we had Hall in there.

Monday he didn't show up for practice.

That night I got home, and there he was waiting for me. He cried and carried on and said he'd do anything to come back. OK. Next day he didn't show up again. I went home and he was there, and he asked me again to take him back.

I said, "Well, Ken, yesterday would have been all right, but now I gotta do something, give you some kind of discipline. See me in my office tomorrow."

The next day he didn't show up again. That was the last straw for me. John Crow wanted me to let him talk to Ken, but I was too pig-headed to let Crow find out what the problem was. Ken Hall was a fine young man, and he was worth saving.

I have tried not to close my ears to a boy's feelings. I know one came in there at A&M and told me he didn't like the way I handled things, didn't like the way I talked, flat out didn't like my approach to the game, and I guarantee you that opened my eyes. I don't say I would have done different, but I sure didn't feel very good about it.

We lost some good boys when we first started at Alabama, too, and if football didn't mean enough to them I was glad I found out, but the prospect of losing a boy now never enters my mind. We hardly get a quitter anymore. I know so many in the past, like Ken Hall, if they had known what I was thinking, what I had in mind — if I had had the sense to tell them — they would never have quit.

And I know now, too, that some who quit didn't mean to. Like Richard Williamson, who was on my staff and is coaching for Arkansas now. He's already a good coach, and he's going to be a head coach one day soon. Richard was a real high-strung kid who would give out of stamina in a hurry, being so keyed up. We had to watch him for fear he'd black out on the field, make sure he got a lot of salt.

He was a terrific competitor and a fine person, and I wanted him to play before he was physically ready. His sophomore year, when I should have red-shirted him, I put him in a couple of games, wasting him, really. Then when we played Georgia in Birmingham on national television he didn't get to play. And it must have hurt because the next night he wasn't at our meeting.

I was afraid he had quit. But the following day he brought his daddy with him and we straightened everything out. If I had stuck to that business about "once a quitter always a quitter" I'd have lost him.

I've said how proud I've been of some of the boys who stuck with me, and I'm sentimental about them I guess, because I've been the proudest when a boy had to take the most discipline and then came back and proved himself. I told you about Bob Gain at Kentucky, who was an All-America tackle, how he hated my guts and told some of the guys he was going over to my house one night and whip my butt, which he could have done left-handed, and then how he wrote me that letter from Korea the night before he went into battle telling me it was all worthwhile.

Bob's problem was that he had gotten by with too much, and he broke the rules so often the school decided not to invite him back that fall. When he found out what they were going to do and heard I wouldn't vouch for him he couldn't believe it.

I said, "Bob, I want to tell you some things you ought to know. We can get you back in school because the dean said we could if I would vouch for you. But I won't.

"In all my experience you're the worst problem I've ever had. You have been pouting around here for a month because you weren't elected captain. I counted the votes, and it wasn't even close. You're selfish, and I don't even want my players around you. Something might rub off."

I told him everything I could think of, and he took it and asked me to give him a chance to get back in.

I said, "If I do I am going to call in the press and your mother and your high school coach" — a real high-class guy and great coach named Carl Hamill, and Bob was scared of him — "and I'm going to tell them all about it right in front of you. And the first day you break that much you're gone, and I'm going to ask them to put everything in the paper."

I said, "Is everything I said here the truth?"

He said yes.

So we got everybody together, including his mother, and I went over the whole business again word for word.

Then I said, "I don't think he's got it in him, but if he does I'll be as proud — more proud of him than you, Mrs. Gain. If he doesn't, it's all going in the paper."

Well, you know how fond I am of Bob Gain. He was already a great player, and he turned out to be the best leader we had at Kentucky. He was the strongest tackle I ever saw. One time Gene Donaldson trap-blocked him out of a play in a scrimmage and I was so surprised I made them run the play again. I said, "I wanta see if that was luck."

They ran it again and Bob almost tore Donaldson's head off, helmet and all.

I said, "That's what I thought."

Gain was this type leader. If a player wasn't putting out, and the coaches couldn't get him to, Bob would go around and threaten to whip the guy's tail. That usually did the trick. Deep down, Bob had a sense of responsibility. Dude Hennessey tells me Gain was big-dogging around about punching me in the nose one night, but when he knocked on the door at the hotel where we were staying all he said was, "Coach, I just wanted to tell you I was going to bed."

It was my lucky night, I guess.

I don't remember the incident, but I do remember toward the end of his last year I invited the seniors to the house for a little party. We had some beer and stuff and they brought dates.

Bob stood at the door and said, "Coach, I can't go that beer. I've got a bottle in my car and if you don't mind —"

"Bob," I said, "my liquor cabinet's right there. I told you when you used to be on your ass, whenever you thought you needed a drink, you could come out here and have one. But make sure it's here." It was shortly after that, two or three months, anyway, that he went to Korea.

I would like to have Gene Donaldson back right now, because I think he'd have been even better — and he was plenty good — in the kind of atmosphere we have at Alabama, where it's go-go-go all the time and there's a lot of publicity and patting on the back. Gene was plenty tough enough. Dude says he used to have a poster in his room of a man being eaten alive, and the freshman players were scared to death of him. He weighed about 195, but he hit like a 240-pounder.

I think now, though, that Gene would have responded better had I been more complimentary. Walt Yaworski probably never heard a kind word the whole time he was in school, not from me or any-body. I could have done a better job with both of them.

Steve Meilinger was another one. I knew he was going to be trouble because I saw a coach slip him a cigarette when I was trying to recruit him. As a freshman he was a loafer, and he dogged around in practice — he'll tell you so — and in his sophomore year I made up my mind I was going to save him or lose him.

I remember this so well, because there were people around. I tongue-lashed him, and I pushed him and shook him and did everything I could think of.

Did he react? You're darn right he reacted. He was great. He was 6–3, 220 pounds, and could fly. He was an end originally, but he played four positions for us, and when he was a senior I stuck him in there at quarterback one night in the rain at Miami.

I'm the luckiest sonofagun. Miami didn't know he was going to play quarterback, but I sure didn't know it was going to rain. The good Lord must have had a hand in it, because all we were going to do was let him fake and keep. The water was up to your ankles, and he just sloshed through everybody, and he even wound up throwing a touchdown pass. We won, 29–0. I don't think Andy Gustafson, the Miami coach, ever forgave me.

Steve could have gone anywhere, he was that good. I really thought he would quit, the way we bounced him around. I remember when he was a senior I talked to Grantland Rice and Harry Grayson about putting him on the All-America team. I knew it was tough, because how could you make All-America if you were an end one week and a quarterback the next? But they went to bat for him, and Fred Russell and Raymond Johnson of the Tennessee papers did, too, and he made it. And deserved it.

Meilinger is a U.S. marshal in Kentucky now, and Mary Harmon and I had dinner with him the night before we played Kentucky last year. He and sixty-six of the old Kentucky players had a testimonial weekend for us. It was the greatest time I ever had. They put on a dinner and a big breakfast and a golf tournament. My former players came from as far off as Boston and San Diego. Gain was there, and Duffy Daugherty was the emcee.

I enjoyed every minute of it, except for a few bad times on the golf course. Steve said, "Coach, if I'd played football the way you're playing golf you'da killed me."

And I sat there that night at the dinner, thinking about the letter Gain wrote before he went to Korea, and ones Meilinger had written, how appreciative they were. How much, as Steve wrote, "they loved me for the things they used to hate me for."

– Twenty-Two –

But I guarantee you I never had a gut check over a boy like I had with Joe Namath. Joe was the best athlete I have ever seen. He is blessed with that rare quickness — hands, feet, everything — and he's quick and tough mentally, too. Anybody who ever watched him warm up could tell that football comes easy for Joe.

A lot of kids have high I.Q.s and aren't good athletes. That's obvious. Others who aren't so smart in a classroom find something like football easy to pick up. Billy Neighbors was like me. It would take us five years to pass an English course, but football was easy. Namath could have made As in school but he didn't study. Nothing came easier for him than football. He could sit down and listen to some football concept for the first time, and snap, snap, he'd have a mental picture of every phase of it.

I don't classify quarterbacks as players. I think of them as coaches on the field. But Joe had more natural playing ability than anybody. Just gifted.

If you know his background, though, you know his life hasn't been so easy, and you know, too, why he wears those dark glasses and fancy clothes and sometimes acts a little brash.

We lucked into Joe. He didn't even visit the campus during the recruiting season of 1961. He was interested only in Maryland and Notre Dame, and we had given up on him. On the last day for signing prospects, Charlie Bradshaw, who was on my staff then, got a call from a friend on the Maryland staff. The guy said Joe lacked a point or two on his boards to get in, and he was afraid he'd go to Penn State or one of the schools Maryland had to play. They didn't want to have to face Joe.

It so happened that Howard Schnellenberger had coached Joe's brother. We sent Howard up in the school plane in a hurry to talk to Joe. Howard got him signed and we flew the letter of intent back to the commissioner's office in Birmingham the day before we started practice. Joe came by bus.

They used to tell stories about Joe's first day, coming out to the field in a beret with a fake pearl on one side, and pegged pants, and big dark glasses. They say he called up to where I was perched on my tower, "Hi, Coach," and I invited him up, which would have been a rare invitation to say the least. I probably did, though. I would have *carried* him up if I'd known then how good he was.

It was all new to Joe — our program, the South. You have to appreciate what he came from. Beaver Falls, Pennsylvania, is in the hill country about twenty-five miles east of Pittsburgh. Joe grew up in a tough eastern environment. Many of his friends were black. Joe was the youngest of five children. His father worked in the mills, but he and Joe's mother were divorced when Joe was twelve or thirteen. He lived with his mother.

There wasn't much money lying around. The way Joe tells it, he ran messages for people around the poolroom, shined shoes, shot pool. He said there wasn't anyone going to hustle him. So you have to say his background was nothing like anything he saw at Alabama. He didn't speak the language. For a long while he was a loner.

I hadn't seen him play until he came to us, but when he walked onto that field I knew we had something special. He had that air about him. He could do it all. He could run, he could play defense. Had he chosen, he could have been a great baseball or basketball player, or a golfer. He could pick up a golf club right now and shoot par. Just an extraordinary athlete.

Joe was never what you'd call a humble person, but most of his talk was light-hearted and quick. Street talk, really. A Vanderbilt tackler hit him pretty good when he was a sophomore and, according to our players, said, "Hey, number 12, what's your name?"

Joe said, "You'll see it in the headlines tomorrow." On the next play he threw a touchdown pass.

Years later some New York writer tried to get a rise out of him about his studies at Alabama. He asked Joe if he had majored in basket-weaving. Joe's quoted answer was, "Naw, man. I majored in journalism. It was easier."

He never had any trouble expressing himself, and many of the things might seem intemperate to some people. He was asked not long ago to compare me with Weeb Ewbank, and he was quoted as saying, "Coach Bryant was always thinking about winning. Weeb is mainly concerned over what kind of publicity you get."

Well, what's in a decision? In Joe's three years we had seasons of 10–1, 9–2 and 10–1. And Joe wound up with a southern accent. I don't know where he developed his fondness for the South, but even now he likes to defend southern football against what he calls "the northern press." A northern writer asked him if as a pro player with all that money he still knew how to "pay the price" on the field.

Joe said, "You can't play for Coach Bryant for four years and not know how to pay the price."

One thing that helped him in his first months at Alabama was that at that time we were blessed with tremendous leadership, the best I've ever seen. Pat Trammell was a senior when Joe was a freshman, and I have told you the impact Pat made on people. Winning that National Championship had to make an impression on a youngster, too. And there were great carryover leaders: Lee Roy Jordan and Jimmy Sharpe and Bill Battle and Richard Williamson to name a few. I think all that helped Joe.

In those days I ate lunch every day with my quarterbacks, to get to know them, to preach my sermons. But if I had done a better job I don't think I ever would have had to discipline Joe. I know he has to be one of the most loyal people I ever met. I remember when he got into trouble there were other players involved, but I didn't know it then. I was walking across campus with him one night, telling him it wasn't much good having friends who let you take the punishment alone.

He said, "Coach, I can't say anything against them. They're my friends." He told me almost the same thing six years later when the National Football League was trying to get him to dissociate himself from the ownership of that bar in New York.

Joe had a great sophomore year for Alabama. In his first game, against Georgia, he threw for three touchdowns and ran for another, and he just blended in so nicely.

George Mira of Miami was the hottest quarterback in the country that year, and he was great, no doubt about that. Mira gave us fits two years in a row. But I told a writer friend who was bragging on Mira one night that "that little boy might be *your* favorite, but I've got one who is going to make more money than any quarterback who ever lived." That was in 1962.

Before we played Oklahoma in the Orange Bowl that year one guy came in wanting to know how to spell Joe's name. "Stick around," I said. "You'll pick it up in no time." We beat Oklahoma, 17–0.

Well, we were coming down to the end of the 1963 season. We had a game with Miami, then Mississippi in the Sugar Bowl, both on national television, and it was right about the time of President Kennedy's assassination. We had taken two weeks off. If it had happened during that period I wouldn't have done anything. We were off and players weren't bound to the training rules.

I got word that Joe and his friends had been down at some woman's store, having a party, breaking training. The woman had told a couple of my coaches about it. This was on Monday, and we were supposed to practice that night. I had planned to fly to Tennessee afterward to see a prospect.

When I heard it I was sick. Nauseated. I checked with my people who were supposed to know, because I had been hearing things all year, and they still hadn't heard it.

I went to the dorm looking for Joe. I didn't want to ask around, I wanted to confront him with it. I couldn't find him so I went into the dining room to have a cup of coffee. He came in and sat down at the table with me and started talking about game plans.

I said, "Joe, let's go back to my room." I have a room at the dorm I sometimes use. "I want to talk with you."

I told him what I had heard, and I said, "Joe, you know I'm going to get the truth, and I don't think you would lie to me."

He admitted it. I didn't know for months that other players were involved. They let him take the rap alone. I told him to go see Coach Bailey, who would give him a place to stay, because I was suspending him from the team.

He said, "How many days?"

I said for the year, or forever, or until he proved something to me.

I said, "I'll help you go somewhere else if you want to, or get in the Canadian league, or if you have enough in you to stay in school and prove to me this was just a bad mistake, I'll let you back on the team next spring."

I went back and called the coaches together and told them my decision and asked if they had an opinion. By today's standards what Joe did was nothing, but I believe if you have rules you abide by them. You can't make exceptions. Every darn one of my coaches said let's do something to save him. Except one. Bebes Stallings.

Bebes just sat there and shook his head and said unh-unh.

He said, "If it had been me, you would have fired me, wouldn't you?"

I said yeah.

He said, "Well, let him go."

I thanked the coaches and asked them to wait outside and told Sam to have Joe wait.

I sat in there two hours. Oh my, I cried. I racked my brains for the right answer. I knew it was more than Joe's career I had to consider.

Finally I called them back in, and called Joe in, and I said, "Joe, everybody in the room except one pleaded for you.

"But black is black and white's white. I'd give my right arm if I didn't have to do it, but if I didn't I'd ruin you and ruin the team, too, eventually."

I said, "You're suspended, and I don't give a damn what anybody in here says. You're not going to play. The university could change this decision if they wanted to, or I could. But if they change it or I change it I'll resign."

And — I'll never forget it — he said, "Aw, no, Coach, I don't want you to do that." The only thing he asked me to do was to tell his mother before it hit the papers.

I called the squad together and told them. I called but didn't get through to Joe's mother. That afternoon I flew up to Morristown, Tennessee, in Red Blount's plane on the recruiting trip, and I reached her from there. Boy, that hurt.

She cried and carried on, begging me to take him back. She's a wonderful lady, too. But I said there was nothing else I could do. And I didn't find this out till years later. Joe had dinner at my house that night with Mary Harmon and my son Paul. Mary Harmon thought of Joe as her boy, and when you think about it there was no better place for him to be at a time like that.

According to the mail, almost everybody objected to what I had done. Letters, telegrams, petitions. I got one telegram from Beaver Falls with six thousand signatures on it.

But taking him back was out of the question. I hadn't done a good job with Joe, I know that, because if I had this would never have happened. But if I had let him go another year we wouldn't have made it as a team, and I may be wrong as heck about this, but I believe Joe would tell you that he wouldn't have made it, either.

We had those two games to play. Could we win without him? No, I didn't believe so at the moment. But after I got to thinking about it, shoot, you can do anything if you want to bad enough.

We outlasted Miami and George Mira, 17–12. After the first four minutes Miami got all the yards. Mira passed for close to four hundred, more than everybody else combined had gotten on us all year, but he ran out of time.

Steve Sloan and Jack Hurlbut were just wonderful filling in for Joe, and we beat Mississippi, 12–7, in the Sugar Bowl, Anybody who had seen our Miami game had to have serious doubts about our chances against Mississippi, undefeated that year. But ours was a team with unbelievable character. And it didn't hurt having Tim Davis, either. Tim kicked four field goals that day.

We lifted Joe's suspension in the spring, and when he came back he just took charge. I could tell he still had misgivings about me, though. Whenever they wanted pictures made he'd kind of shy away. But it didn't affect his play one iota.

We won another National Championship that year, sweeping ten in a row, and of course that was the year Sonny Werblin and Weeb Ewbank came to Miami for our Orange Bowl game with Texas and made Joe a rich man.

I actually had very little to do with it. It was rumored that I got $25,000 for delivering Joe to the Jets, and if the guy who started it said it to my face I'd spit in his eye. If it had been offered I would have taken it, all right — and given it to Joe.

Joe did ask me to help earlier, and I tried to come up with a figure for him. I said, "Ask for $200,000, and see if they'll give you $100,000." Something like that.

He said, "What if they say yes?"

I said, "Let's go get you a lawyer. This is too big for me."

Mike Bite of Birmingham handled it for him. Mike is a good lawyer, and a friend of mine. Joe had been drafted by the Cardinals, also, and the bidding must have been terrific. The only thing I said to Joe on the relative merits of the two clubs was that Weeb Ewbank had won two championships at Baltimore, and if Joe still was interested in winning he might give that some consideration.

They made the announcement right after the Texas game in the Orange Bowl dressing room. Joe would get $40,000 cash, and $400,000 parceled out so the taxes wouldn't kill him, and a couple of automobiles. It was by far the richest contract in pro football history. Knowledgeable people also say it was the deal that made the American Football League.

Well, that was the good part. The bad part was that Texas beat us 21–17. Joe had been hurt earlier in the season against North Carolina State, a knee injury that has plagued him ever since, but he came off the bench and almost pulled it out. We were behind 21–7 at one point. Just before the game ended Joe got us to the Texas goal, and on a fourth-down quarterback keep he came that close to winning it. Tommy Nobis met him head on. Our guys thought he scored.

Afterward one of the writers asked me who called the play. I said I had. (I always call the ones that don't work.)

He said, "How can a $12,000-a-year coach call the plays for a $400,000 quarterback?" I admitted he had a point.

The next day they had a big press conference at the Bal Harbour

Inn. Joe showed up in a pink sport coat. I sat with Weeb Ewbank at the head table. I told Weeb if it was true like people said that it takes three or four years to develop a pro quarterback, and it took that long with Joe, then he wasn't as good a coach as I thought he was.

Werblin and the Jets' line coach, Chuck Knox, who is now head coach of the Los Angeles team, were also at the table. Everybody made a little speech. I told them I was "thankful I had the privilege of being one of Joe's coaches. He has meant a lot to the state of Alabama, and to the university." I said, too, that he was "the most talented young man I have ever seen."

When he got to New York Joe enjoyed the kind of life I imagine he always dreamed about in Beaver Falls. He had his buddies — Joe Hirsch, the writer for the *Morning Telegraph*, as his personal handicapper, and Ray Abbruzzese, his old Alabama teammate and Jet defensive back, as his bartender. His apartment was decorated by the same guy who did Frank Sinatra's. He was quoted as saying, "I don't care what a man is as long as he treats me right. I like everybody." That's about as close to a personal philosophy as I could give you on Joe.

I stayed over in Miami for about ten days after the Orange Bowl, getting used to being a plain old coach again. When I was checking out of the Seaview Hotel there was Dr. Rose, the Alabama president, at the desk. I hadn't seen him since the game. He hugged me, and when we were walking out he said: "Tell the truth, Paul. You didn't call that quarterback sneak on the goal line in the Orange Bowl, did you?"

"Yeah, I did." Whether I called it or not was immaterial; my quarterbacks are an extension of me on the field.

He said, "Well, I would never have done that."

I said, "I wouldn't, either, if I'd had ten days to think about it."

Since then Joe Namath has become the celebrity I predicted he would be, but he has never called me anything but "Coach" before or since. Never "Bear" or "Paul." I have to think, too, he is a better man for that long-ago suspension.

The only time I have interfered in his life since Sonny Werblin came into it was to try to take some of his money on the golf course, which is very difficult to do, my game being what it is. I took some lessons when I was playing with him in the Hope Classic one year and my old buddy Julian Lackey told everybody that "taking golf lessons for the bastard" — meaning me — "is like a hog going to a beauty parlor."

I did try to talk Joe out of quitting football when he ran into problems with the NFL over his lounge, the Bachelors III, in June 1969. Joe didn't want anybody to dictate to him, and I can understand that. When I got him he was going out the door for the press conference.

I said, "Joe, if these friends of yours really care about you, they'll *make* you get out of that partnership."

He said, "No, sir, Coach. I know I'm right. I've got to do this."

We talked about twenty minutes, and I finally asked him, "Joe, have you gotten too big to pray?"

He said, "No, sir, Coach. That's all I've been doing for two nights."

For a while I thought it was going to be a very abrupt end to a great career, but Joe got it straightened out and I was glad to see him playing again. Even with two bad knees he's the best in the business. I only wish those Jet fans could have seen him the first couple of years at Alabama, when he was whole.

I think this. The Joe Namath I knew then is not that much different from the Namath that makes the headlines and gossip columns now. He's just being packaged differently. When he comes to Alabama, the first person he goes to see is Jim Goostree, our trainer, and then the equipment man, and the other people who meant something to him. He never misses.

And I'll never forget the last game of his senior year, in the dressing room after we'd beaten Auburn. We were the only two still in there. And he said something that made me about as proud as I've ever been.

He said, "I want to look you in the eye" — that's one of my pet expressions — "I want to look you right in the eye and tell you you were right, and I want to thank you."

I wouldn't take a jillion for that.

- Twenty-Three -

How much is a year of a man's life worth? I don't know, but *The Saturday Evening Post* took ten years off my life, and I billed them $10 million for it. I guarantee you, if I had collected that much — which I didn't — it would not have paid for the suffering they put me through.

I get mad today just thinking about it. I used to wake up nights worrying about the way it was killing my wife and children. I'll never know how much it hurt Mary Harmon, because she hides her feelings better than I do.

The irony of it, the thing that makes you want to cut somebody's throat, is that the people who were guilty of the whole thing, who got it started and wrote the stories — they just got paid.

On October 10, 1962, *The Saturday Evening Post* came out with a story by a reporter for the *Atlanta Journal*, Furman Bisher, about brutality in college football. The story — "College Football Is Going Berserk" — tried to make a case against me and my program. They hadn't been satisfied by the way the same writer crucified one of my players to get at me the year before.

The story reopened the wounds of the Graning incident and talked about how we did things — knocking people around in prac-

208

tice, teaching excessively rough football, "brutal" football. Bisher was supposed to be an expert on all these things because he'd been to my practices maybe twice in his life. (He will never be to another one.)

It was funny, because that very fall I'd done a radio tape with Bisher in my office, and he was complimenting me on getting so much out of my personnel. My feeling was, and still is, that it's ridiculous to believe you can teach brutality and be successful with kids, to get them to give so much.

The story quoted me as saying I kept a player out of practice this day that the writer was supposed to have been there because "he's so tough we don't let him scrimmage during the week. He's liable to hurt somebody."

That was either a misquote or he took a kidding remark and twisted it to his own purpose. Either way, it came out wrong.

In the first place the trainer and the team doctor tell me who can or cannot practice. We often hold key players out to keep *them* from getting hurt, not hurting somebody else. Second, if I was afraid a player would hurt somebody, do something illegal, I wouldn't let him play. I've already told you what I think of penalties and players who draw them. Every player on any of my teams knows that.

I might have said the player was being kept out that day, and he might have been injured, but I sure as hell never indicated he was too mean or tough to practice. I did appreciate the fact that he was like most of those little skinny-legged guys we had then — a contact player. If he wasn't he wouldn't have been playing for me.

I'm not going to get so humble that I won't stand up for what we were doing then. Call it brutal if you want, but we were teaching the best football in America in those days. Guys like Jimmy Sharpe and Lee Roy Jordan would have jumped down an elevator shaft if I'd asked them to. You don't get that kind of loyalty if you're teaching something wrong. It's common sense.

Billy Neighbors was quoted as saying at the time, "Why don't they ask the boys who play for him? We could tell them." Bobby Jackson, in the same story, said, "Has anybody at Alabama killed anybody?" And Gary Phillips said, "There's a difference between being tough and being dirty. We had an end who got three 15-yard penalties Coach Bryant's first year. He never played again."

I still maintain that none of this would have happened, or been carried to such lengths, if Bobby Dodd wasn't trying to get his people in the frame of mind to pull out of the Alabama series, and out of the Southeastern Conference. He'll tell you so. And if I'd been a little more alert to the whole thing I'd have been in the Tech dressing room right after that game taking care of it, or making sure the next week that it didn't get worse.

The *Post* story also made an issue of a statement I made my first year back at Alabama. We'd lost our first game that year, and I had gone on television and said there would probably be some rumbling but this was my team now and the best thing about getting beat was you always get rid of the "riffraff." The implication was that I called players who quit, or who I didn't want anymore, "riffraff."

I wasn't talking about my players, I was talking about people, and I'll say it again if we lose a couple of games this fall. We'll get rid of the riffraff, the hangers-on, the few people who take up your time getting in your way and who would turn on you in a minute. We have them, Notre Dame has them, everybody does.

And I can tell you exactly when that riffraff business started. It was in my last year at Kentucky, 1953, when we went down to play Rice and got behind in the first half when I thought we should have been ahead.

When I got back to the dressing room I was about to throw a fit, so I said, "All right, I want all the riffraff out of here, so I can talk to my players."

Smokey Harper used to get a kick out of telling the story, because the "riffraff" included the governor of the state and a number of dignitaries. They all scurried out of there like little pigs, and "riff-raff" got to be an expression I used. If it was an unfortunate one I can't help it now.

Well, I had always made it a practice not to get into arguments with newspapermen, because if you do you're an idiot. You can't argue with the printing press. I have very close friends who are newspapermen, and 99 percent of those I've met are good people trying to do a good job. If a newspaperman writes something wrong — and I always think it's wrong if it's something ugly about me — I may think he's wrong, but he may think he's right. We've both got a job to do, but we don't have to think alike.

I know I got a lot of attention for the way I did things at Kentucky and A&M, and a lot of newspapermen who were on me then are good friends of mine now. Like Clark Nealon down in Houston.

I also know I antagonized a lot of them over the years. I used to say, "I've got the product, they come to me. I don't have to go to them." But I never said, "Sportswriters can be had with a bottle of whiskey and a steak dinner," because I know better.

At Kentucky we were trying so hard to get publicity I even made one writer my "consultant," the only time I ever did that. I figured if he was on the payroll he'd get off my back, but he still second-guessed me all the time. He finally went into promotion work and found out how tough it was to get publicity.

I wound up with some good support in Kentucky, especially from the late Larry Boeck of the *Courier-Journal*. The guy on the other paper was impossible. He was a big man in the fraternity Dopey Phelps was in and he didn't like the way I handled Phelps. I don't blame him — I handled Phelps poorly. I used to complain that Purdue and Indiana got more space in the Louisville papers than we did. But we had some believers by the time I left.

Our winning at Kentucky probably had an adverse effect on my successors there in their press relations. Instead of the once-a-week coverage I got, they were scrutinized every day. I think Charley Bradshaw, who had been one of my players and assistant coaches, would have done a good job if they hadn't gotten down on him so quickly. He followed Blanton Collier, and by then most of the groundwork we laid had dissipated, and Charley didn't win. I was surprised they cut him up, though. If it had been me I could understand it, the chip I had on my shoulder then.

At Texas A&M we had a terrible press for a long while. I guarantee you if that guy in Fort Worth wrote the things now that he did then I'd either sue him or shoot him. Jack Gallagher in Houston got to be a friend of mine, but until I got to know him I thought he was the biggest pain around. I felt so alone at A&M, without a supporting big-city paper, and I knew I had to prove myself fourteen thousand times, which was all right, too. Nobody had a better press than I did my last year there.

At Alabama, for the first time, I was in a situation where the press was basically for you, because it was for the university. When

I first arrived Auburn and Georgia Tech got most of the attention, which I could understand because Alabama hadn't been winning. I resented the fact that Benny Marshall of the *Birmingham News* would cover the Tech game instead of ours, but I understood it. We eventually turned it around.

Mary Harmon still gets upset if somebody seems to be writing too much about Auburn. I tell her Auburn's a good school and if they've got something worth writing about over there it oughta be written, even if we do beat 'em most of the time. The Alabama press is for Alabama schools, and helps them, and Charley Thornton, our publicity man and assistant athletic director, treats them fairly and makes it a point not to slight any of them. He's no child. He's a pro and very able. I let him handle it.

I say it all the time. The coaching staff may have a team fired up once or twice a year, other times it's the atmosphere on campus, the student body, friends back home *and* the press. Usually the local writers want you to win as badly as you want to. They'd rather write about a winner any day. And what they write can help you. Somebody like Charles Land or Alf Van Hoose or Bill Lumpkin or Bill Easterling might write about the team or an individual at Alabama or Auburn, and what appears in the paper can stimulate and motivate.

Writers help us immeasurably, without really trying. They'll write something that, in the truth of it, will get a boy — or the whole team — riled up. It wouldn't matter if we were the underdog or the overdog. It's a funny thing about reading something in the paper. If the coach tells you it's one thing. If you read it in cold print the effect can be much greater.

I could always get my message across with Benny Marshall. I'd give him a clue and he'd go with it. One of the greatest stories I ever read was one he wrote just before that 1962 Sugar Bowl, when we were in Biloxi practicing, and everybody was sick, including me.

About 11:30 one night there was a tiny little knock on my hotel room door.

I said, "Come in!" loud as I could, hoping to scare 'em off. And Benny walked in.

I didn't say much, I was so sick and feverish and all. But the next day he wrote a piece in the paper that won the game, and he never knew it.

He wrote about the old man being sick, and hurting, and his wife and son laid up at home. But the old man would show up for sure, he said. It had to make an impression. That was the 10–3 Sugar Bowl victory over Arkansas, and you may not see it that way but I'm positive we wouldn't have won if Benny didn't write that story.

You say, well, you just use the press. That's right. What's wrong with it? I use newspapers, television, bulletin boards — anything I can to get our players to look and listen. I'll never forget little Mickey Herskowitz, always coming around trying to get stories at A&M. And me always trying to give him something to impress a player with. Except I wasn't as good at it then as I am now.

One Sunday Mickey was in there and we were chatting and he said, "I'm doing a piece on Lloyd Hale. What can you say about him?"

I was trying to get Lloyd to be a little tougher on defense at the time. I said, "Mickey, just say, 'Lloyd's defensive play doesn't quite measure up to his offensive play.' "

I thought about it for a minute, and I said, "Naw, don't say it that way. Say, 'Hale's a fine offensive player, but his linebacking could stand improvement.' "

I didn't like that either. I said, "Wait a minute. Say —"

And Mickey interrupted, "Damn, Coach, you're beginning to sound like an English professor."

I took my feet off the desk and looked Mickey in the eye and said, "All right, dammit. Say, 'Hale's a good offensive player, but he's a piss-poor linebacker.' " Good old Mickey saved me from that one.

So I don't hesitate to call Charlie Land or Alf Van Hoose, because they can help. Sometimes writers from other areas can do it, too. A couple of years ago a Florida writer put something in his paper about the Lord being on Florida's side. Our good Christian boys didn't believe it. They had that clipping plastered all over the walls. We beat Florida, 17–14.

Because of that kind of thing I used to have a rule that my players couldn't talk to the press about anything to do with football. Anything that could hurt our chances. They could talk about pretty girls, what kind of pie they like, what a lousy coach I am, anything, and I love them to be interviewed. But they don't have to be a good interview to make All-America. I know I made wrong statements lots of times with the help of a whole staff of publicity people. How can I expect them not to, especially right after a tough game? Now we have a rule that they can talk to the press after a game, but only after a cooling-off period.

I'll tell you what can happen. We had this Trimble kid playing for us at A&M — the one whose brother was later on our Alabama team — and we beat Texas in that game in Austin, the first and only time A&M ever beat Texas on their field. One of my favorite expressions is "mamas and papas." I've about worn it out now; I've got to get a new one. But I'm always saying how important it is to have "good mamas and papas."

Anyway, everybody's happy and hugging around, and they've thrown me in the showers, and somebody asks Murray Trimble what he thought of the Texas team.

Murray said, "Well, not much. They probably don't have good mamas and papas."

I like to died when I saw that in the paper. Can you imagine whose dressing room wall that went on the next year? And who beat us the next year in a big upset?

I know this policy has been gravel in the craw of a lot of writers. It used to kill Jack Gallagher. At one Orange Bowl game a fellow who was then on the *Miami News*, Tommy Devine, called me a "whipcracking, narrow-minded tyrant" because of the restrictions I made him work under. I didn't like it much, but I can understand it.

The thing about a few newspapermen is that they'll put words in your mouth if you let 'em. I have to watch my tongue. I've gotten to the point where after a game I try to generalize until after I've seen the films. I might say, "Old Joe made a nice play there," but I'm leery of saying he "played well," because you're never sure.

After a Mississippi game one year I was walking down the street with Jay Rhodemyre, one of the best players I had at Kentucky. Jay's dead now. We were going to the train to take us back to Lexington, and I said, "Jay, I never thought I'd see you play so poorly."

He said, "Coach, I thought I played pretty well."

I said, "If you did I didn't think so."

We got home and graded the films, and Jay graded higher than any player we ever had. How would it have looked if I'd criticized him to the press after the game?

The reverse has happened. We were playing Georgia in Lexington and I bragged on a boy who had made an exceptionally fine block. But I said what a "great game" he had. When we graded the film, it turned out to be the only block he made all day.

One thing about it, I'll beat everybody second-guessing. That's the first thing I do on my Sunday television show. I have three or four notes jotted down, things I'm going to belittle myself about, things we did poorly. And sometimes I get other little goodies in there. I tell about John So-and-So's daddy being at the game, and how I wish I could get him to play a little better. It's corn, but it wins. A boy's out there listening with his girl or something, he's going to pay attention.

Well, any other time I would have just shrugged off that first *Post* story. I have more confidence in myself and my program than to go tearing off in all directions.

I should have just considered the source and dropped it. I'd never been impressed with Furman Bisher. I remember the first time he came to Tuscaloosa, when we first got there in 1958. We took him and his wife to dinner, and Mary Harmon looked after Mrs. Bisher and spent a lot of time showing Furman her scrapbooks. If I'd known what he was up to I'd have given him thirty minutes and excused myself. He picked a sentence out of here and one from there, whatever he could find to make me look bad.

I suppose a man who has had so much controversy in his life would learn to live with it, but things were going so well, things that should have made these years the happiest of my life. We'd won the first National Championship in 1961 and the coaches had elected me Coach of the Year. That is a great honor just because it is the coaches who give it.

Then the brutality story came out, and it was like a blow on the neck. I remember we were flying back from Knoxville after the Tennessee game. I was sitting with Red Blount, a member of the Alabama Board of Trustees. Red was egging me on, telling me I ought to sue, and I got to thinking what an injustice it was and how it would hurt our program.

215

So I talked to my lawyer friend, Winston McCall, and demanded a retraction. None was given. On January 4, 1963, we filed a libel suit for $500,000.

Well, you challenge somebody on one pack of lies and you wind up with a bigger pack of lies. It was a mistake. If I hadn't sued the *Post* on that one I don't believe there would ever have been the second story. They must have started working on it right after we filed the suit.

– Twenty-Four –

The second story came out in the *Post* of March 23, 1963, but the rumors were coming to me long before that. I got calls from Alf Van Hoose of the *Birmingham News* and Fred Russell of the *Nashville Banner*. They were in Florida, where they were covering baseball, and they warned me that something was coming.

Eventually I found out who was compiling it: Furman Bisher, although his name wasn't going to be on it.

Then Mel Allen called me. He was in Fort Lauderdale with the Yankees, and he was very disturbed and said if anything happened he would help me get Louis Nizer in New York as my lawyer, if I wanted him. I even got a call from Don Hutson, my old roommate.

The story they were getting in bits and pieces was that Wally Butts, the athletic director and former coach of the University of Georgia, and I had fixed a game — bet on it.

Bisher, or somebody, was supposed to have a photostat of a $50,000 check I had written as a payoff. Besides the Georgia game, I was also supposed to have thrown the 1962 Georgia Tech game. We lost that 7–6, our only loss that year and the first in twenty-seven games.

The clincher, though, was Tom Siler of the *Knoxville News-Sentinel*. Tom called me asking for a statement.

I said, "Hell, Tom, I can't say anything. I haven't even seen it."
He said, "Well, *I've* seen it. And it's a helluva story."

Another newspaperman told me it had to be authentic if Siler said so, because Siler had been with Bisher in Florida. Then I got a letter from Wally Butts. He'd heard it, too.

So I went to see our President Rose and the athletic committee to tell them what I was hearing. Dr. Rose immediately began an investigation of his own, and I can't blame him for that. He had to know.

In the meantime I had to go to Washington for a clinic. Bud Wilkinson and I had been talking politics, and he was telling me what an impressive man Bobby Kennedy, the attorney general, was, and he wanted me to meet him. Bud was trying to get me interested in running for something, and he thought Bobby Kennedy could give me an idea of whether I could win. Bud got us a date with Kennedy for the next morning, but Kennedy's office called to change it to 2 P.M. I couldn't make that because I needed to be home for something and asked Bud to express my regrets.

I left town but early the next morning Bud called me. "Bobby's sorry he didn't get to meet you," he said. "If I were you I'd try to see him first chance I got."

One thing led to another and it wasn't long after that I was back in Washington and got another appointment with Bobby Kennedy. By then rumors were hot and heavy. My publicity man said we'd get the full story in a few days. And that very morning a Washington paper had a report that two southern coaches were involved in what could be the biggest scandal in college football history.

So I went in to see Mr. Kennedy, and I think he was one of the most impressive men I ever met. I had met his brother Jack, then the President, in December 1961, when I was at the Waldorf Astoria in New York for the Hall of Fame dinner. I had presented President Kennedy with an Alabama football letter. I told him he was the first President in history to get one, and he asked me if I'd let him come down and play a couple minutes.

Bobby had that same magnetism. Later he came to Tuscaloosa to speak and we had dinner at Dr. Rose's mansion, Bobby and Ethel and Mary Harmon and I, and Bobby and Ethel spent the night in my room at Paul Bryant Hall. A lot of the players remarked how impressive they were. I've recently been on a couple of programs with Mrs. Kennedy and I still feel that way.

Anyway, I went in for our meeting, and when we started to talk politics I said, "Mr. Kennedy, before we go further, if you've seen the morning paper, they're talking about me. What they're hinting at is that Wally Butts and I fixed a football game."

He said, "Well, what the heck could Wally Butts do for you?" I said, "That's a good question."

He said he thought there was nothing to it, because he hadn't heard anything. He said, "Something that big would have come by my desk."

So we had about a half-hour visit, and later, when the story broke, people found out I'd been there, and I read where a writer asked Mr. Kennedy what we talked about.

He said, "Well, I think you should ask Coach Bryant." I appreciated that.

I will never tell how I got it, but shortly after that I came into possession of the page proofs of *The Saturday Evening Post* story, a sort of advance copy of the magazine, a makeready, I believe they call it. A good friend of mine arranged to get it, picked it up in Birmingham, and brought it to me.

This was still days before it hit the newsstands, and the *Post* was just then alerting its dealers to be ready for something big. But there I had a copy of it in my hands at four o'clock in the morning outside my office. I didn't wait to get it inside, I read it by the headlights of my car. And I couldn't believe it: "The Story of a College Football Fix," under the by-line of Frank Graham, Jr.

The story said that an eavesdropper named George Burnett had somehow got cut into a telephone conversation and heard Wally Butts pass on confidential information to me to help Alabama beat Georgia, 35–0, on September 22, 1962. The headlines called it the most "shocking" sports story since the Black Sox scandal of 1919. It said that Wally and I had "rigged" the game in order to bet on it by my using information provided by Wally about his own team. It was so crammed full with lies and half-truths I couldn't believe it.

Well, Mary Harmon was down at Lake Martin, where we had a little summer cottage. Dr. Rose had a place down there, too. I was so riled up I got into my car and drove right down to his place. I had a driver but I wouldn't let him drive. I was afraid he wouldn't drive fast enough. It's about 120 miles from Tuscaloosa to the lake house, and I had never driven it in less than two hours and twenty minutes. Until that morning.

I got there about 6:30, and Dr. Rose's wife, Thommie, was already up making coffee. While we waited for Dr. Rose to get up, I showed the story to her, and she threw a fit. She said I ought to sue them or shoot them or something.

I said, "Honey, we can't get overexcited. We've gotta plan this thing out." It was funny in a way. I had to calm *her* down.

She said, "What kind of sons ——" And she's a lady, but she said that. She said this can't wait, and went on back and woke up Dr. Rose.

When he came out he was as flabbergasted and as upset as she was.

He said, "Paul, let's get your lawyers."

I went on over to my house on the lake there, and I was nauseated. I knew there could be vicious people, but not like this. I got over there, and my folks started crying, and for a long time — hours, it seemed — we just sat there, shocked.

But I knew we had to do something, because you just can't stand there and take it. Dr. Rose was on my side, I knew that, and I wanted to tell my players. I drove back to Tuscaloosa and called a meeting at Friedman Hall, where we always meet every day at noon just outside the dining hall. I quieted them down and got the story out. I said, "This ——," and I named the Atlanta writer and what I thought of him, "has done this, and I want you to know what has been said before anybody else tells you."

I read them the whole story, pausing over the points I thought needed to be elaborated on. I knew from the beginning they believed me, and a few of them came to me afterward and said so. But I know, too, it must have been a terrible shock.

Before the day was over I was in Birmingham, another 60 miles away, in conference with Winston McCall, my lawyer. Between him and Dr. Rose and I, we decided we'd announce it before the *Post* did, beat them to the punch, go on television and lay it right on the line.

I called my agent, Frank Taylor, and my television sponsors,

Sloan Bashinsky of Golden Flake Potato Chips and Preacher Franklin of the Coca-Cola Bottlers, and told them.

I'll never forget it. It was an awkward time for me financially. The market had been bad for me, and those things always happen at the wrong time. I told them I wanted to go on statewide television for thirty minutes and I'd just have to pay them later. Both of them said, listen, you go on and there won't be any commercials and it won't cost you a dime. Boy, that meant something.

Dr. Rose, meanwhile, consulted with the university's Board of Trustees and Harry Pritchett, a neighbor of his and a good friend of the university and a golfing buddy of mine. We called in Bernie Moore, the commissioner of the Southeastern Conference, and we got Benny Marshall and Alf Van Hoose and Bill Lumpkin, the newspapermen, and then Butts, who hadn't seen the story yet, and his folks. These were the people we felt should know what was going on.

Butts, as it turned out, had already learned part of it. On February 23 he had been called in to meet with the Georgia athletic board, who were mostly old friends. Or *were* old friends. They told him Burnett's story, and showed him Burnett's notes, the notes allegedly taken while listening to what he said was this conversation between Wally and me. When they suggested a lie detector test Wally got very indignant, according to what he told me, and I don't blame him. He'd been a Georgia man twenty-four years, and now they were doubting him. Instead, he resigned.

But now Wally knew that Burnett had sold his information to the *Post*, and we showed him the story. This was Friday, March 15. It was decided he would go on television the next day in Atlanta, and I'd go on television Sunday afternoon in Birmingham.

In the meantime different members of the Alabama Board of Trustees were calling around, trying to find out what they could. One guy over in Georgia told one of our trustees that he heard somebody had seen a check of mine for $50,000. Harry Pritchett called my business partner in Tuscaloosa, Jimmy Hinton, and asked him if I bet on football games.

Jimmy said, "Hell, no. Of course not. Paul plays poker, and he likes to go to Las Vegas, and he's tough to win money from on the golf course, but he sure as hell don't bet on football games. What's this all about?"

Then Bernie Moore's son-in-law, a Nashville attorney, told Bernie he'd talked with one of his clients, a big bookie who knew everybody in the world who bet on football. The bookie told Bernie's son-in-law "Bear don't bet on football."

Well, we were going on the air at four o'clock, and Sunday morning I was up there in my suite at the Bankhead Hotel in Birmingham trying to iron out what I wanted to say. Dr. Rose came up, and Bernie Moore, Red Blount, Harry Pritchett and Tom Russell, who owns millions in land where we have our cabin and is on the Alabama Board of Trustees.

And they questioned me. "Now, Paul, could you be wrong? Is there anything you haven't told us, or remembered, about a check or anything?"

And I said, "Red, I went through all my checks. The bank has photostatic copies. There isn't one I can't account for, and they're available if you want to look at them." The biggest I could find was one for about $2,000. There have been ones a lot bigger lately, because I deal in bigger figures now, but they couldn't find one that was even close to $50,000.

I told them about phone calls, of course, and later I even got a list of them from the phone company.

So we kept talking, and one of them said, "Well, Butts didn't help any, because he wouldn't take the lie detector test." Wally did take one later, but I realized then what they were getting at. They wanted me to take a lie detector test. If they had *asked* me to take one I'd have said go to hell, just like Wally did. But it wasn't a question now of believing me.

I said, "Look, that might be a good idea, me take a lie test, and I'd love to take it. I won't be able to tell you exactly what I said to Wally on the phone — and there's no doubt I've talked to him many times on the telephone — because I don't know for sure what I said. But I can tell you I haven't fixed any game, or bet on one."

Red Blount said, "You mean any game or just this game?"

And I said, "I haven't fixed *any* game. Ever. And I haven't bet on one since I was a kid." (I already told you about that five-dollar pool we got up for the Tennessee game that time.)

222

Well, you could just see them lighten up, like I had taken a big load off.

Within two hours they had the lie detector set up in the Tallulah Bankhead suite at the hotel. Tallulah's father was a U.S. senator and the family owned the hotel. They're tearing it down now.

An expert in uniform, Walter Kuhen, who's now a federal judge, and an ex-FBI man, who lectured at the Keeler Polygraph Institute in Chicago, were there to give it to me.

Everybody was trying to get to me, reporters and TV people were waiting, and we were holding off so I could take the lie test. Dr. Rose was there, with his assistant, Jeff Bennett. Bernie Moore, the SEC commissioner; Winston McCall; Jeff Coleman, the secretary of the alumni association; Frank Lee, president of the Alabama alumni, and Red Blount. We began the tests some time after ten, and we were done before two.

Well, it didn't bother me two cents' worth, the test itself. But when they put me in that chair with all those straps it was like getting into an electric chair. They started the questions: "You from Fordyce, Arkansas?"

Well, it's supposed to be my hometown, but it's not, really.

"You play football at Fordyce High School?"

Yessir.

"You bet on the Georgia Tech game?"

No sir.

"Your wife named Mary Harmon Bryant?"

Yessir.

"You have two children, one named Paul Junior, one named Mae Martin?"

Yessir.

"Did you bet on the Georgia game?"

No sir.

And so on, dropping them in like that.

I took a series of four tests, and it wasn't until we were through and they'd gone off to check the results that it hit me. I'd read somewhere about these things not being absolutely foolproof, and I thought to myself, suppose those sonsofguns come back up here and say I've been lying? I knew I hadn't, but what if the machine had?

I started trying to determine who'd believe me anyway, and I knew Dr. Rose would, and those men on the board, but who else? I was sweating. You got to have a plan for everything, and I had made up my mind what I was going to do. I was going to bow my head and go back to my players.

The polygraph men came back to the room and walked straight over to where I was sitting, and one said, "You didn't quiver. That line didn't jump a fraction."

You can imagine the load it took off me. That period of doubt only lasted about fifteen minutes, but it seemed forever. I know I'll never take another one of those tests about anything, because it didn't dawn on me until I'd been in that harness an hour and a half what could have happened.

By then I was getting so keyed up I was having trouble being coherent as the 4:15 television deadline approached.

At about two we left the hotel and went to the television station. They set me up at a corner table, with a nameplate: Coach Bryant. Frank Taylor, who directs my television shows in the fall, handled the details. Preacher Franklin was there, in case I needed anything, he said.

At 3:30, the newspapermen and wire services were admitted. They would be the studio audience.

You talk about gut checks — this was one. We were going to have the biggest audience in the history of the state, no doubt about that. My family would be watching down at the lake. I had a speech prepared, and it was checked by my attorneys so I wouldn't say anything I could be sued for, being so mad and all. Dr. Rose was standing there with a towel, wiping my head, I was sweating so bad, and I apologized for being so much trouble.

Two minutes before we went on they brought in the speech rolled up to put on that TelePrompTer thing for me to read. Dr. Rose's voice, not him in person, came on the air. He made the introduction, and then I started trying to read this thing, and I couldn't. I was half-crying. Then I just quit trying to read and I went after them.

I wouldn't be able to remember all I said, being so keyed up, but they kept the tape and I can give it to you almost verbatim. In the interest of space, I'll leave out some of the repetition. But I challenged everybody. I said,

"Ladies and gentlemen, I have been accused in print of collusion or attempted collusion with the athletic director of the University of Georgia to fix or rig a game we played last fall. Our boys won the game by a score of 35 to 0. I welcome this opportunity to tell the people of Alabama that these charges are false in every sense of the word.

"Never in my life have I ever attempted to fix or rig a ball game, either as a player or as a coach. Certainly such charges have been derogatory to my integrity and character, not only to myself but to the University of Alabama . . . [but] one of the worst things to come of this is that it is a reflection on the performance of the University of Alabama football players.

"In these charges there's a statement that we had information on the Georgia football team. Certainly we did. We have information about every team we play. This comes from scouting, rehearsal and study. . . . Ladies and gentlemen, that is what coaches do the other nine months of the year after the football season is over. We study films of schools, films of our team, films of all college teams.

"We exchange films. We study films of players, their abilities, their weaknesses and their habits. We study coaches and their techniques. The games they played with us previously and the games they played with other teams. For instance, the latter part of the season when we were contenders for a bid to the Orange Bowl, and it was common knowledge that our opponent would be from the Big Eight Conference, we scouted all the contenders for the [Big Eight] title . . . and all of you who saw the game against Nebraska on television know that except for one play we proved we knew their offense [and] their defense. . . .

"The *Post* article taken in total infers that Coach Butts and I . . . attempted to fix the score . . . [and] bet on the game. This I absolutely deny. I did not bet on the outcome of the Georgia game or any other football game. . . .

"Ladies and gentlemen, I have nothing to hide. I volunteered and [took] a lie detector test before a recognized professional expert in order to assure my friends of the truth of what I say. This report completely supports me and has been delivered to Dr. Rose and the commissioner of the SEC, Bernie Moore. I repeat. I have bet on no football game, and this denial includes the vicious rumor . . . that I bet on the Georgia Tech game [in 1962].

225

"It is necessary that I bring to your attention something about the relationship between *The Saturday Evening Post* and me. Last fall this magazine wrote a false and contemptible article very damaging to my character and integrity as an individual. . . . Because of the damages it has done to me I have filed a half-a-million-dollar libel suit against this magazine and the author of the article.

"With this in mind it is more obvious . . . that this . . . is another malicious attempt to destroy . . . my reputation for honesty and integrity, in order to affect the outcome of this suit. . . When you read this article, you'll probably get mad like I am. . . .

"There's a great deal of discussion at this time about the freedom of the press. I think that this article and the one last fall are the greatest abuse of [that] freedom I have ever seen. . . ."

I went after them for almost the full fifteen minutes, and then Dr. Rose got on and backed me up with a short speech. He said after a "careful and thorough investigation" (this was three weeks after he had first heard the rumors) he had found no evidence of any kind to substantiate the charges. He finished by saying that "a real injustice has been done to the university and Coach Bryant."

We announced we were suing the Curtis Publishing Company for $5 million. Later, when there was no retraction — in fact, instead of a retraction the April 27 issue of the *Post* had an editorial stating that they were standing by the "fix" story — we filed suit for $5 million more, bringing the total to $10,500,000, counting the original suit for the first story.

When the telecast was over I almost collapsed, I was that spent. They all clustered around me in the television studio, handing me Cokes and being attentive. Everybody was relieved.

But the suffering hadn't started.

— Twenty-Five —

Oh, my, the nightmares.

Waking up in the middle of the night, wringing wet with sweat and lying there unable to sleep or to think about anything else. Many a night, *many* a night, getting out of bed and sitting in a chair for hours, worrying. Not worrying about the outcome, because I sure as hell knew I didn't fix any game, but just frustrated and mad and worried over what it was doing to my folks.

I had nightmares almost every night for two years. I'd go to bed with one pair of pajamas on and have to change to another, and then sometimes another.

I'd get up and sit, and I could see those dreams, not always sure whether they had happened or not. I slept alone. I didn't want Mary Harmon to know what I was going through.

The night before we played Mississippi in the 1964 Sugar Bowl I had dinner with Winston McCall and Bill Sellers, and we discussed the case and decided to bring in another lawyer, a mean one who knew libel law backwards and forward, Francis Hare of Birmingham. I felt he would really round out the staff. Hare is a tough sonofagun, I'll tell you. A little spindly guy with a high voice who can really get after you. We knew he could help make things happen.

I woke up at four o'clock the next morning, with my pajamas soaked, and I looked out the window of the hotel and it was snowing. Snow on the ground, snow in the air. A freak storm in New Orleans. I thought, "Damn, we've had it now." It was bad enough I had had to suspend Joe Namath, but now we were going to have to play Mississippi — a big, rugged team — in the snow. It didn't turn out that bad, of course. The game, I mean. But it gives you an idea the kind of nights I had.

I'd worked so hard to discipline myself, trying to keep my mind off the case when I was working or studying or doing something, and trying not to mention it around the house because of what it was doing to Mary Harmon. You mention it now, even now, and it upsets her.

When I did a series on my life for *Sports Illustrated* two years later she wanted to leave out all mention of the *Post* and what we went through. Just throw it all out like it never happened. I had a time explaining to her that it was a very important part of my life, something I couldn't wish away. But I'm sure if she could she would remove every trace.

So much happened along in there to make her frightened. Between the first *Post* story and the second, one week when we were away for the Auburn game, somebody broke into our home, hacked a hole in the back door with an ax or something, and went through everything we owned, trying to find something. I'd like to know what. Every piece of clothing, shoes, shirts. Whole drawers of things dumped out on the floor. Pulled things away from the walls, emptied out desk drawers, just systematically ransacked everything.

Took the closet where we kept our silver and emptied that out and left the silver. Passed up jewelry, money, anything of value. Only things they took were a couple of Paul Junior's sweaters, a red jacket and socks, and several pairs of my cuff links that I had a strong preference for.

They were looking for something, all right, and I sure wish I had been there to help them. Later we had good reason to believe our phones were tapped, and the FBI took care of that, but imagine the feeling *that* gives you.

In the months that followed we had to put on three or four extra secretaries to handle the mail. Must have been a jillion pieces. Some of the letters were nasty — I didn't even look at them — but ninety-nine out of a hundred were backing us, so many of them from government officials and clergymen and officials of one kind or another. A lot of them were from out of state, including a large number from Georgia.

Richmond Flowers, then attorney general of Alabama, conducted his own investigation. He got some football coaches — not mine — to look at films of our games and came out with a real strong statement supporting me. His son, Richmond Junior, was on the Tennessee squad — a real fine boy — and I told folks he was entirely too good to play for anybody but me. He's with the Giants now.

Anyway, the McClellan Committee sent a man in for about twelve weeks investigating for the U.S. Senate. And so did the Internal Revenue Service. I didn't care. They could have called in Perry Mason if they wanted to, and it wouldn't have bothered me.

The McClellan man was part of that antirackets committee investigation into the gambling aspects of sport. He wanted to find out if I was betting on football games. We had to set the investigator up with some office space, and he practically became a fixture. He was an eager beaver, I'll tell you. He wouldn't even go to lunch with Mary Harmon and Niel Morgan's wife, Mary, during that time. He'd say, "No, I can't, I can't."

Finally when it was over — he found nothing, of course — I invited him to the house.

He said, "I'd love to. I could sure use a drink." I think he was as relieved as we were. We never heard from him again.

The Alabama state legislature made its own investigation and had Dr. Rose and me and some of my boys in for questioning, and there were resolutions passed backing me. You better believe you find out who your friends are at a time like that. A year later some of those legislators were responsible for passing the resolution that allowed the university to name the athletic dormitory Paul W. Bryant Hall, after a living man.

On April 16, the legislative committee issued the following statement:

"To this point we have been unable to find any creditable evidence of illegal, corrupt, unethical or unsportsmanlike conduct on the part of Coach Paul Bryant; nor have we found any such evidence to indicate that the 1962 football game between the University of Alabama and the University of Georgia was rigged or fixed in any way. We have found no evidence worthy of belief to indicate that Coach Paul Bryant received any information from Coach Wallace Butts that had any effect on the game."

Well, the story was so wrong, so filled with errors, it's ridiculous to try to go over the whole thing, but let's just consider a few major points.

There's no doubt, first of all, that Wally Butts and I had a telephone conversation. They got the time and probably the day wrong, because I was supposed to have left the field to answer the phone, and my kids then would tell you the only time I did that was when there was a death in the family.

But there's nothing new about athletic directors or coaches calling one another, and sometimes for long conversations. The greatest for that, and I said this on the stand when I went over there for Wally's trial, was Bob Woodruff, who's at Tennessee now. When Bob was head coach at Florida he would call, and if you were eating supper you could just forget it. You could lay the phone down, pick it up again in five minutes and grunt. He'd still be talking.

On the same day this call was supposed to have been made — or the day before, I forget which — I talked to Darrell Royal for forty minutes. I probably average two calls a week to Darrell right now, mainly to discuss the wishbone offense. We trade information. Duffy Daugherty and I talk all the time.

And if we're playing somebody like Charley McClendon of LSU or Steve Sloan of Vanderbilt I'll call them the week of the game. Pat 'em on the back, tell 'em how good they are. Try to soften them up. All I'm trying to do is beat 'em, of course. If anybody had plugged into my phone the week before the 1963 Orange Bowl game they'd have heard me and Bud Wilkinson talking about all our deficiencies.

But as far as getting information is concerned, do you think I'm going to listen to somebody from the other side when I've got my own men going to his games every year and to his spring practices? We swap those films and everything else.

Why wouldn't I listen to Wally? First, my men know more about it; Wally Butts as athletic director probably wouldn't see more than a dozen Georgia practices all year. Second, Wally was for Georgia.

When I was at Kentucky and Wally was coaching he'd visit with me on the day of the game, and we'd sit around talking, feeling each other out. When we went down to his place his wife, Winnie, always had those collards and hog jowls and black-eyed peas for me, the things I've loved since I was a child.

I remember Bob Woodruff coming out to the house when we played Florida one year. We sat around on the floor listening to a game, and everything that sonofagun said I tried to figure out why he said it, because we were playing that night.

But you'd be stupid to interpret anything from it. You can't get to worrying about what you haven't prepared for, you sure can't change your plans, because that will get you beat quicker than anything. Shoot, the fellow I talked to more than anybody for a long time there was Bobby Dodd. Now my regular calls go to Darrell Royal and John McKay.

In this business you get all kinds of tips — rumors and letters and telephone calls and things — and if you listened to them you'd never have time to prepare for the stuff you really know.

I remember one time at Texas A&M some student took a lot of secret movies at LSU's practices and tried to give them to us, and I wouldn't even look at them. I got a letter or a call one time from somebody telling me he had watched Auburn practice and Auburn was running the shotgun offense. I didn't believe it, and that week we probably spent about five minutes on defense for the shotgun, which we normally do. We went over to play Auburn, and darned if they didn't use the shotgun practically the entire game.

So you can be fooled either way, and you're just better off ignoring everything and getting to work.

Wally Butts had been a very close friend of Coach Thomas's. Wally and I actually didn't get to be good friends until Coach Thomas died. Back when I was Thomas's assistant they'd be together, and I'd run get them Cokes or some lemonade or something and try to listen in on their football talk.

I know I learned a lot from Wally over the years. He knew more about the passing game than anybody. He had those great passers — Frankie Sinkwich, Johnny Rauch, Zeke Bratkowski, and, of course,

Fran Tarkenton — and led the SEC in pass offense almost every year.

Later, when I was stationed at Georgia Pre-Flight in Athens, Mary Harmon and I lived three blocks from Wally and Winnie. We coached against each other eight times after that. My teams won five.

But, with all respects to Wally, you sure don't like to get slowed by telephone calls when you're busy and trying to get ready for a game. Sure, he might have told me at one time or another how much better the material was at Georgia now than when he was coaching there, but I didn't pay attention to that, because every coach feels that way when he looks back. I felt that way after I left Kentucky, and I felt the same after I left A&M. And Wally always had a few tears handy. It was his nature.

If you were gullible enough you would fall for Wally's moaning every time. He convinced a sportswriter named Scoop Latimer one time that Georgia was no match for Furman even though Georgia was a three-touchdown favorite. He told Latimer how Charlie Trippi had this bad leg, and Johnny Rauch was throwing poorly, and the receivers were all dropping the ball. He said he'd probably have to use his fifth team.

The next day Latimer predicted in the paper that "Furman will thrash Georgia." Wally *did* wind up using his fifth string that day. When Georgia was ahead 70 to 7.

As for the specific call this fellow in Atlanta was supposed to have heard, if there was a call, I can't say for sure what was said, and I wouldn't try. I do know Wally and I had been discussing a certain rule interpretation, because he was on the football rules committee and the committee had decided to do something about butt blocking and butt tackling, which is putting your head right in a ball carrier's gut. He called me to explain it because, he said, he didn't want a good boy like Lee Roy Jordan, our center and captain, to get thrown out of the game for doing something he didn't know was wrong.

I invited George Gardner, head of the SEC officials, to come to our practice because of Wally's warning, to give us his understanding of it. And some good came out of it because I had always taught my players to hit until they heard a whistle. I changed because an official might be late blowing his whistle, or might not get it to his mouth quickly enough. So I modified my instructions to say that when a guy goes down, or if he touches a knee and he's stopped, *you* stop, too. If you hit a man after he's been stopped you should be penalized.

Insinuations were made about a lot of things, and my gambling was one of them. I've never tried to hide that. I'd be a fool if I did. I'd tell anybody that wants to know I've cashed checks at racetracks and in Las Vegas and I play the stock market.

The insinuation was made that I bet on the 1962 Georgia Tech game, that 7–6 loss. The story suggested I had thrown the game because we had a first down on the Tech 14 with about a minute to play and instead of kicking a field goal we threw a pass that was intercepted.

Well, we were a passing team that year, and anybody with half a mind for football can look at the films and see that the receiver on the play was wide open. The ball hit his hands and bounced up in the air, and that's how Tech intercepted it. He makes the catch, and we're on the 3-yard line with plenty of time to score a touchdown and in surer position for a field goal. He misses, and we've still got three downs.

Tech had as good a defensive team as there was in the country that year, and we weren't very good running the ball. We had Namath, and what runner can run better than Joe can pass? But as often happens in a case like that, your blocking suffers. You do a lot of backing up and rubbing bellies, trying to pass-protect. You're not down there knocking them out of the way like you do with a ball control team.

Actually, the big mistake I made in that game was going for 2 points after our touchdown with Jackie Hurlbut as quarterback instead of Namath. They knew Hurlbut was going to run it. With Namath they wouldn't have been sure. They'd have been a step or so back and that's all he'd have needed. Even at that, Hurlbut only missed by a hair.

My first mistake that day was trying to pull something new — trying to use Namath and Hurlbut in the same backfield. We were leading the polls by 200 votes, with nobody close, and I should have played it straight. I don't in any way excuse my poor judgment.

The next week was miserable, trying to get back up and ready for Auburn. We never had a sorrier series of practices. Finally on Friday I had enough, and called a meeting in the film room.

I said, "I want you gentlemen to know something. I've been telling you a damn lie. I didn't lose that game last week, I was just trying to keep the press and our people off your ass. Let me show you this."

And I ran the picture of the 2-point play after our touchdown. I said, "I've looked at every man on this play. There isn't a clean block to be found. If *one man* had made a clean block we'd have scored. If you had to do it over, what would you do?"

And I started right down the line, pointing at them. Challenging them. I said I was tired of making excuses for 'em.

The next week they beat Auburn, 38–0, and shut out Oklahoma in the Orange Bowl, 17–0.

I won't dwell on the story's errors in football judgment, because there were so many. But to point out one particular mistake, they said we beat Tech "on a last-minute field goal in 1961," which is interesting mathematically, because the score was 10–0.

Of course, neither Bisher nor anybody else ever came around to ask me about all this stuff beforehand. A couple of years later Bisher made a big brave thing of coming to our publicity office and sitting there waiting to get a pass to our practice. The head of university security sat with him to protect him, and I went about my business. It was a little late then for him to want to see me.

People ask me how I feel about those people who started this thing. Well, how would you feel? They tried to destroy me for a lousy $6,000. I wouldn't make a speech for that now. As for Johnny Griffith, the Georgia coach then, I never did think much about him one way or the other because he was quoted so many different ways.

From 1960 to 1964 our boys beat Georgia, 21–6, 35–0, 32–7 and 31–3. A point was made that I had said that the 1962 game was going to be tough, that we'd have to scratch for our lives to win. And that's right, I really thought we would. Georgia had fine personnel that year.

But what I say today about a game might not be the way I feel tomorrow. I never lie to a newspaperman; I might just mumble around and belch, but I never lie.

There's no doubt I sometimes sound like the voice of doom. But I'm not going to say what some guy wants me to in an interview, I'm going to say what *I* want to say. And if it's something that will help my team, I'll say that, too. I say what I think. I'm an optimist, but I'm also a realist. I can't assume we're going to play 200 percent and the other team is going to play 60 percent. That doesn't mean what I think won't change.

Two weeks before our Orange Bowl game with Nebraska on New Year's night, 1966, I didn't think we had much of a chance and I said so. But the night of the game I was standing on the field with a writer friend watching Nebraska work out, and I put my arm around him and said, "Listen, I may be wrong, but I think we're going to outquick these people and beat them pretty good." We did.

The *Post* story made an issue of one other point. It said our defensive players were calling out Georgia's signals as if they knew what was coming. That's old stuff. Much of the terminology in football is similar, and if you know something about a team — you *oughta* know something if you've been scouting them — a lot of times you can holler things and throw them off. It's effective, and we've done it a lot.

I know one year we were playing Andy Gustafson's team in Miami and my kids would say, "Look out, Joe, here it comes," or something like that. The first time we did it our linebacker ran through a hole and made a big play. After the game one of their guys who had an old high school friend on our team said to him, "You rascal, you knew everything I was doing."

My boy kidded him and said, yeah, that's right. But of course we were just guessing.

Ray Graves did a real good job at that sort of thing when he was coaching the Florida team, having his boys calling out things, getting the other team worried. It's psychological, and it's effective.

The summer wore on. At a pretrial hearing in Atlanta, the *Post* admitted that Furman Bisher supplied the information for the article, for $1,000, according to the court record, though Frank Graham, Jr.'s by-line appeared on it. It was also disclosed that Mr. Burnett's desire to tell the truth was helped along by a $5,000 payment by the magazine for telling what he said he heard.

It was later revealed — this is a matter of record; I'm not making it up, even though it sounds farfetched — that the magazine never saw the notes Burnett said he took when he eavesdropped on our "conversation."

— Twenty-Six —

On Monday, August 5, 1963, in Judge Lewis Morgan's court on the third floor of the U.S. Post Office and Court Building in Atlanta, Wally Butts's trial began. I took my dinner bucket and went over to testify.

I remember being over there the night before. Wally's lawyers, William Schroder and Allen Lockerman, bought me a steak and we were sitting around talking, and I could tell they were leery of me because I was so belligerent and bitter. I wasn't going to be any witness, I was going in there after them. Wally's lawyers were afraid I'd be too hostile, but they agreed to put me on anyway.

I remember that *Post* lawyer, trying to put words in my mouth the next day, and I'd say, "I didn't say that, *you* did."

There are many things, specifics about a football game, you forget. But they had a blackboard set up in the courtroom, and when I got on that blackboard I could make football plain, because then they were talking my game.

I don't remember the exact words, of course, but I have the transcripts — three bound volumes — and it's all there.

They asked me about a defense we employed, one that was supposed to have been related to the notes the eavesdropper took, and I explained how we were actually hurt and surprised early in the game by a Georgia formation. The lawyer said, "When [Georgia] did go into the so-called . . . pro-set, that had the effect on Lee Roy Jordan, [he] is your best linebacker, I assume —"

"He was our best football player, sir."

"That formation took him out of the play?"

"Yessir."

"Was something done to take care of the situation . . . ?"

"Well, we are not stark idiots. . . ."

I explained the adjustments we made. If I'd known so much about Georgia we wouldn't have had to make adjustments.

They asked me about a note the eavesdropper took that said, "best since Trippi," referring to a Georgia back named Porterfield.

I said, "Sir, I don't know. I have heard Coach Butts brag on Georgia's players, and they all get better after you quit coaching. Mine will get better, too. But I never heard him compare anybody with Mr. Trippi."

They asked me about the alleged sixteen-minute phone call, how the operator was supposed to have said, "Coach Bryant is out on the field, but he'll come to the phone." This was supposed to have been on Friday, September 14, eight days before the game, according to the *Post*. I said it was three blocks to the practice field from that extension. I timed it. It would take thirteen minutes to get back and through the gate and to the office.

I said by all means I had had conversations with Wally Butts, "because that's my business. That's my hobby. . . . I know I've talked to him about his football, particularly his passing game, because he's the greatest passing coach this area has ever known, and most of us, what little we know about passing, we learned it from him. . . . I've talked to him a lot of times about football in general. You can't get two coaches together when they don't talk about that."

When they cross-examined, they asked me about a later call I made to Wally on September 16, the week of the game.

"You put this call in to Coach Butts, didn't you?"

"I don't know."

"You don't remember whether you —"

"I don't know the call was placed."

238

"You don't know you made the call, and you don't remember anything that was said?"

"I remember plenty of things that were said sometime, sir. I don't even know the call was made. I am not sure all these notes weren't made after the call was made."

"I move to strike that, your honor. That is not in response to my question."

And the judge said, "Well, let's get the session down to what the facts are."

I was asked if Coach Butts and I were in a business together, Continental Enterprises. We had been, but we both lost our tails in it, along with a lot of coaches in the area.

He said, "Who got you into that?"

I said, "Nobody got me into it. I got myself into it."

He hinted around that Wally talked me into buying. I said he didn't.

I said, "I might have talked *him* into it as far as that goes."

He said he was talking about a deposition I had given in Birmingham on May twenty-seventh.

I said, "Well, it's the same now."

He asked me about another conversation of September 16. Our telephone records indicated there had been one. I said the call may have been in reference to Lee Roy Jordan, on that butt-blocking rule.

He insinuated that if I could remember that I could remember other things. He said, "You remember that conversation?"

I said, "Yessir. I sure do. You mention Lee Roy Jordan and I'll remember it pretty good."

He asked me about a letter Dr. Rose wrote to the Georgia president when the rumors first broke, quoting Dr. Rose as saying, "Coach Bryant informs me that calling this" — the thing about Lee Roy — "to his attention may have favored the University of Alabama football team, but that he doubts it seriously. He did say that it prevented him from using illegal plays after the new change of rules."

"Is that correct?" the *Post* lawyer said.

I said, "No sir. We don't use illegal plays. . . ."

Well, it went like that for a few minutes, and I could tell the *Post* lawyer didn't like my answers. He didn't extend the cross-examination very long.

Wally's lawyers got three of our players up there, Jimmy Sharpe, Charlie Pell and Lee Roy Jordan, and all three testified that there were certain things Georgia did in the game that actually surprised us. Jimmy Sharpe was real strong about what had happened in the game, and that if any late information had come in we certainly hadn't made any changes in our defenses the last week of practice.

Lee Roy testified that we had to adjust at halftime in order to get him back in the middle because Georgia's offense was keeping him out of the action.

They asked him — the same as they did Sharpe and Pell — if there was any way that two coaches could rig or fix the outcome of a football game without the players' knowledge.

Lee Roy said, "No, sir." Sharpe and Pell said the same.

Georgia's own coaches ripped the story apart. John Gregory, the head defensive coach, went over the notes point for point on the stand, and according to the transcripts called them "useless."

Charlie Trippi, who was then the offensive backfield coach in charge of planning, said that after reviewing the things the eavesdropper had written down the first thing he would do with them is "tear them up, because they are baseless." Trippi said that "we give more information to the press every week to promote the game than is being expressed in these notes right here."

The amazing part was all the lies the *Post* was caught in. Things made up. Things twisted. The story said that "the Georgia players, their moves analyzed and forecast like those of rats in a maze, took a frightful physical beating." Charlie Babb, a star Georgia player, was asked if that was true. Babb played fifty minutes of the game, according to his testimony.

He said, "Nosir. We didn't take a physical beating from Alabama. They don't play that type of ball game. They play a hit-and-run defense. They analyze your plays as quick as possible, and they are gone."

He was asked if he felt each Georgia move was being analyzed. He said, "No."

He was read a statement the story said he made to Furman

Bisher that "the Alabama players taunted us, 'You can't run eighty-eight pop,'" a "key Georgia play."

"They knew just what we were going to run and just what we called it," Babb was quoted as saying.

He was asked if the quote was accurate. "That is *in*accurate," he said. He said that the conversation he had had with Furman Bisher wasn't even about the 1962 game, but the 1961 game. "What I said was not related at all to the 1962 game."

He said Georgia didn't even have a play called "eighty-eight pop."

Sam Richwine, the Georgia trainer, was quoted in the story as saying "[Alabama] played just like they knew what we were going to do, and it seemed to me a lot like things were when they played us in 1961, too." He said the quote was "inaccurate."

I wasn't there for all this, of course. I'd taken my dinner bucket and gone home. But I've read the transcripts and the stories about the trial, and some of the things that came out are still hard to believe. These, for example:

George Burnett admitted in cross-examination that he never showed his notes to Frank Graham, Jr., who wrote the article. That the article was published without the *Post* ever having seen his notes.

That the very first sentence of the article was wrong — it wasn't Friday, September 14, 1962, when he was supposed to have picked up the phone in his insurance office and dialed a number of an Atlanta public relations firm and somehow got cut into this alleged conversation between Wally and me. It was Thursday, September 13.

That he never saw the article prior to publication, that no one from the *Post* checked him on the accuracy of the statements attributed to him. That he never said, as was written, that "Butts said that Rakestraw, the Georgia quarterback, tipped off what he was going to do by the way he held his feet." Instead, Burnett said he "didn't say anything to Mr. Graham about Mr. Rakestraw's feet."

He said he never mentioned anything about a "rigged" or "fixed" game, or it being "a sellout." Or that Wally and Bryant were "corrupt men."

When they got to Johnny Griffith, the Georgia coach, it was even more incredible. He said, as Babb had, that he never felt Georgia's moves were "analyzed and forecast like those of rats in a maze," or that his team "took a frightful physical beating." Nor did he know where they got that information.

He said he did not say, as was quoted, "We knew somebody had given our plays to Alabama."

He was asked if he said, as quoted, "We knew somebody had given our plays to Alabama, and maybe to a couple of other teams we played, too. But we had no idea that it was Wally Butts."

He said, "Nosir, I did not."

He was asked if, as quoted, he had said that "my players kept coming to the sideline and saying, 'Coach, we been sold out.' "

He said, "No."

And then the worst of all. The words that appeared as a subtitle at the top of the story, and then as the last line in the body of the story. Griffith was quoted, "I never had a chance, did I?" He was asked if he said that.

According to the transcripts he said, "No," he did not, "not to the *Post*, or to anyone else."

Such lies and distortions as these that the trial brought out made my friends in the newspaper business, respected men like Benny Marshall, tell me they were ashamed to know of such shoddy journalism. I think "yellow" is a better description.

And so many questions were left unanswered. Why, for example, did the Atlanta newspapers sit on the story for weeks, when one of their own men was compiling it? They waited for it to break in Birmingham. Even after *Sports Illustrated* tipped it off on March 13, the Atlanta papers said nothing.

The game was played on September 22, 1962. If the conversation was heard on September 13, why did Burnett wait until January 4 to take it to the *Post*? Here's a coincidence for you: January 4 was the same day I filed suit against the *Post* on the first story, Bisher's "brutality" story. What about that? And if Burnett was trying to help Georgia, why didn't he go see Johnny Griffith on September 14?

Well, like I said on the stand, taking their money was too good for them. They ought to be jailed or something, and I meant it and still think it. As I said, I know that story took ten years off my life. They probably spent a million dollars embarrassing me. I was never worried about what they could pull at the trial, because I knew I didn't bet on, or fix, a football game.

On August 20, 1963 — I was long gone from Atlanta by then — the jury returned a verdict for Butts and a record-breaking libel judgment of $3,060,000 — $60,000 in actual damages, $3 million in punitive damages. They say that Bill Schroder's summation was so good there was hardly a dry eye in the place. I read later that the *Post* people couldn't believe their ears when the figures were announced.

Judge Morgan eventually reduced the judgment to $460,000. He considered the jury's amount excessive, but he said that "the article was clearly defamatory and extremely so. . . . The guilt of the defendant was so clearly established by the evidence in the case as to have left the jury no choice but to find [the Curtis Publishing Company] liable. . . ."

Niel Morgan and I were having coffee in the drugstore opposite Bryant Hall when the word came over the radio. Niel actually cried with relief. We flew right up to the lake to tell the folks, and then I called Wally and kidded him a little. I said, "What happened to the rest of the money, Wally?"

There were appeals, of course, stretching out Wally's ordeal, but he finally got his money. I don't think for a minute it was worth it. I don't think for a minute that the story and the heartache it caused did not take Wally Butts to an early grave. He died in December 1973, but in those last years, the few times I saw him, he was no longer the tough, jaunty little man I'd come to admire and enjoy. No judgment could pay for that.

My case never went to trial. On February 3, 1964, I settled out of court for $300,000.

Matthew J. Culligan, the president and chairman of the Curtis Publishing Company during that period, said in his book that the settlement saved Curtis "at least $2 million."

Hindsight is better than foresight every time, and maybe I'd have been $2 million richer, or even the full $10 million richer if I'd stuck it out. Today I would. Then I couldn't. I doubt I'd be alive to collect if it had gone any longer, all it was taking out of me and my family. They strung Wally out four or five years. I wouldn't have lasted.

I'd have loved to have had the trial if it had just been me and them, but I could see how it was wearing everybody down. We'd probably all be dead. And all that time I was trying to run an athletic program and coach a football team. At times I thought I *was* going crazy. In that light I wish I could have settled a year before.

Knowing all the lies that had caused it in the first place had made me wary. You begin to think anything can happen, and anything can be said. One of the things that crossed my mind was they'd bring in some sensational witness who would testify to some lie, that I'd done this, that or the other.

My trial was scheduled for February 4, 1964. A week before it was to begin, Dr. Rose, Harry Pritchett and Winston McCall came to my place very solemn and serious.

Pritchett said, "Paul, what would you settle for?"

That was a bad question because I was ripe for anything. I'd gone the gauntlet.

I tried to figure what it would take for Mary Harmon and the children to get by if I died the next day. Based on Wally's verdict, and the way his case had stretched out and was still pending, I gave them a very modest figure.

The next week we went on over to Birmingham. Our lawyers and the *Post*'s agreed the night before the trial to a $320,000 settlement — $25,000 for the brutality story, which I split with Darwin Holt after lawyers' fees, $275,000 for the second story and $20,000 for expenses. They said they'd send me a check the next day.

I said, "I don't want a check, I want the money."

The judge kept his court open till after dark getting it all settled.

That night Mary Harmon said she slept "all night for the first time in a year."

The next morning Winston McCall came to our table at the Parliament House, where Benny Marshall, Carney Laslie and I were sitting, sat down, and handed me two cashier's checks. The total came to $196,000, which was minus lawyers' fees.

I called my banker and told him to line up my creditors. And after I paid them off I had a little left over to buy a new suit and Mother a new dress.

It was on radio and television immediately. Both my children were home, Mae Martin and Paul. Mae Martin said she was mad because she had been keeping it a secret and here it was all over town. Dr. Rose made a statement expressing his pleasure. He said the money the Curtis Publishing Company paid to settle "fortified the vindication given Coach Bryant by the verdict of the jury in the Wally Butts case, and the conclusions of Judge Morgan."

Well, I'll always feel they got off cheap. And I'll always be bitter over some of the things that I can't quite forget. Like the fact that the NCAA and a so-called SEC executive committee investigated Wally and me, but never investigated the people who were to blame for all of it — the *Post*, and the eavesdropper, and the writers. Some people actually wonder if I was "sorry" that the *Post* wound up going out of business. Hell, no, I'm not sorry. I wish I could have done more to hasten its departure.

It would have been helpful to know Matthew Culligan's feelings, but his book did not come out until 1970 — *The Curtis-Culligan Story*, which the jacket called "the inside story of the decline of the Curtis Publishing Company."

Mr. Culligan didn't give the *Post* much credit for its handling of what he called "the ghastly Butts-Bryant libel case." I found it fascinating reading, to say the least, learning firsthand what was going on up there. It was almost as absurd as some of the things that were revealed in the trial.

Culligan told of learning for the first time what his people at the *Post* were up to when Clay Blair, then managing editor, came to his office with proofs of the story.

He said Blair "seemed comical" in his actions, that he closed and locked the door and said, "Hold onto your hat," and laid the proofs in front of him in his finest dramatic manner.

These are all Culligan's words:

"Though Blair seemed almost ridiculous, what I read was not. I am sure I gasped when I read the headline — 'The Story of a College Football Fix.' I may have trembled with excitement when I looked at the artwork and read the captions. When I dove into the story itself, I was startled, angered and sickened by its content. I looked at Blair when I finished and asked: 'My God, can we print this?' "

He said if they "had taken more time, called in other counsel, done more research, either the story might not have run at all, or sufficient changes might have been made to make it nonlibelous and unactionable."

On the trial itself, Culligan said, "The Curtis defense was a comedy of errors." Well, it wasn't very funny to me, but it was ridiculous, I grant him that.

According to his account, Culligan said that as the libel action in Birmingham approached the *Post* people "were very much depressed because of one inescapable conclusion — if Butts had received an initial jury verdict of $3.06 million in Atlanta, then Paul (Bear) Bryant would, we felt, get a huge jury judgment in Birmingham."

Mr. Culligan sent me an autographed copy of the book.

It's pathetic, really. One of the last lines of the "fix" story said that "careers will be ruined, that is sure." Evidently from Mr. Culligan's account a number of careers at the *Post* were ruined. So was the magazine.

You can total up the relative costs. They paid Burnett $5,000, according to testimony. For notes they never saw. Burnett's friend, Milton Flack, a promoter who tried to peddle the story to three places, got $500. And $2,000 went to the writer, Frank Graham. And another $1,000 to Furman Bisher for his "information."

And they paid Wally Butts $460,000 and me $320,000.

But more than that, according to Culligan, the judgments "hurt both the magazine and Curtis deeply. For the first time in the history of the Post, since the days of Benjamin Franklin, the honesty and integrity of the magazine were exposed to serious question."

You don't think it was an expensive story?

Most of what has been said since then has been in the form of kidding or banquet jokes about telephone calls and magazine subscriptions, and I remember even Wally brightened up and said he'd been told by a few coaches that he could call them anytime — collect. None of it is really very funny, of course, but you learn to live with it.

As far as giving you any instructions on how to fix a football game, I can't do it, because I don't know how in the world you could without the players knowing. And if you think you can fool your boys you're crazy. I remember Pat Trammell came to me one year after my television show. He was a doctor then. He said, "We aren't going to lose another game, Coach."

"Oh, no? Why not?"

"Well, I heard you talking to Bowman last night on television, and he got the message."

"What message?"

"Don't you remember? You said, 'If that boy starts blocking like he can run he'll sure get my vote.' You were talking to Steve, and you knew he'd be listening."

I laughed and said, "Yeah, but I didn't know *you* knew it."

I'll tell you one true story about the game Frank Howard of Clemson and I tried to "fix," if you want to call it that. We were rival coaches in an all-star game down in Texas. Howard had been going around talking about how much better his single-wing was than my T formation, and I was getting back at him in the papers, saying the single-wing went out with gaslights and outdoor privies. Everybody thought we were really mad and it was a grudge game.

So we're in a taxi going over to the game together, Carney Laslie, Frank, his assistant and me. Frank said, "Hail, Beah, one of us gonna look pretty silly if the othuh whups his butt by a big scoah. Maybe we oughta have a signal we can flash so that when it gets bad and the othuh fella sees it he'll call off his first team." If anybody has a worse accent than me it's Howard.

I said OK, and we agreed the signal would be to cross our arms. And I winked at Carney.

Well, we go into the fourth quarter, and we've got a couple of touchdowns on him and our big back, Billy Quinn of Texas, is ripping into 'em pretty good.

The crowd's yelling, but I can hear Frank Howard. "Beah! Beah!"

Out of the corner of my eye I can see he's got his arms crossed, but I don't let on. Old Billy Quinn gains some more yards. Frank's really yelling, now.

"Beah! Hey, Beah!"

But I'm not looking. Carney Laslie comes over to me and says, "I think Howard's giving you the signal, Coach."

I said, "Yeah, but we gonna beat him a hundred."

About that time Billy Quinn breaks loose and goes to their 3-yard line, and the crowd goes silent just as Howard really lets go. Everybody in the place can hear him:

"Hey, Beah! *Look* at me, you lyin' sonofabitch!"

At the Hall of Fame banquet in New York, President Kennedy and General MacArthur listened as an old football coach told of the pride in having players like Pat Trammell, behind me on the podium.

When Pat Trammell died it was the saddest day of my life. His widow, Baye, accepted a plaque in his honor.

Our series with Georgia Tech was spirited from the start. Coming from behind 0–15 to beat Tech 16–15 at Grant Field in 1960 got me a free ride, but made no friends among the fans in Atlanta.

The flak — whiskey bottles, mainly — got so bad by 1964 that I wore a helmet onto the field before the Tech game.

When I received word that the *Saturday Evening Post* was going to publish the "fix story," I went on television to challenge the lies.

After we beat Tech for the last time, as a postscript to the "fix" episode Bobby Dodd, an old rival and an old friend, shook my hand.

On this occasion, Shug Jordan of Auburn was being carried off in triumph, a pleasure he has not had often since we came to Alabama. Shug deserved my salute.

I had to discipline Joe Namath with a suspension during that critical period, but he remains to this day the greatest athlete I've ever seen.

Quarterback Steve Sloan, now the coach at Vanderbilt, is a young man that both the Reverend Billy Graham and I can be proud of.

With Steve Sloan leading the way, we whipped Nebraska soundly in the 1966 Orange Bowl game to climax the uphill climb to the National Championship. For me, it was also another easy trip to the dressing room.

The pleasure of the off-season is enjoying it with fishing, hunting, and golfing buddies like Jimmy Hinton, my business partner.

After what I considered a long slump, we bounced back in 1971 to go undefeated, beginning with this 17–10 victory over Southern California and my good friend Coach John McKay (*right*).

An old coach has pleasures now that he would never have imagined in his youth. Like being fitted with a special Bryant hat by my granddaughter Mary Harmon Tyson under Sonny Werblin's approving eye.

Fritz, our long-time companion, with his real master, Mary Harmon, who is still the prettiest gal I ever met and the kind of wife every coach should be so lucky to have.

Even from the top of my tower I still get chills watching my Alabama team do something well. And as long as I'm part of the game, I'll have a few things to say if they don't.

· Twenty-Seven ·

We had one more piece of unfinished business that year. We had to go to Atlanta to play Georgia Tech for the last time. I won't deny my bitterness toward Tech. And Atlanta, too, for that matter. I felt everything that had happened — the brutality issue, the first *Post* story, my suit, the "fix" story, the Butts trial, all the heartaches — had sprung from the Graning incident, from the way it was twisted to suit a rival viewpoint and then blown out of proportion by an unfair press.

The 1964 Tech game was to end the series. Bobby Dodd was pulling out. He said the Graning incident had nothing to do with it, that he just had to get away from so many tough games in November, and I believe him. But the implications were made and my program attacked, and I was bitter.

I will try to recollect as much of my thoughts and words as I can over that period because I believe they have a direct bearing not only on my actions at the time, but also on my philosophy of football. The 1964 Alabama–Georgia Tech game was like a laboratory test. So bear with me.

At the outset, I have to say I was sorry the series was ending. It had become an important one in college football, but I felt with two-platoon football coming in it was just as well we were going to end the series. If you have a lot of ability — which Tech usually had — you don't have to get in really good shape to win with the two-platoon. Tech was also handicapped by having a little higher entrance requirement than most.

It was just as well, too, because sooner or later I was going to get killed by a flying whiskey bottle in Grant Field. The visiting team sits right in front of the students, and on four or five occasions whiskey bottles were thrown at me.

In 1962, our last previous trip there, when Tech beat us 7–6, they not only were loud and ill-mannered, rocking the stadium with boos, but I was hit twice with bottles and one went right by my ear onto the field. Nobody did a damn thing about it. I may be older and more humble, but I am not soft on that memory.

I have to say this about Atlanta, though. I went over there a few years ago on a special invitation when they were honoring the Alabama boys on the San Francisco baseball team, and I wasn't sure if I'd get lynched or what in Atlanta Stadium. I got a standing ovation. Not long after that I played in a pro-am with Namath and Tommy Jacobs at the Atlanta Country Club, and they applauded every shot I made. Even if I just kept it in the fairway. Or putted and it stayed on the green. I'll never forget because two boys came up to me, asking for autographs and chatting real polite-like. They were Furman Bisher's sons.

Anyway, we had won our first eight games in 1964, on our way to that second National Championship. I couldn't expect my players to share all my prejudices about the Tech game, but I expected them to be ready to put the bonnet on them, and I suppose my adrenaline was working overtime because on Wednesday I was overwrought and we had a terrible practice.

I finally called them all together in the middle of the field, and according to Carney Laslie I made the greatest talk he ever heard. I wish I could remember all I said, but I can't. I know Carney used to be after me to make the talk again, but all I could remember were the bare essentials.

The sun was beating down, and we were all sweating and tired and dirty, and all I really did was put myself in their shoes.

I said, "Gentlemen, the coaches tell me you're tired and sore, and

257

feel bad, like I may be working you too much. Well, I'm tired, too. But I'm fifty years old. I got an excuse.

"I know what you're going through, and I know what you're thinking. When it's hot like this, and you've been out here two hours, and I'm standing up on that tower yelling at you, you're thinking, 'Yeah, you big bastard, let's see you get your ass down here and do better.'

"And when I just made you run another wind sprint, and you're down at that end of the field, you're thinking, 'If that s.o.b. makes me run one more I'm coming up there and kick his butt.'

"But you put it off. You put off kicking my butt for another day. And you come back the next day, and you pull on those clammy jock straps, and you got the jock itch, and it's miserable, and the uniform smells, and your shoes smell, and you're tired before you go out. And that's not much fun. And then I'm on you at practice, and I'm on you in the meetings, and you think of all the good lines you could say to tell me off. But you wait."

I said, "Then on Friday you begin to feel a little different. Practice is over. You breathe easier. And on Saturday when you put those silks on, and everything's clean and fresh-smelling, and you go out to warm up and the fans are yelling for you, and that little old ugly girl is up there, and your mama and papa, and you feel like you're going to wet your britches ten times — well, that's what it's all about."

What I was telling them, see, is exactly what I went through. Just like when I used to cuss Coach Thomas under my breath. "You little s.o.b., I'd like to see you do this." But I didn't tell them that. The difference was when I was younger I *could* do it, and did it. Got down there with them.

I said, "And after the game there are three types of people. One comes in and he ain't played worth killing, and he's lost. And he gets dressed and out of there as quick as he can. He meets his girl and his mama, and they ain't too damn glad to see him. And he goes off somewhere and says how 'the coach shoulda done this or that,' and 'the coach don't like me,' and 'I didn't play enough.' And everybody just nods.

"And the second type will sit there a while, thinking what he could have done to make his team a winner. And he'll shed some tears. He'll finally get dressed, but he doesn't want to see anybody. His mama's out there. She puts on a big act and tells him what a great game he played, and he tells her if he had done this or that he'd be a winner, and that he will be a winner — next week.

"And then there's the third guy. The winner. He'll be in there hugging everybody in the dressing room. It'll take him an hour to dress. And when he goes out it's a little something extra in it when his daddy squeezes his hand. His mama hugs and kisses him, and that little old ugly girl snuggles up, proud to be next to him. And he *knows* they're proud. And why."

Well, I wish I could remember all of it. I'd give $10,000 for a tape because I'd like to say it again some time. Ken Donahue, one of my coaches, used to make notes of things I said, and he asked me to repeat it and I couldn't.

But I'll tell you what Jerry Duncan said. Jerry was an All-Conference tackle on that team. He said if we had played Tech that afternoon we would have won 50 to 0.

The timing was right, see. You go into your boss's office to ask for a raise, the timing better be right. You walk into the kitchen and give your wife a smack. Sometimes it's just the thing to do, and she eats it up. Other times it don't mean a thing. You might as well kiss the refrigerator.

So I told them they were going to forget about being tired, forget about being sore. Because we were going to beat Georgia Tech.

And that night at our meeting I told them why. I didn't speak more than five minutes and I never raised my voice. All I said was that I had been playing and coaching against Georgia Tech for twenty-five years, "before most of you were born."

I said, "Tech hits hard, but they don't hit hard all the time. They play tough, but they don't play tough all the time because they don't live tough like we do."

I said all that stuff about "Dodd luck" and "Grant Field luck" was horse manure. The fact that we had beaten Tech five out of six was proof of that.

I said, "You make your own luck, even at Grant Field. But let me tell you this. That will be the most hostile crowd you've ever seen. Two years ago they threw everything at us from ice to bourbon bottles. I don't mean to insinuate they're not good folks. They probably got good mamas and papas, too. But I think some of them have forgot their training."

I said that helmets would be worn on the bench at all times, and that I might wear one myself.

And I wasn't telling *them* what to do, but "while I am in Atlanta I'm not going to read any newspapers."

We turned on the projector to show the Tennessee–Georgia Tech game, and I had one last thought.

I said, "They're afraid of you. They don't think they can beat Alabama. They couldn't do it when they thought you were just ordinary folks, and they know now you're not ordinary folks."

Tech hadn't been as good that year as they might have been. They were not quite as talented as usual, and it was one of those years. And as I said, and won't go back on now, you're not going to get ready for Alabama by playing volleyball at practice. I told a writer friend at dinner that night that if this were two-platoon we'd lose, "but when it's eleven men and sic 'em, it's a different game."

Dude Hennessey was our scout for Tech that year. He had fifteen pages in the game plan. Dude didn't expect Tech to run much. He said, "I don't think *they* think they can run on us." He said if he was wrong he would leave at dawn on his recruiting trip north. I told him I'd be there to see him off.

The only change we made was in the offensive backfield. We put both fullbacks, Steve Bowman and Les Kelley, in the starting lineup. They were our leading ground-gainers, and since we had no outside speed to speak of, we wanted to make their defensive backs feel something when they had to make a tackle. I didn't think they would care much for that.

Alabama people bought the ten-thousand seats Tech allotted us for the game before the season started, and I read where scalpers in Tuscaloosa asked $100 apiece for tickets.

Well, you never know what your players are thinking, how much a game means to them, but occasionally you get an inkling. We had a senior on that team from Enterprise, Alabama, a 6-3, 204-pound, big-jawed boy named Gaylon McCollough. Gaylon was one of those kids you love to have, who not only plays well but has a high B average and is a member of the Fellowship of Christian Athletes. He was going on to med school, and is practicing medicine in Alexander City now.

I got this secondhand, from a magazine story that I saw later, but this is the way Gaylon McCollough was quoted before that Tech game:

"In the spring, and then in the early fall when it's two a day and dog-eat-dog, you don't think you'll ever make it. You lie up in your bed at night and you think, oh Lord, if I could only get out of here, if I could only get a day off. Every play is full out, and every workout is like a war. You go into every play like it was your last, you come back to the huddle keyed up for another.

"Then all of a sudden it's over, and the season's on, and it's fun. And now here we are with two games to go and a chance to go to another bowl game and win the National Championship and you know it's not every man gets this kind of chance. I could have gone to Tech to play. I came here because I wanted to play for Coach Bryant, and that's the truth. I wouldn't trade it for anything."

And I wouldn't trade *that* for anything.

I'm not what you would call a superstitious guy, but I indulge in a few. I wore my lucky red and white tie to Atlanta. Mary Harmon sat next to me on the plane, a twin-engine Southern Airlines propjet. Four-engine planes and jets couldn't fly out of Tuscaloosa then. Mary Harmon likes to sit nearest the front on the right side. She thinks that helps, too.

She was wearing the Alabama brooch I had bought her my first year back, another asset. She told one of our friends on the plane that I had forgotten to wear my blue sweater that got us through twenty-six games before the 1962 Tech game. She made it sound like it was pretty dumb on my part. Julian Lackey's daddy even wrote me a letter about it, and he didn't mince words: "You dumb sonofabitch, you forgot your sweater!"

"He had to borrow another one," Mary Harmon said. "We lost."

On the bus ride from the airport to the Biltmore Hotel the driver started giving us his little speech, pointing out this and that Atlanta landmark. I wasn't in the mood.

I said, "Thank you, but we got the tour when we came over here in 1962. Just get us to the hotel."

Jerry Duncan overheard me. He told one of my coaches later, "Damn, Coach Bryant is really keyed up."

The next morning at our team meal at the Biltmore I made my last pitch.

I said, "Most of you will live another fifty years or more. I hope it's seventy, but if it's fifty that's still a good life, and what happens today you'll have to live with the rest of the way. You can't get it back if you don't win. It's sixty minutes and over. The losers are the ones who say, 'Oh, I wish I could play it again.' You can't play it again."

I wasn't talking very loud, so they were on the edge of their chairs.

"Well, you're not really going to have to play sixty minutes. None of you. The longest play in a game is six and a half seconds. The shortest play is less than two seconds. That's barely a wink of the eye. You'll average five seconds a play. Five seconds of total effort, going all out, giving a hundred percent. You oughta be able to hold your hand in a fire that long.

"If you're lucky enough to play seventy plays, that amounts to about six minutes. Six minutes of your time. Out of fifty years, six minutes doesn't seem like much. But a loser will regret it the rest of his life.

"You've worked a long time for this. You've been playing since you were in the seventh grade. You go out there in front of all those people and don't give a hundred percent every play then you're cheating yourself, and your recruiters, and your parents, and your high school coach, and everybody who ever helped you. This is what you have been working toward."

I got on the blackboard then and went over the things I always cover on game day. The things that can happen. The intelligent use of time-outs, and of the wind. The kicking game and the specialty teams. The clock plays. The penalties.

"I know you've heard all this before, but I want to remind you what can happen.

"In any big game there are five or six or seven key plays that will decide the outcome. If you put out for five seconds on every play, you'll get your share of those key plays. You never know when they'll come, so you have to go all out every time.

"If you're reckless, and give that extra effort, and every play try a little harder, you'll see in the films on Monday that it was you who made those five or six plays that win. Play 'em jaw to jaw, and you'll win in the fourth quarter.

"I don't think this game is as big for us as it is for Tech. We're on a longer road. We've got a bigger one next week, and the week after. Because the next game is always more important if you're going to the top. And that's where we're going."

I've given up trying to tell how a team should act in order to win. I used to think I could tell, but I have to admit I couldn't that day. I thought going out that I might have overdone it. But something happened when we got there that loosened everything up.

Before every game, before we go into the locker room to dress, we take a walk around the field in our street clothes. Just stroll around and look the place over. Test the grass, look at the scoreboard. This is usually early, when there aren't many fans there, and it's really just a way of relaxing. A ritual, I suppose.

Everybody got off the bus and went through the gate toward the field. I was in back. But at the gate they stopped, waiting for me. The stadium was no more than a quarter full, but Tech's student body was already there, in full voice. Yelling and screaming. Things like "Go to hell, Alabama, Go to hell." That was the nicest one. The scoreboard showed 'Tech 90, Bama 0.'

I said, "You all wait a minute." And I went back and got a helmet — I don't know whose — and put it on. And in I went, leading them onto the field.

The Tech students couldn't miss it. And I just took my time walking all the way around the stadium. They yelled their heads off, but I didn't pay any attention. I must have stood in front of the Tech bench five minutes, making believe like I was checking things out, making sure they could see me real good. They called me every name in the book, but I was ignoring them.

Finally I walked on off with the players. And I could feel it. There was no way we were going to lose that game.

When we came back out to warm up, Bobby Dodd and I chatted for a while under the south goalposts. By that time I had taken off the helmet and put on my lucky brown hat. As it turned out, we didn't need a whole lot of luck.

We had field position throughout the first half. As I said, Joe

Namath had been hurt earlier in the year, and Steve Sloan started at quarterback. He drove us down to the Tech 11 on the first series, but we had a touchdown called back.

Howard Schnellenberger was next to me on the sideline. He said, "If they're smart, they'll ram it right to us."

Tech did have some early success with counters and reverse traps inside our ends, but every time they got near making something they'd pitch out or try a rollout. We covered those pretty good.

Late in the second quarter (less than a minute to play, actually), with neither team having scored, I put Namath in. He was still limping. His first two passes were poorly thrown, for him. On third down he came back with the same pass he had used on the previous play and David Ray caught the defensive back leaning. He took Joe's pass on the dead run and was to the Tech 1-yard line before they caught him.

On the next play Bowman scored, and we pulled an onside kick that got the ball back. Namath passed to Ray Ogden to the Tech 3. Two plays later he threw to David Ray in the end zone, and we were ahead 14–0.

In the second half Ray kicked a field goal to become the all-time collegiate kicking champion, and we got another touchdown and won going away, 24–7. Tech didn't score until the last minute of play.

Bobby Dodd was very gracious afterward, and I shouldn't have been surprised. He said, "It's no disgrace to lose to the best team in the country."

I couldn't match him in class. When the Atlanta press came in, I said, "I didn't think Tech would score."

I have never seen such carrying-on in a dressing room. Everybody was crying. Old Pooley Hubert, the first great Alabama player, was in there crying and hugging me, and Red Blount, and I don't know who all. We dressed and left immediately for Tuscaloosa.

Normally I ride the first bus, but for some reason I got on the third bus that day. The "Blue Darter" they called it. The Blue Darters were the third team, the guys who had to play both offense and defense. In one-platoon we had a first team that was superior on offense, and a second that was better on defense, then the third that went both ways. Mary Harmon sat with me. She always rode the Blue Darter.

I never had so much fun. Every one of them was whooping and hollering. Mary Harmon said it was always that way on the bus that I'm not on.

We were home before dark. We put our bags up and went over to the Indian Hills Country Club to join Jimmy Hinton, my business partner, and his lovely wife, Jean, for dinner, and everybody was drinking and having a time. Jean must have still had that helmet scene on her mind, because she came over and hugged me and said, "You are the cutest man I've ever known."

I said, "Honey, how can a fifty-year-old man be cute?"

I still kid her about it. Whenever I see her, I say, "Jeannie, girl, am I still cute?"

And she says, "The cutest I've ever known."

- Twenty-Eight -

I don't doubt for a minute that those '64, '65, and '66 Alabama teams will be remembered as much for their size as for their achievements. The first two won the National Championship, and the third should have won it because it was undefeated and untied and the best team in the country that year. I don't care what the Notre Dame people say, we were the best.

But I suppose by then the voters were tired of seeing us up there, and hearing Bryant brag on his quick little boys.

Well, they *were* quick. The quickest I've ever seen. John McKay makes fun of me, talking about how we "outquick" people, but that's what we did. We certainly weren't big enough to do it. Our biggest offensive lineman was Cecil Dowdy, an All-America tackle at 206 pounds. Our fullback, Les Kelley, weighed more than that. He was a strapping 208-pounder.

Jerry Duncan, John Calvert, Bruce Stephens, Frank Whaley, Mike Ford, John Sullivan, Paul Crane, Mike Reilly, Wayne Owen all looked like high school players. They weighed less than 200 pounds, and they were all starting linemen. We had linebackers like Bob Childs who weighed less than 180, and most of our defensive backs — Dickie Thompson, John Mosley, Bobby Johns — were in the 170-pound class. Most college scouts won't even look at you nowadays if you don't weigh 240.

Frank Howard, the Clemson coach, didn't believe our weights. Before our game he complained in the papers that we had doctored the figures, making our boys out to be smaller than they were. When Clemson came to town I got our equipment man to fix the scales so they would weigh 50 pounds less, and I got the police to go out and pick Howard up at the hotel and bring him over for a visit.

Sure enough, as soon as he walked in he started bitching about my "program weights."

"Hail, Beah," he said, "you ain't foolin' nobody."

I said, "All right, Frank. If you don't believe it let's go down there right now and check 'em out."

Ordinarily Frank Howard weighs about 270. He doesn't pass up many meals. So I made him get on the scales himself, in front of some of my boys, and the scales read 220.

Howard said, "By God, Beah, they're accurate after all!"

The 1964 Alabama team did not have great players. Guard Wayne Freeman made All-America, and Namath was on that team, his senior year, but he was hurt most of the time. He was sprinting out against North Carolina State on a run-pass option, pulled the ball down to run, and his knee just gave way. Nobody touched him.

Steve Sloan picked us up from there. Sloan had been great filling in for Joe as a sophomore, and he was great that year. How we ever got him to Alabama, knowing he would be in Joe's shadow for two years, was a miracle, as good as Steve was.

He had been all-everything as a schoolboy athlete in Tennessee. Everybody tried to recruit Steve, and I thought Tech had him.

But Bebes Stallings said, "Let me take a run at him."

If you didn't want to come to Alabama, or to play for me, Bebes thought you were crazy. So he went up to Cleveland, Tennessee, to Steve's home, and found what I expected. Steve had been told by Georgia Tech and Tennessee people that it was futile to go to Alabama. Who wants to caddy for the best quarterback in history? That was their pitch.

When it came to a decision, the Tech, Tennessee and Alabama scouts were all there together, in Steve's house. Steve asked to be excused. He said he wanted to go out and pray about it. If you know Steve you know that's the way he does things.

He came back in thirty minutes and said, "I want to thank all of you. I appreciate it, and I'm flattered. But I am going to Alabama."

I couldn't believe it when Bebes called me.

As it turned out, I couldn't have been closer to Steve if he had been my own son. He's close to me now, too. He's trying to beat my ears off as the Vanderbilt coach, but I can forgive him for that. I remember after his senior year, when the Atlanta Falcons came in to try to sign him for $50,000. I said, "Shoot, I'll give him more than that to coach my freshman."

The scout went back and told Rankin Smith he would have to dig deeper. Steve wound up getting a good contract, but he hurt his arm, and when I saw he wasn't going to play in the pros I asked him to come coach for me, which he did. And, to no one's surprise, he turned out to be an excellent young coach.

But outside of Steve Sloan, Paul Crane, Wayne Freeman and a few others, most of that 1964 bunch were average players. They just didn't know it. Four times in the last five games they came from behind to win. I used to say they were my favorites, the way they scratched and clawed.

But the 1965 group was even more amazing. We were favored to win it all again that year, but right out of the box Georgia beat us 18–17. Movies showed that Georgia's winning score came on an illegal play — a flea-flicker late in the game. The receiver was on his knees when he lateraled to the boy who scored the touchdown. The ball should have been blown dead, but those things happen.

After the game I told our players the good Lord was testing them, "to see if you can come back and be champions. I think you can, but it'll take a lot of work. I don't think the good Lord's testing me because I know I've got it."

The next week, according to Jerry Duncan, I almost killed them in practice. The first night a couple boys quit.

Every day I reminded them if it meant enough, if they cared enough, we could come back and win the National Championship. In those days we never even mentioned the SEC. We took that for granted.

We beat Tulane pretty good, but the week of the Mississippi

game I had to go down off the tower a couple of times and jerk a few of them around.

Finally I said, "Aw, go on, get out of here. I'm sick of looking at you. Go get your girlfriends and hold hands or something, because there isn't a football player in the bunch."

When they got in the showers the manager went in and told them to come back out, I wanted to talk to 'em.

I said, "Gentlemen, the way it is now Ole Miss is going to beat your ass. But I think I can save you. I want everybody on the practice field at 5:30 tomorrow morning. Any player who is late is through, and any coach who is late is fired."

That must have been one of those nights Dude Hennessey slept on the rug.

At five I was already out there, waiting for them. I had on street clothes and my boots. I didn't make them practice more than fifteen minutes, but they performed, I'll tell you.

Mississippi had us 9–0 at the half. I didn't get mad, I just went to work on the blackboard. I said we had made some mistakes, but we would get them straightened out, and we'd win in the fourth quarter.

With six minutes to play we trailed 16–10 and had the ball on our 11-yard line. We drove the length of the field. Three times we came up with fourth-down plays. Sloan got the winning touchdown. He had great receivers in Ray Perkins and Tommy Tolleson, and Bowman and Les Kelley were fine runners, and they just made one clutch play after another. I told them afterward, "I've been into the arena with a lot of teams, but I've never been prouder than I am of you. You've made up your minds you're not going to lose."

I'll never forget that game because the head of our security police, Chief Joe Smelley, met his match that weekend. Chief Smelley's dead now, but for a long while he was a familiar figure around the Alabama team, and an imposing one — close to 300 pounds in full uniform. He got his feelings hurt that year because some newspaperman in New Orleans wrote that "nobody gets near Bryant and his players because of that fat cop."

Chief Smelley came into my office with the story balled in his fist, madder than a skunk. "You see what this no good —?"

I said, "Yeah," and I couldn't help laughing.

Chief Smelley's counterpart at the Mississippi game was a tall fine-looking policeman. He was Chief's kind of guy, a devout bourbon drinker. The night before the game, they went out on the town together, and the next day when I saw Chief Smelley he was in sorry shape.

He said, "I done met my match," and he nodded over to where the Mississippi chief was standing in the hotel lobby. "Just look at that sonofagun." The guy looked like he just walked out of a fashion magazine. Chief rolled his eyes and shook his head.

The only wrong turn we made the rest of the year was in Birmingham, when we were tied by Tennessee, and that was my fault. We gained enough yards to win three games. But I had put in a play just for that game and called for Ray Perkins to come in motion on a switch, from one side of the line to the other. The idea was to force Tennessee out of its seven-four defense.

When Ray Perkins runs he grunts, and as he came down the line Paul Crane, our All-America center, heard the grunts and mistook them for the quarterback's signals. He snapped the ball. Twice it happened, and both times we lost the ball deep in Tennessee territory.

That was the game when Ken Stabler threw a fourth-down pass out of bounds, deliberately, with seconds to play and the ball on the Tennessee two. I don't blame Kenny. I had sent in a kicker and holder with instructions to call a clock play on third down, a "quick 99" it was called. If the pass didn't work it would stop the clock and give us time to set up for a field goal.

But we got screwed up in all the confusion — on the field and on the bench — and Kenny ran instead of passing and didn't get it out of bounds. He lined them up, and threw the ball away to stop the clock. There were four seconds left. And we were fresh out of downs.

When we came off the field the dressing room door was locked. I was so mad I gave it a slam with my shoulder and it came off the hinges.

I got them inside and told them I was more disappointed with my performance than I was with theirs. I said, "If I had to do it over, I would have stayed home and just sent the team to Birmingham. You would have won if I hadn't been here. That was the most disorganized bench, the most disorganized game plan, the most disorganized everything I've ever seen.

"But I want to tell you once more. You can still be National Champions if you want to be. If you don't, then I've misjudged you."

You say, well, you couldn't have believed what you were saying. But I did. And so did they.

We won our next five in a row, finishing the season with a 30–3 victory over Auburn. Each week we gained ground on the leaders, picking up votes until there were only three ahead of us — Michigan State, Arkansas and Nebraska. When the bids were extended it was obvious that the National Championship would be decided in the bowls: Michigan State against UCLA in the Rose, Arkansas against LSU in the Cotton and Nebraska against Alabama New Year's night in the Orange Bowl.

I put it up on the board for the players, charting how it would happen. UCLA would upset Michigan State, LSU would upset Arkansas, and we would play Nebraska for all the marbles. It wouldn't happen again in a million years, but that's exactly the way it went: UCLA 14, Michigan State 3. LSU 14, Arkansas 7.

That night at the Orange Bowl I took Steve Sloan aside and said, "Steve, we're not going to win the National Championship by lucking out 7–6 or something. We have to win big. I don't care where you are on the field or what the score is, I want you to play like you're behind."

He had to be surprised because I had never said anything like that before. It wasn't my style.

Well, I've already said we beat Nebraska 39–28, and I may be wrong, but I don't think any team of mine ever enjoyed themselves more in a game. Just wild, reckless fun.

I could tell you a lot about it. How we threw a screen pass off a tackle eligible play on our first formation and gained 35 yards.

How Ray Perkins made fingertip catches all night — he must have caught ten.

How well Sloan passed, and Bowman and Kelley ran.

How we gained more ground running the ball in the fourth quarter than Nebraska did the entire game.

How tough our little boys defended against those big fine-looking

Nebraska players. I can still see Johnny Mosley trying to get his arms around one of those tree-trunk legs of Tony Jeter, the Nebraska end. Holding on for dear life.

And how it was really no contest. When the votes were in the next week we were National Champions again.

But I would rather devote some of this time to Jerry Duncan. If any player typified that bunch it was he. I've said it before. Jerry Duncan and Dee Powell, who played for me at A&M and is on my staff now, were the toughest kids I ever had, mentally and physically. The only one I knew like them was Jim Tipton, who played with me at Alabama and is a retired Air Force general.

I have seen Jerry Duncan cry and beg our trainer to let him practice when he was hurt. If he didn't get any satisfaction he'd come to me, and I'd have to say, "Jerry, I can't overrule the trainer." He still came out to watch. He didn't want to miss anything.

And it may surprise you, but Jerry Duncan — our star offensive tackle — was a halfback when he came to Alabama. From Sparta, North Carolina. We stumbled onto him. I was in Raleigh at a clinic, and his coach came to see me to tell me they wanted him to play for us. I told them to send him on.

As a halfback Jerry Duncan would never have been a regular, at least not with the backs we had then. But our only good lineman was Cecil Dowdy, and we were desperate. I told our coaches we would just have to put people in there who wanted to play. Fill the holes with athletes, no matter their size. Two of those tapped for jobs were backs, Johnny Calvert and Jerry Duncan. Neither one complained.

And with Bruce Stephens and Jimmy Carroll and those others, they made the darnedest line you ever saw. They were so quick nobody could touch 'em.

This is the kind of competitor Jerry Duncan was. In 1966 our defense against punt returns was phenomenal. Opponents were averaging less than a yard per return, and it looked like we were going to break the record. But against LSU, Jerry came down on a punt and missed a tackle and the ball carrier made 8 yards, killing our chances. Jerry came off the field in tears. Literally crying like a baby.

Well, because Duncan was a good athlete, and had been a back, we put in a tackle eligible play that year. If you're not familiar with it (you never see it in the pros, and it's no longer legal in the colleges), a tackle eligible is a play where the man outside the tackle lines up a step back from the line, making the tackle an eligible pass receiver. A well-disguised tackle eligible can surprise most defensive backfields.

It was Duncan who caught that first one against Nebraska for 35 yards. He got two or three more that night, and the next year I don't know how many he caught, but every time we ran the play he was wide open and we made a mile. And that usually made the other coach want to throw up.

A couple of years later the NCAA rules committee outlawed the play. I won't say it was because of our success with it, but I think that's a possibility. Johnny Vaught was on that committee, and I don't know if it affected his decision or not, but against Mississippi that year Danny Ford caught one for 25 yards that set up a crucial touchdown.

I was disappointed in the decision for a couple of reasons. It's an exciting play, the tackle eligible, and there's nothing wrong with a coach having to work a little harder, though I don't know any coach who can defense it consistently — me included.

I was disappointed, too, because of young men like Jerry Duncan. Around Alabama in 1966, when mamas and papas were buying their kids Alabama T-shirts for Christmas, with a favorite player's number on them, there were a lot of 12s (Namath's) and 10s (Steve Sloan's) around, but the seller of the year was number 65. Jerry Duncan's number. Can you imagine a tackle getting that kind of attention? It was deserved, of course, but think what it did for the kids who played those positions, who weren't skilled enough or fast enough for the more glamorous jobs.

The 1966 Alabama team was the best I ever had and got done in by the ballot box. We were locked out of the National Championship by Notre Dame and Michigan State, who got more attention by playing a 10–10 tie.

That's my prejudiced opinion, of course. I said at the time that Notre Dame didn't deserve it because they actually played for a tie in that game, and if you don't at least try to win you don't deserve the championship. I have to admit now that Ara made the right decision — if he won it, which he did, he was right.

The only close game we had in 1966 was the Tennessee game, and we could easily have settled for a tie that day, and I'll get to that in a minute.

The final vote went to Notre Dame, but I wish we could have played either one of them that year. Someone made the comment before the season that I had a hard time "painting a pessimistic picture," which was right. Of the forty-seven men who played against Nebraska in the Orange Bowl only nine were seniors, and the rest of them must have liked what was going on because not one quit the team and not one flunked spring examinations.

I remember toward the end of that Nebraska game Howard Schnellenberger, my offensive coordinator, was standing next to me. As the score kept mounting on both sides I said, "Isn't this the damnedest way to win a football game? I promise you this will never happen again."

That spring we hardly worked on anything but defense. And in 1966 we shut out six teams, including LSU and Auburn, and just got better and better. In our last two games we beat Auburn, 31-0, and flat out overwhelmed Nebraska in the Sugar Bowl, 34-7.

It was as complete a team as you'll ever see, with the exception that it did not have much size. It had quickness, though. And balance. And good passing, power running, option running, receiving and good defense. Ken Stabler had served his apprenticeship behind Steve Sloan, and in many respects he was a facsimile of Joe Namath. A left-handed Namath. The players called him "Snake," after his quickness, I guess. He had that good release the better passers have, and he was quick with his feet.

Like Namath, Stabler was an outstanding all-around athlete. We signed him originally with the proviso — his — that he could pitch baseball in the spring. He was good enough to get big league offers, and he would probably be pitching for the Dodgers or somebody right now if he wasn't making it in pro football.

So we had great quarterbacking in Stabler, and great running in Les Kelley and Frank Canterbury and Gene Raburn, and excellent receivers in Perkins and Homan and Wayne Cook, and you could just go down the line of talented young men — Dowdy, Ford, Bob Childs, Mosley, Mike Hall, Bruce Stephens, Bobby Johns. So many.

As I said, the only close game we had was with Tennessee at Knoxville, and I made a big enough mistake before that game to have blown it for us. It was rainy and misty, a miserable clammy gray day, and I let myself get talked into receiving. The team and the coaches always want to receive, which is understandable, but I knew better and I should have said the hell with that, we'll do it right.

But I gave in, and Tennessee kicked off, and on our first play from scrimmage Kelley fumbled the ball on our 26. Tennessee got it and scored.

They kicked off again, we fumbled again, and they kicked a field goal.

So we were down 10–0 and we barely had our feet wet. It was still 10–0 at the half. Stabler hadn't completed a pass. I went in there clapping and smiling anyway. I told them that was Tennessee's half. The next would be ours.

In the fourth quarter we put a drive together and scored, and I had a choice of going for 1 or 2. If we got close again, I wanted to be able to kick a field goal and do more than tie. So we went for 2. Stabler hit Wayne Cook with a little old play-action delay pass and it was 10–8.

When we got it for the last time there were less than four minutes to play and we were 75 yards from the Tennessee goal. And it was raining.

And Stabler strung together one of the prettiest drives you ever saw. He got 2 yards and 5 yards and 3 yards, just inching along. And he completed two passes, for 14 yards to Kelley and for 20 to Perkins, and when we got close and they bunched up he slipped outside for 11 to the Tennessee 15. We worked it down to the 5, and then to the 1, and on fourth down Steve Davis kicked the field goal that made it 11–10.

The bench was whooping and hollering so much I barely got a kickoff team out there. The kick went out of bounds on the Tennessee 27, and they chose to take it there. And sonofagun, Dewey Warren completes a long pass, and then Charlie Fulton throws a halfback pass to that big tight end Tennessee had and he goes all the way to our 13.

They were on the 2, with 16 seconds to play, when they called time out and sent in their field goal kicker.

I sent in Donny Johnston, a preacher's son from Birmingham who specialized in rushing kicks. We were set up to rush from our right. Ray Perkins told him, "Donny, you block that kick and I'll give you my tickets the rest of the year."

Donny didn't block it, but he came in there so hard I think he forced the kicker to angle it right. It was barely wide, over the upright actually. It took a lot of guts for the referee to call it in front of 56,000 wet Tennessee fans. If it had been straight I think Donny Johnston would have blocked it, though, as close as he came.

Well, I said that day that you can't tell about left-handed crap-shooters and left-handed quarterbacks. Snake Stabler had been great, and he was great for us for three years, but I've always felt I made a mistake with Kenny that hurt us later on.

In the spring of 1967 I had to discipline him, much as I had had to discipline Namath. It was over a combination of things. They just kept piling up and I couldn't overlook them. I finally suspended him from the team.

But that fall — 1967, his senior year — I took him back. We made an agreement. If he lived up to it, he could play. And he did. And he was a fine player, no doubt of that. But I've always felt my not being firm with Kenny — and I think he's a warm friend of mine now — had a bad effect on our morale.

I'm glad I took him back for *his* benefit, but I think it might well have started us on that downslide, because for the next three or four years we weren't as tough and as disciplined as we had been. I don't blame Kenny. I'm the chairman of the board. I'm the one who's responsible.

A lot of things were going on in those days, and I did a poor job of coping. We had problems on campuses nation wide, and rebellions against coaches at a lot of schools. I couldn't believe it when the drug problem hit us, and I'll get to that.

So I blame myself for not keeping closer touch. For not being aware. It was four years before we were back where I thought we should be — contending for the National Championship — and if

I hadn't been so busy going off in all directions it wouldn't have happened. I told you what that freshman said about coming to Alabama because of me, and then not having seen me but twice since he got there. That shocked hell out of me, I'll tell you.

The thing was, I was being flattered to death. I got more attention than an old country boy could handle. Honors and television specials and things. And to top it off I got an offer to coach the Miami Dolphins that would have made Mama a rich young lady and saved me forever from going back to that wagon.

– Twenty-Nine –

I've had several opportunities to coach professional football teams, and I'm not going to fluff my feathers about that. But a lot of people have wanted to know why I didn't or wouldn't, and I'd like to set the facts straight.

When I was at Kentucky in 1950, George Marshall, who got me my first job at Maryland and had been on my side a long time, wanted me to come coach the Washington Redskins. Actually it was the second time he'd asked me; the first time was so flattering because it came in October 1948, right after we had lost three straight games. His coach, Turk Edwards, had resigned. I told him then I wasn't old enough to talk back to some of his players, and I declined.

George Marshall may have had a lot of enemies, but I wasn't one of them. He had done a lot for me. I scouted for him when I was practically starving, and he sent me money, and in 1948 I was having my troubles and he knew it.

Marshall was a very charming man and a great host. I'd stay at his house when I was in Washington, and I loved going to New York with him. But I had also remembered something Doug DeGroot told me. Doug used to be a great friend of George's. He said, "Don't ever work for him. George changes overnight." I don't know if that was true or not, but I didn't want to find out.

Anyway, by 1950 he figured I was old enough.

I met him in Cincinnati and then again in Washington, and I guarantee you what he laid on the line was tempting. He offered to sell me a percentage of the club, and since I couldn't afford it, he said he'd loan me the money. I was to be vice-president in charge of football at a salary a whole lot more than I was making.

Well, you never know. Maybe if he'd catered to Mary Harmon a little more, or maybe this or that. He offered her $20,000 to help buy a house if I signed, then he shooed her off to the department stores so we could talk. The two of us went and had dinner with Leo D'Orsay and Leo drew up the contract.

He put down $18,000 a year for eight years, a big salary then. The $20,000 for Mary Harmon's house. And the option to buy the part of the club Harry Wismer owned. Harry had agreed to it — something like 18 percent, for $2,800.

I don't know how much 18 percent of the Redskins would be worth today, but it would be a bundle. Red Blount and some of our guys tried to get George to sell them the club later, and he'd laugh and act like he was interested, but I doubt he ever was.

I had D'Orsay put in the contract that George couldn't have a telephone to the bench, couldn't come around there second-guessing, and just about every other thing I could think of to make me safe from interference. He agreed.

But when it was done I backed out, and the two best reasons I can think of are these.

First, I have always been so highly motivated that a purely professional atmosphere, a straight-cash reason for playing or coaching football was foreign to me. I was used to coaching college boys, whom I knew could be motivated, and I think sometimes I might have done better with high school boys for the same reason.

The second reason, the real clincher, was something George didn't say. I knew for sure I didn't want to be in a position to get fired, and pro coaches are not always the most permanent people in football. Consider what happened to Paul Brown.

I said, "George, I want you to understand, I'm a big fan of Sammy Baugh's. I have known him for years and think he's wonderful. But suppose, just suppose, I didn't get along with Baugh, or someone of his stature, and I wanted to sell him. What then?"

He said, "Aw, Paul, that won't ever happen."

That's all he had to say. It *might* happen, and any team that has a coach who plays second fiddle to a player is not the team I want to work for.

One possible opening that kind of appealed to me at the time was at Green Bay before Emil Fischer died, before they got Vince Lombardi. I knew Mr. Fischer quite well through Don Hutson and used to see him down in Florida. He sent Babe Parilli to talk to me, but I wasn't really interested and it tailed off.

During the 1966 season a friend of mine, John Plummer, called from Atlanta. He said he was feeling me out for the people who had the Atlanta Falcons franchise, and when I realized what John was talking about, I said, "Listen, I appreciate your interest, but there isn't enough money in the U.S. Mint to get me into the same town with Furman Bisher."

I said when I went to Atlanta I took my lunch bucket, because I didn't want to spend a dime there. I was still bitter over the *Post* thing.

Three real stingers came in the next year from different groups, not offering me a job in pro football, you understand, but stock, long-term contracts, fringe benefits, a bunch of things. In the long run one offer would have amounted to around a million dollars. If something had happened and I needed a lot of money in a hurry I might have been tempted, although I doubt I would have coached. I'd probably have one of my own handle that, somebody like Parilli, or Blanda, or Walt Yaworski, or Ermal Allen.

One of the groups wanted to put a pro team in Birmingham and applied for a franchise in the old American Football League. Now they are trying to get into the NFL. They're all good friends of mine and friends of college football, and they think pro football in Birmingham is inevitable, and they're locals. If anybody gets it I hope it's them. (I'm talking about an NFL franchise, not the World Football League. Time will tell on the latter.) Nevertheless, like I told this bunch, heck, I'm for the colleges, I'm on the other side.

A few years later I was in New York and I went to a Jets game with Sonny Werblin. I'm genuinely fond of Sonny and respect him. He probably thought I was big-dogging it, but Jimmy Hinton, some other friends and I had some money to invest, and Jimmy had mentioned buying into a pro football team.

So I put it to him. "What do you say to $10 million for the Jets?"

I'm sure he doubted that my group could come up with $10 million, but we could have. That afternoon. It was that simple.

Sonny said he wasn't interested in selling the Jets. "But if you and your friends got that kind of money, buy the Miami franchise. You can't go wrong."

He said we could probably get it for half as much, and that in the long run it would be worth more. Sonny's one of the smartest men I know. We're in business now on a couple things, including those hats I wear. He was right about Miami, but we didn't do anything, or even try. The Dolphins were drawing less than 30,000 then, and now they're averaging 80,000 and have won two Super Bowls in a row. What do you suppose that franchise is worth today?

The offer I got the biggest kick out of was made by Charlie Finley, the owner of the Oakland Athletics. Charlie's a longtime friend of mine and I've always enjoyed the way he shakes up baseball. Those wild uniforms, exploding scoreboards, balls popping out of the ground, donkeys running around. After that 1966 season he started talking about getting a football franchise for Birmingham, and guaranteeing me $100,000 a year for ten years to coach it. He said he'd give me an option for 35 percent of the club — "if we get one."

I said, "Yeah, Charlie, but suppose you don't get it?" (Pete Rozelle wasn't about to let him own a baseball franchise *and* a football team.) I said, "If you don't, what could I possibly do to earn all that money?"

Charlie said, "Hell, Bear, you can still ride a mule, can't you?"

Well, it's ironic. I got my last real offer to coach in the pros from Joe Robbie, the Dolphins' managing partner, in the winter of 1969. What he said appealed to me. When we got to terms, I put it up there pretty good. I had been accustomed to living a lot better than I'm entitled, and by the time we got all the goodies lined up I actually agreed to go.

We drew up the contract in a hotel room in Birmingham. I got my lawyer, Winston McCall, to rewrite Robbie's original. We put in everything I could think of, making the total value so good I'd have had to make about $1.7 million over a five-year period to equal it. A stock option, a place to live, cars — the works. The most important item was $10,000 for Mary Harmon to go back and forth to Tuscaloosa during the season.

I don't know how many times I talked with Joe Robbie. Twenty, maybe. I went down at Christmastime with Mary Harmon and spent three weeks as guests of Carling and Connie Dinkler at the Palm Bay Club, and Joe kept talking and I kept listening. Some of the Dolphin owners entertained us. Earl Smalley and Harper Sibley are friends of mine, and Sibley took us down to his place at Ocean Reef. Joe showed us the quarters we'd have at the Jockey Club, and it's a swank place, all right. He said we could live there or they'd give us a house. My head was turned.

While I was there I had Joe Namath in, and I got him to go over the Dolphin personnel with me, man for man. Joe could tell even then, two years before they won anything, how good the Dolphins would be.

We were talking casually — I hadn't told him my reason — and I said, "Joe, who's the best young quarterback in the league?"

"Bob Griese."

"Who's the best running back?"

"Larry Csonka."

"C'mon, boy, I want to talk to you."

We went up to my apartment, closed the door, and I took him into my confidence. Told him everything.

He said, "Shoot, Coach, you could win here left-handed."

I had lunch with Howard Schnellenberger, who was then with the Rams. Howard wound up with the Dolphins before he became head coach of the Colts, but had been one of my boys. Playing for me at Kentucky and coaching for me at Alabama. He gave me the same answers Joe did.

I thought, Boy, if I can't win with this I oughta be in jail.

That night I told Joe Robbie I'd take the job, but that I had to get the approval of my people first. And when it came down to the nut-cutting, I couldn't do it.

I went before President Mathews — Dr. David Mathews — and the Alabama Board of Trustees to tell them I would like to leave. I said it was time for a change, and it would be good for everybody.

I had gone to school with every man on the board except one, and we talked. I wanted to be released from my contract, which had ten years to run. But I wanted them to have a say. Deep down I thought they might be glad to get rid of me. We'd lost a bunch of games. A lot of talking was done, and pitches made.

Red Blount finally said, "Well, if that's what you want to do, go on, if you can get us a good 'un."

I said, "What are you talking about, 'good 'un'?"

President Mathews said, "Well, he has to be under forty-six. . . ." and he started naming off the qualifications. He made it pretty damn tough, I'll tell you. I could think of only three or four coaches who would qualify. One was Darrell Royal, and another was John McKay. And a third was Charley McClendon.

Dr. Mathews said that made sense. An even swap. "Somebody as good as you."

I knew Darrell wasn't ever going to leave Texas, or Charley McClendon Louisiana State, so I called McKay at USC.

He was coming back to be with us the next day in Mobile, and I thought he might be interested. I was under the impression he might like to get away from a private school where the fringe benefits aren't as good, and maybe try a country place after being in the city so long. Once, in a light remark, he had indicated he might want to. I know better now. I called, and he said we'd talk about it when he got to Mobile for the Senior Bowl and NCAA meetings.

I said, "This can't wait, John. This has to be settled in the next *hour*."

And of course it was.

The next morning at about six I called President Mathews. I said, "Is it too early for you to have a cup of coffee?"

He was laughing. He said, "I been up an hour myself."

I went to his office and I said, "You know, you're the smartest young man I ever saw." He's still under forty. Darned if you're not right" — and I started laughing — "I can't get anybody as good as me."

That night Mary Harmon and John and Corky McKay and I met in Mobile, and we went out to the airport with Admiral T. R. Jackson, head of the Senior Bowl, to meet some friends and greet the new

Junior Miss America. And who's the first guy off the plane? Joe Robbie.

He kinda eased through the gate, checking things out like a movie gangster, and I went over and shook his hand. He said, "You want to find someplace to talk?"

I said, "Aw, c'mon, Joe. I'm sorry and I apologize, but I'm not interested in a new deal. I just can't do it. There's no way I can leave Alabama. So forgive me, just c'mon and be one of us and have a good time."

And he joined us and stayed there a day with those Alabama people, having a good time. And he never mentioned it again.

When it was all over, I really felt guilty. I had tried to convince myself that it was the challenge that interested me. Nobody had ever done it both ways, won in college and the pros, and I knew I could do it. But I think now it was more the money, because I kept thinking about four bedrooms, seven baths, Jockey Club, and Cadillacs and Lincolns, so many things. Things I didn't need or already had.

It was ridiculous. And I knew it. Never again.

And don't you know they've said their prayers a million times in Miami about getting Don Shula instead of me? They couldn't have done any better. Maybe I would have won, but he did win.

I have to laugh. I heard later that Csonka said when he was in high school in Ohio, being recruited by Syracuse and everybody else, he thought it would be great to play for me at Alabama. But he was afraid I'd make a tackle or a guard out of him, as big as he was.

Larry's right. I would probably have cost him a million dollars.

I will say this, pro football is a fine thing for guys who are good enough and want to go on and play and make some money. I remember when I played at Alabama and got out of school, I was offered that $115-a-game deal to go with the Detroit Lions. Even that was more than I was worth. I took the coaching job instead for $1,250 a year, but that gives you an idea of the difference between what they're getting now and what they weren't getting then. The point is, I like to see my boys make something, and professional football is a place to make it.

As far as the two products are concerned, I'm not going into a long spiel about why college football is better, even though I think it is. Certainly there are some points you can argue with. Tradition, for one. Like McKay says, "Whoever heard of the University of the Rams?" It means something to a college fan to know that these kids represent you, and the school you attended. And are in it for more than just a big salary and a fancy pension plan.

I don't know about you, but I still get a kick out of the antics and enthusiasm of college kids. Cheerleaders hopping around, and bands playing, and the alumni up there whooping and hollering and raising hell. I still get chills when they play those old fight songs and the Alabama alma mater. If that's corny then I'm corny.

From a technical standpoint, the pro game is a great game. Fifty million people can't be wrong. The pros excel in every department, and should because they're postgraduates. But I prefer the college game because there's more diversity to it, more room for error.

The pros have gotten stereotyped, and they know it. This year they made a whole flock of changes in their rules, hoping to bring some excitement back to the game. They moved the goalposts to the end line, where the colleges have them, and made field goal kicking a greater risk by ruling that every missed goal beyond the 20-yard line goes to the other team at the point of the kick. They did a few other things, too, to help the offense, and some of the coaches complained — mainly because they'll have to do more coaching — that it meant the pros "would be just like the colleges." As if that were something bad.

Well, anybody who had eyes could see our Sugar Bowl game with Notre Dame was ten times as exciting as any Super Bowl in recent memory. The total offense for both teams that night was 738 yards. The average for six NFL playoff games was 557 yards — almost 200 yards difference. You don't think fans appreciate that? They were shaking the Sugar Bowl from the opening whistle. Ohio State and USC in the Rose Bowl totaled 855 yards.

The big difference between the two games now, of course, is that we run the quarterback. A good run is still the most exciting play in football, and you see more good running attacks in college football. A couple of years ago the Dolphins set a rushing record in the NFL by averaging something like 210 yards a game. Everybody thought that was amazing. The same year we averaged 324 with the wishbone — and Oklahoma averaged 370.

One of the reasons we get more is that we do more. We have a greater variety of offenses. Many are four-back offenses — every back is expected to run the ball at one time or another. That goes for the Texas wishbone, which we copied, and Notre Dame's multiple-winged T, and USC's power-I. The pros use a two-back offense, the so-called pro set, with a quarterback who passes, period. And one back who is really just a third receiver.

The only thing about the pro game that is more complex is that, within their basic four-three they play more varied defenses. Do more things with zones and coverages and keying. They can do it because they can spend more time on it. That's all they have to do. They don't have to worry about keeping their grades up or going to class.

But neither do the pro defenses have to face a new offense every week. They see virtually the same one all the time. John McKay says he'd love to spend his retirement years coaching defense in the NFL, because he would never have to defend against an option play. The option is the toughest play we have to defense. The pros never see it.

Styles change in the colleges a lot quicker than in the pros, because we have to adapt to new talent coming in all the time. As a result we aren't nearly as afraid to risk failure. Joe Namath wasn't the same type of quarterback Steve Sloan was, or Babe Parilli was, or George Blanda was, so we did things differently when we had Joe. Now we've got Gary Rutledge, Richard Todd, and Robert Fraley, and they're different than the others. But there are times when you flat out can't find a quarterback and you have to make do.

For a while every college team had a good passer, a "pro-type" passer. We were throwing more. It could be Namath's $400,000 contract started some of that — everybody wanting to throw the ball and make their fortune. And we had to get somebody to catch it, so we had good receivers.

But lately there has been a return to the tough running game, primarily because of the success teams like Texas had with the triple option. The wishbone offense. Quarterbacks couldn't just drop back and throw anymore. They had to be guys who could also run like halfbacks.

I don't know what these option quarterbacks are going to do when the pros get them. The pros don't want them to run because they have a ton of money invested and they're afraid they'll get hurt. I'm sure that's why they don't use option offenses. The wishbone, say, or the power-I. It's too bad, because they're missing out on a lot of excitement.

The greatest thing the pros have going for them is longevity. I'd love to have Paul Warfield for eight or ten years. Or Larry Csonka. Think what we would have going for us and Alabama if we had had Joe Namath there all this time.

The pros are together as a group longer, they have more time to perfect their business. I've always said they do their best job at pass protection, and that's understandable, because how many times, how many years, did Jim Parker of Baltimore rear up protecting for Unitas? How many years will Larry Little and Bob Kuchenberg and Norm Evans rear up protecting for Griese? That's the big difference, getting to do things over and over until they're right.

I think, too, that the top professional teams play a spirited, tough game, the ones fighting for the championship, and you pick out certain coaches, like Shula and Paul Brown, and they will always have their teams playing that way. I don't care if it's high school, college, or what. But, like I tell my players, you watch, and by the middle of the season the contenders are still in there hitting, but other teams just push and shove and rub bellies. They're not that way now because of TV. They fight like hell all the way.

Unless some of my boys are playing, I don't get much kick out of the pro game itself, because they're gonna run pretty much the same plays and throw the ball — read the short man, come back to the sideline, hook, do those things time after time — and it's just a matter of who can do the same things better.

I don't get to see much pro football, except occasionally on TV. I don't see anything new in it, but if you ask me if I learn from the pros I would say I learn from everybody. Pros, colleges, high schools. I have been watching some of those Canadian games on television lately and I'm beginning to think I like that twelve-man offense. It would be interesting to see a twelve-man offense against an eleven-man defense. Except that I doubt I could get anybody to coach the defense.

Sure I learn. And whenever I'm around my ex-players — Namath, Perkins, Blanda — I'm quizzing them, wanting to know what's going on, what they're doing new or different. I get Namath on that blackboard every time he comes around to tell me about this or that defense.

I believe this: When the first good team does what Baltimore was forced to do when Unitas got hurt — take a good running back like Tom Matte and put him at quarterback so he can run and throw — and what Chicago is doing occasionally with Bobby Douglass, it will move those defenses out of that four-man front in a hurry.

They used to kid a lot of college coaches about playing dull football. Well, if I was a pro coach I would try whatever it took to win, no matter how dull it might be, even if I got fired doing it. But I wouldn't get fired, because nobody kicks when you're winning, dull or not.

They make fun of old Woody Hayes and his 3-yards-and-a-cloud-of-dust offense, but he wins, and he fills those 80,000 seats at Ohio State. When I went out to Texas A&M I heard a lot about the aerial circus in that league, how wonderful it was, and we hardly threw a pass that first year, hanging in there, getting beat every game by a couple of points or a touchdown. People started saying why don't you throw, why don't you open up? I said, because if we throw we're liable to get beat 50–0.

The weaker you are the more conservative you play. You try to make fewer mistakes, and maybe then you'll luck into a win. You try to make your team do something they're not capable of and you get murdered. We only threw twenty-seven passes (both teams) in the Sugar Bowl game with Notre Dame, but the offenses were so diversified it looked like we were throwing the ball around all night.

In college you recruit, and you adapt to what the boy can do. At Kentucky we had Parilli, and he beat every passing record they had, and we had Blanda. And at Alabama we had Namath, Sloan, Stabler and Scott Hunter. Nobody complained about us not passing in those years because we had players who could. I remember one year, though, when we couldn't and didn't, and a Philadelphia writer said to me, "Your teams are so colorless, Bear. How come you don't pass more?"

I said, "How come you don't get in your car and go out and run red lights?"

In 1956 SMU threw the ball all over the place. They threw almost three times as many passes as we did at A&M, ten for touchdowns, but they had four times as many intercepted and won only four games all year. Nine of our passes went for touchdowns and we didn't lose a game. Which team had the better passing attack? That was the best passing the league had seen in years, and nobody even realized it.

The point is, if you've got a good running team you'll *be* a better passing team, and then you can win throwing. Vince Lombardi introduced that idea to the pros. Don Shula has perfected it. If you're playing a team as good as yours, and you *can't* pass, then they have you outgunned. You are toughest to defend against when you can spread the defense out. It's like catching a rabbit. The wider the area the tougher to catch. But if you don't have a passer, bring that flanker or split end in where he can block, and keep it simple.

There's no question the college game is better than it ever was, which makes the pro game better, too, of course. There has to be a place for both, because you can't destroy one without destroying the other. Certainly in some areas where there are just so many entertainment dollars it's a bad situation — like around San Francisco where there are so many teams: pro football, college football, pro baseball, and pro basketball. The Oakland Athletics have a fantastic record and don't draw flies. Just not enough dollars to go around.

But winning is *always* popular. USC has drawn extremely well in Los Angeles despite the competition, because McKay's teams win. Pro football has done a great job merchandizing its product, and some teams draw even when they don't win, and even when they're not very interesting. You have to wonder how long it will last.

Every owner in the National Football League squealed like pigs this year when Larry Csonka, Jim Kiick and Paul Warfield announced they were jumping to the new World Football League. I don't get too upset about that. We at the universities lose ten or fifteen of our best players every year, and have a complete turnover in personnel every four years. We've learned to live with that. It makes better coaches out of us.

The only thing that bothers me is that the new league is playing on weeknights. Our feeling in Alabama has always been that weeknights — Thursdays and Fridays — are for the high schools. Saturday is for the colleges, Sunday is for the pros — and the Bear Bryant television show.

Cut into the revenue of the high schools and force them to give up the game (it's expensive at the high school level, too) and you'll kill it for everybody — high schools, colleges *and* pros.

I know this much. Alabama football will survive anything, because we play the most interesting football there is — we win. But if the pros get too greedy they will ruin the college game. Pete Rozelle has one of the sharpest minds there is, and so far he has shown enough respect for the colleges to reconcile most differences. They better keep listening to him.

Thirty

College football, which has gotten so big, certainly needs a governing body, and the NCAA does a creditable job. But I don't think it is organized properly. The pros have twenty-six teams and when they want to change something it's twenty-six votes. We have 126 so-called major colleges, and the range of the electorate is staggering. Everybody has a different objective.

The schools at the top are competing for bowls, for television money (vs. the pros in some cases), and, not the least, for Number One, because that's an intangible worth even more in identification, support and respect. USC has 90,000 seats to fill. Davidson has 8,000. Their objectives are totally different, yet they operate under the same rules and restrictions. And vote on the same issues.

Alabama draws close to 600,000 spectators a year. It would take Davidson, with that 8,000-seat stadium, which it doesn't fill, forty years to make the kind of money we do. I don't mean to single Davidson out; there are fifty just like it who are voting on the same issues we are. If their budget is, say, $50,000, and ours is $2.5 million, it stands to reason they won't want to do the things we do. They can't.

The figures at the bottom of your balance sheet should be reasonably consistent with the people you're competing against. Such as the ones in your own conference. They're the ones you should meet with to decide the number of scholarships, the extent of the grant, the recruiting rules and the number of practice days and games you can play.

The rules are pretty silly for some of us. I certainly don't think it would corrupt the University of Alabama, or break its bank, if it wanted to give a high school coach a ticket to the game on Saturday. Or to take him out to dinner. As the rules stand now we aren't allowed.

College administrators who don't have successful athletic programs are always saying, "Cut down on football scholarships." You can't upgrade your own program by dragging down another's to your level. The University of Miami is in a struggle right now with the Dolphins for the entertainment dollar. Miami needs *more* scholarships, not less.

The mystery to me is why they always want to cut the football budget. Football pays the freight at most schools. Pays for itself and every other sport. Why would you try to shut down the counter that's keeping you in business?

In 1958 the Alabama athletic budget was $300,000, and in the red. Last year it was $2.5 million, and when we were through paying everything — including the mortgage on the new buildings — we were several hundred thousand in the black.

In 1970 we sent USC the biggest check it ever got from a football game, including its Rose Bowl shares. I think it came close to $175,000. We had increased our capacity to 72,000 at Legion Field, and we just kept letting people in that day. Police estimated there were 30,000 people still outside when we kicked off.

That wasn't our biggest payday. For a time our biggest one was against Louisiana Tech in 1966. If that surprises you — why Louisiana Tech instead of, say, Louisiana State — I'll tell you how it happened, and why our success is so popular with our rivals.

Tulane had dropped off our schedule and we were having a devil of a time getting a game, finding an opponent that didn't have blacks. We finally got Louisiana Tech, and we got Southern Mississippi to move to Tech's spot on the schedule and put Louisiana Tech first. I got their athletic director, Joe Allett, to agree to juggle his schedule around, and when we got down to money I said, "Joe, tell me what you want."

He said, "Shoot, I don't know, Bear. The most we ever made was $15,000."

I said, "OK, we'll give you $15,000."

What happened? We had a sellout, with thousands more trying to get in, and we had record receipts. More money than we could count. I felt guilty.

I went to our athletic board and said, "Listen, let's send Louisiana Tech $10,000 more." They agreed.

Shortly after that I got a letter from Reed Green of Southern Mississippi. He said, "Old Buddy, I understand you gave Louisiana Tech $10,000 extra. You wouldn't have had that game if it wasn't for us."

So I went back to the board and said we should send Southern Mississippi something, too. They got $10,000 without playing anybody.

I'll give you one more lesson in game contracts. We had a sellout against North Carolina State in 1961, when State had Roman Gabriel. But they had agreed to a $25,000 guarantee. I felt a little ashamed that they didn't make more money, so a few days later we sent them some more.

Ten *years* later I was at an all-star game in Texas, sitting in the lobby of our hotel one night with a group of coaches. One of them was Earle Edwards, the N.C. State coach.

John McKay was there, and a few others, and I thought it was a good time to point out how generous we were. So I told them about sending N.C. State that extra money.

Earle Edwards's eyes kept getting bigger, and when I finished the story he said, "Well I'm a son of a gun."

He said, "All these years I've been thinking what a cheap bunch you were in Alabama, bringing us down there with a great player like Gabriel and then keeping all the money."

What happened was the athletic director had put the second check in the athletic fund without telling Earl. Earl checked it out when he got home, and wrote me. He said his athletic director must have been ashamed for anybody to know what a stupid contract he had written.

So if you ask me what football means at Alabama in dollars and cents I can tell you it means a ton. The program is self-sustaining. We don't get any of the taxpayers' money. Football supports all the other sports, and we're giving more scholarships in the others than ever. The Coliseum — basketball arena, athletic offices, etc. — cost about $2.8 million and is being paid for principally by athletic funds.

We gave the University $500,000 to raise faculty salaries. We gave them another $200,000 for general use, and a pledge of $100,000 a year for academics.

Paul Bryant Hall houses 130 athletes, and originally cost $680,000. We added a rec room that cost $300,000. It all came out of the football program. We advanced the money — about $700,000 — for two airplanes that all the departments use. They turned out to be a great investment.

Outside of that, I can't think of a thing football has done for Alabama.

When they talk about cutting athletic budgets, I say, where? You got to cut people then, and that means coaches and players, and how can you do it? Where are you going to cut if you're trying to improve your program, have a well-rounded setup everybody can enjoy? If you want to sacrifice the whole thing, then cut football. Deemphasize.

People say, "Well, you shouldn't be in the entertainment business."

I'm not. In Alabama football is a way of life.

You have to have the NCAA as a police force, of course, because without it you would have anarchy. There used to be a lot of abuses. Due to its popularity, football breeds that sort of thing. A Carnegie Foundation report on American College athletes spoke of "alumni subsidies" and "slush funds" years ago. The report said:

"Into this game of publicity the university of the present day enters eagerly. It desires for itself the publicity that the newspapers can supply. It wants students, it wants popularity, but above all it wants money and always more money.

"The athlete is the most available publicity material the college has. A great scientific discovery will make good press material for a few days, but nothing to compare to that of the performance of a first-class athlete. Thousands are interested in the athlete all the time, while the scientist is at best only a passing show. And so it happens that the athlete lives in the white light of publicity."

I didn't memorize that. I read it in the *New York Times* last year. The report was made in 1929.

For years there were no rules. The NCAA was run in a closet in the Big Ten office in Chicago. And after they moved to Kansas City, and Walter Byers became full-time director, there were still a lot of iffy things going on. I told you about those tryouts we used to have, bringing in boys by the busload. Carney Laslie used to say that's how we won at Kentucky, and that's probably right. It wasn't illegal then.

When I first admitted in *Sports Illustrated* a few years ago that our alumni had paid athletes at Kentucky and Texas A&M, the ethics committee of the Football Coaches Association was said to have been "exercised" by my statements. They were considering "a study."

I don't know if they studied or not, but I said then I didn't care if they took it to the United Nations, I had nothing to hide. I still feel that way. I think if more of our problems in intercollegiate athletics got out in the open we could look at them a whole lot tougher, and solve them.

Why it has gotten so bad now could very well be what we're talking about — schools trying to operate big-money budgets, in the red, and desperate to win. We're supposed to be in this for more than the money, but when administrators start squawking about the costs and the coach hears nothing but complaints, I can understand his collar getting tight.

Some rich alumnus offers to help, and before you know it they're flying parents around, and opening charge accounts, and tampering with grades, and forging transcripts, and paying players, and promising jobs, and doing every other damn thing they can think of to survive.

Frank Broyles says that "if something isn't done the lid is going to blow off," and I say it's going to have to take some listening and some understanding on both sides. Come to a conclusion on what football means to your school, how much it is worth in publicity and esprit de corps, and then live with your conclusion.

One thing we have in college football today is excellent officiating, and this is a plus for the NCAA. I've gotten so now I don't even pay attention to who's officiating the games. That doesn't mean I won't holler at them and kick up a fuss if I think they're wrong on something, and my coaches grade them in the films afterward. But I'll never do again what I did one year when we went down to play SMU in Dallas, because it was embarrassing to me and demeaning. Well, it was stupid.

The game was over, which is too late to be popping off anyway, but it had been very poorly officiated. We had lost, and the players were in the dressing room crying when I went back out there to talk to the press. I was so tired I sat down on the steps and they clustered around.

The first question I got was that old stock thing, "What was the turning point of the game?"

It just so happened the officials were walking by at that moment and I pointed to one of them and said, "When that sonofabitch right there walked on the field."

If it hadn't been for the SMU coach, Matty Bell, who was friends with the official and me, I probably never would have gotten out of Dallas. But the tough part was when Mary Harmon and I went out to Matty's house for dinner that night. Who turns out to be his house guest but the official.

The point is that you just can't cry when it's no good crying. I didn't say anything, and wouldn't, about the touchdown Georgia made that beat us in 1965, because we didn't know until the picture came out in the papers and we checked the films that the boy who caught the pass was down on both knees when he caught it. If I had known that I would have probably stopped the game, or thrown a fit, or done something, but the next day was too late. The only thing to do then is to say, well, they just beat us.

I remember a few years ago we were playing Florida at Tuscaloosa, and the officials made a mistake on the down. The ball was on about our 2-yard line. If it had been on the 40, where a 15-yard penalty could hurt us, I wouldn't have done what I did. I couldn't get their attention so I just ran out there and put my foot on the ball and stopped the game.

I said, "The ball ain't gonna be snapped until we get this thing straightened out." I was very calm about it.

The official realized his mistake and changed his decision, which showed courage on his part. But the next day would have been too late for me to protest.

Almost the same thing happened at Mississippi State one year and I didn't risk it because the ball was at midfield. If I had run onto the field they might have penalized me the 15 yards. Backed up against your 2-yard line it wouldn't matter much.

Against Colorado in the Liberty Bowl a few years ago we had a little whoopy pass that was thrown behind the line but was actually a forward. I explained it to Pat McHugh, the referee, before the game, just in case we used it.

We pulled it at our 6-yard line and it was incomplete. Colorado fell on the ball. And the next thing I know they're lining up and giving it to them.

So I charged out and stopped the game.

I said, "Pat, I explained that play to you before the game. Why the hell do you think I took the time to tell you about it?"

He said, "Coach, you're absolutely right, and I'm sorry. You get the ball back. But I'm going to penalize you half the distance to the goal for coming on the field."

I said, "If that isn't a damn gyp. You're penalizing me for something you screwed up!"

The logic made no impression. He still penalized us.

When I was at Texas A&M in 1956 we went over to play Paul Dietzel's LSU team in Baton Rouge. Six of our starters had the flu, including John David Crow, who was upset he couldn't play because he was a Louisiana boy. That was Dietzel's second LSU team, and a good one. I can still see Paul on the sidelines, that big toothpaste grin of his.

Baton Rouge happens to be the worst place in the world to be a visiting team. It's a dug-out arena, and you get all that noise. It's like being inside a drum. The officiating suffers because of it. I have five starters from Louisiana on my team now and they know about that noise and what it can do. Last year we couldn't hear the signals at all. We just guessed at them.

On the first play of the game, Bob Marks, who's on my staff now, intercepted a pass and ran it back to the LSU 19-yard line. You never heard such booing and carrying on. I wanted them to hold up play till it subsided, but I couldn't get the officials' attention.

Roddy Osborne ran a play anyway, and with the noise nobody could hear him and we jumped too soon. Five-yard penalty.

He tried again. Same thing. Five more yards.

We were offsides four times in a row.

On the next exchange we completed a pass out of bounds near our bench, and I ran over and grabbed the official, George Hecht.

I said, "All I want is a fair deal. Make them keep that damn noise down."

The fans must have thought I was arguing about the pass being in bounds or something, because when George gave us the ball and a first down they nearly tore the stadium apart.

Bobby Joe Conrad, subbing for Crow, eventually got us a touchdown on a pass, and Dee Powell blocked a punt for a safety and we won, 9–7.

The following Monday I got a call from the Touchdown Club of New Orleans, wanting to know how I felt about cheating LSU out of the game.

I said, "What do you mean, 'cheating'? If you had kept the damn students quiet we would have won it in the first quarter."

He said, "The films show your left tackle was over the goal when you completed the touchdown pass. That made him an ineligible receiver downfield."

I said, "Well, I hope the hell he *was* downfield. Give them my regards in Baton Rouge." And I hung up.

I couldn't wait to go back and look at the films. Sure enough, when the receiver caught the ball one of our linemen, Ken Beck, who happened to be from Minden, Louisiana, was deeper in the end zone than the pass receiver. I was tickled to death.

That winter Dietzel invited me to speak at his banquet and I went down. When I got up to speak I got a few boos, and I thanked them all for inviting me.

I said, "And I want you to know I'll be glad to come back any time and help Coach Dietzel with his officiating problems."

— Thirty-One —

For years, because we didn't have black players or play against teams that had black players, we were criticized around the country for having an "insulated schedule." One that on the surface appeared weaker than others. I would debate that anytime, but there is no need now because the problem has long been solved.

We have black players, and we play against them, and that's progress. For a while I used to say it didn't matter. That five or ten years from now folks won't look back and say, well, he beat so-and-so, they'll just say, he won 200, lost 40, tied 2, or whatever. I still feel that way, but I don't have to defend a vulnerable position anymore.

When you've been raised around blacks, and had them as close friends, and even had a few fistfights with them as I did, you sure should have no trouble accepting integration. I don't say I agree with everything Martin Luther King said, but I saw the wisdom in most of it.

When I was at Kentucky I told the president, Dr. Herman Donovan, that we should be the first in the Southeastern Conference to have black players. I told him he could be the Branch Rickey of the league. But I didn't get anywhere.

You say, well, you were being selfish. You were just trying to get good players. That's right. I was. I wanted to win, and there were a couple of black boys then who could have helped us a lot. One who went to Illinois was the best athlete in the state that year, and the other was the son of our cook.

You don't change people's thinking overnight. Not in Kentucky, not anywhere. Shoot, when I was back in Arkansas some of those ignorant country boys thought it was awful that Al Smith was running for President. Smith was a Catholic, see, and Catholic was a bad word. They didn't know any better. When folks are ignorant you don't condemn them, you teach 'em.

We began to break down the resistance in Alabama when we played Penn State in the Liberty Bowl in 1959, and then Oklahoma and Nebraska in the Orange Bowl later on. We had to be proud of the way our boys conducted themselves, the good comments we heard. By the same token, Steve Sloan and Paul Crane told me during a golf match one summer that Nebraska's Freeman White had impressed them. All three of those boys were members of the Fellowship of Christian Athletes. What bothered me about it at the time wasn't what Steve said, but what he did. He sank a character-building putt on the 18th hole and I choked on mine, a little bitty three-footer that lost the match.

I have no doubt we would have gone to the Rose Bowl in 1961 when we were unbeaten and National Champions if the Los Angeles papers hadn't raised the specter of segregation. Tom Hamilton told Jim Owens we were in, and Jim called me from the Los Angeles airport. "You got it. They're going to extend you the invitation."

But about six o'clock both Owens and Hamilton called and said if I had anything else on the fire to grab it. Later I heard the Los Angeles papers were making it out to be an invitation to the Ku Klux Klan. I resented that, but I couldn't do anything.

We were in a damned-if-you-do, damned-if-you-don't situation. Our SEC opponents were as tough as any in the country, no matter what color the players were, but when we looked around for a team to play outside the conference it had to be from the South. I would have much preferred to play Michigan State or Illinois or somebody, because we'd have beaten them, too, and it would have been easier getting our boys ready to play. Southern Mississippi was as good as Illinois, but our guys wouldn't have gotten excited over the match. And you'd have to give the Southern Mississippi players a saliva test, they'd be so eager to get at us.

I think it cost us the National Championship in 1966, because we had played Louisiana Tech in Birmingham instead of Tulane, which had dropped us, and though Louisiana Tech was as good as anybody in the Big Ten that year (except maybe Michigan State), it didn't have the prestige.

I'll never forget, we were playing Auburn in Birmingham on national television in December, and I got this black who was always around and had been helping us for several years and had him put on an Alabama wardrobe. I told him I wanted him to "stand by me every minute. I may need you."

He said, "Yessir."

I knew they were going to put the camera on me sooner or later. I wanted them to see that black face over that Alabama shirt. I'm told they had us on about twenty times that day, and he was right there next to me every time. We shut out Auburn, 31–0. When the final votes were in the next week, Notre Dame still won the National Championship.

After the civil rights issue got so hot in Alabama the way to get elected was to holler "nigger." That's what some politicians thought, anyway. John Patterson was running that kind of campaign against George Wallace. We were for Wallace. Mary Harmon had loaned him a toothbrush when we met one night in a hotel in Birmingham, and they've been close ever since.

Anyway, we got the bid to play Penn State in the Liberty Bowl, and Penn State had a few black players. I wanted to go anyway because we were just getting our program going good. I told Governor Patterson I'd need his support.

He said, "Shoot, Bear, I'm just trying to get votes. Go on up there and play 'em."

Which we did, and got beat, 7–0, by Rip Engle's team. It should have been worse. After the game there was a little party for the players, and a big black tackle named Charlie Janerette came up to me and said he wanted to shake my hand. He said, "Coach, that's one of the nicest bunch of sportsmen I have ever played against."

I said, "Charlie, I don't know how to take that. I think I'd rather you told me they were mean and ugly. Maybe we'da won."

When Governor Wallace made his stand at the schoolhouse door, I had a clinic scheduled in Montana, and I flew out a day early. I was in Chicago, eating at a fancy restaurant near O'Hare Airport. It was so crowded I had to leave my name to be called, and I didn't think to use another name.

I ate, and I'm not sure what the tab was, but since they knew who I was I left a tip that was more than I could afford. About $20.

The waiter said, "I don't want your money," and walked away.

He was a white guy, too. I put the money back in my pocket. If he wanted to cut off his nose to spite his face that was all right with me.

So for years I had to hold off trying to recruit blacks. We finally had some in school, and I said if they were eligible they were welcome to try out. There were a few I recommended to other schools, but the time wasn't ripe. I had one high school coach see me about his boy's chances at Alabama, and I said he'd be welcomed and treated fairly, but if it were me I'd send him someplace else, because we were still two or three years away.

I said I wasn't worried a bit about our players, but we had to play two games in Mississippi, and for that and other reasons it might be too tough on the kid. I wanted him to be treated and to act like any other Alabama player. And I damn sure wouldn't stand for him showing up with a bunch of photographers and some big-talking civil rights leader trying to get publicity.

Two or three years later we recruited Wilbur Jackson down in Ozark, Alabama. His daddy was a railroad man, at the same job thirty-five years, and Richard Williamson of our staff went down to offer Wilbur a scholarship. He invited Wilbur up to see the campus, and when he came in I laid it on the line.

I said, "Wilbur, this is all new to me. You got to have problems. Our white ones have 'em. I can't tell you you won't, or what they'll be. But before you go to anybody else with them, you come to me." From that day on I never had to raise my voice at Wilbur. Not in four years.

So we signed Wilbur Jackson, and early the next year John McKay and I were in a hotel in Houston on a Sunday afternoon, visiting with Johnny Mitchell, my old friend from Texas. I had a list of prospects on the West Coast that I was asking McKay about. I knew I couldn't beat him if he wanted any of them bad enough, but I was checking anyway.

Finally he laughed and said, "Well, hell, Paul, the best one out there isn't even on your list, and he's got the same name as him" — and pointed to Johnny Mitchell — "and he's from Mobile, Alabama. And I want him."

I excused myself after a minute or two and went into another room and called my office to find out who this Mitchell was. It all checked out — John Mitchell, an end from Mobile, then in junior college at East Arizona State.

It so happened that Johnny was home vacationing at the time. Two hours later my recruiter in the area had him in a room in Mobile, and I talked with him long distance from Houston. He was very receptive.

I said, "John, you'll be the first black we ever started, and that should mean something to you." (Wilbur, a sophomore, did not figure to start. We still had him at flanker then, which was our mistake.)

Then I asked to talk with John's mother.

I said, "Mrs. Mitchell, John and I have talked this thing out, the problems that might arise. But you just trust me."

All this happened on a Sunday afternoon. We just barely got him because Miami came in there strong that very night and he told me later they almost won him.

As I've always said, the best thing you have going for you in recruiting is a boy's mother, and I made a friend out of Mrs. Mitchell. And she got a friend in old Papa.

I'll never forget, we were playing Texas in the Cotton Bowl, and I hadn't met Mrs. Mitchell in person then. Only on the phone. We were standing out front of the hotel, in one of those milling crowds, and she was next to me but we hadn't been introduced. I didn't know if it was she. A black newspaperman came up and started talking smart, like he was looking for something. He said, "How many black players you got on your team, Coach?"

I said, "I don't have any. I don't have any white ones, I don't have any black ones. I just have football players. They come in all colors."

Mrs. Mitchell got a good idea of my feelings that day. She told the reporter who she was, and we talked, and I guarantee you we respect each other pretty good now. They had a banquet for John at Mobile last year, and he spoke for twenty minutes about what it took to come to Alabama, and he cried, and he wound up by saying he was so thankful to the good Lord for sending him there. I tell you that made an impression on me.

John Mitchell was our first black starter, our first black captain, our first black All-American (in 1972), and our first black coach. He's on my staff right now. He's a gem, too.

But John McKay never forgave me. We started Mitchell that same year in the opening game against Southern Cal. On the kickoff he came down and almost dehorned the USC ball carrier. We won, and went on to win eleven straight.

McKay finally got even last year. I had been kidding about Mitchell, and I went too far. He sent Willie Brown in there and took a black kid right from under my nose, a kid who was living in Atlanta but whose mama and papa were from Tuscaloosa. I thought sure we had him, but on the last day Willie Brown showed up. Turned out to be the boy's first cousin.

Meanwhile, we converted Wilbur Jackson — a 6–2, 210-pounder — from wideout to running back. We had to. He dropped every pass that was near him. But he had that long stride and great balance and when we went to the wishbone we moved him to halfback. He wasn't just good, he was great. He averaged 7.7 yards a carry his junior year, and 7.9 his senior year.

Last winter he was picked in the first round — by San Francisco — in the NFL draft.

I really can't tell you how many blacks we have now, but they're my boys and I love every one of them. I've had no problems, and, to my knowledge, neither have they. The great majority have been good players, and the whites on the team have bent over backwards to get them accepted. Which may be a mistake because it's not natural that way.

Somebody asked me if I hired Johnny Mitchell to "coach the

blacks." No, I didn't. I think I can coach a kid as good as anybody, black, white or green. But I wanted the best young coach available, and John was it. And if a good coach happens to be black, I want him. Not just in football, in all areas. Other coaching jobs, ticket takers, secretaries. We can't be stupid about this thing. If they're good, we'd like to have them, and it will make everybody happy.

I'm sure there are people in Alabama who resent them being on the team. People who will never accept them. But I think our won-lost record since they've been included has opened some eyes.

When USC came in here and beat us so bad in the opening game in 1970, Jerry Claiborne made the remark that their big black fullback, Sam Cunningham, did more for integration in the South in sixty minutes than Martin Luther King did in twenty years. Sam gained about 230 yards and scored three touchdowns that night and like to have killed us all.

I think you have to have good athletes to win, and when the blacks are good they should be playing. I would rather have them for me than against me. If Willie Shelby and Wilbur Jackson and Woodrow Lowe and Mike Washington were playing for somebody else they'd be worrying us to death, and that's just naming four. Or Calvin Culliver. He's going to be an All-America fullback, and I want him on my side.

The trouble seems to occur when you have blacks who aren't playing, because they'll have fifty thousand people telling them they're better than the white boy who's ahead of them. You're not going to be right all the time. I'll tell you how it goes. I had a white boy in St. Louis, a hot prospect I got, tell me that he heard from one of my players that I favored blacks over whites, that if it was close the blacks would get it. Well, I won't dignify that kind of remark.

I don't believe you are better because you're black or because you're white. But some of the blacks now are like I was when I came out of Arkansas. They don't want to go back to what they came from. Like Bo Schembechler told me before I had even one, "They won't quit you. They got nothing to go to."

Do I treat them alike? No. You can't. When I was a young coach I used to say that. "Treat everybody alike." That's bull. Treat everybody *fairly*.

Everybody is different. If you treat them all alike you won't reach them. Be fair with all of them and you have a chance. One you pat on the back and he'll jump out the window for you. Another you kick in the tail. A third you yell at and squeeze a little. But be fair. And that's what I am.

The only sad thing I've seen, and as I say it's new to me, is that the blacks segregate themselves. I'm not going to get upset over it because that's the wrong psychology, and because other coaches who have lived with this longer than I say it's the same everywhere. But except for Johnny Mitchell, Wilbur Jackson, and a couple others, they go into that dining room and group up. I won't make an issue of it as long as they get along with everybody, and so far they do.

Sylvester Croom was a good center for us last year. His daddy is a preacher, one of the three top black leaders in Tuscaloosa, and a warm personal friend of mine. He's one of my advisers on local affairs, and I go to him when I need answers.

Sylvester made a statement after the season that made me feel we had to be on the right track.

He was quoted as saying, "The blacks on this team love the white guys as much as they do the black guys."

Don't you think that made me proud?

— Thirty-Two —

The black question, if you want to call it that, didn't bother me a minute compared with that three-year slump we went through in '68, '69 and '70. For the first time since coming back to Alabama I felt like my program was missing, and that I might be losing my touch. Some coaches might not consider those years so bad, because we went to bowls every time. But we also lost five games twice, and that's bad. And it was my fault.

Everything that's bad with Alabama football is my fault. That's the way it's supposed to be. Who else you going to blame? You can't blame the kids. You can't blame your assistants. You can't blame the president. Who else?

Our selection of players hadn't been sharp in the late sixties, and that was sure my fault. And we did some other things I wouldn't exactly recommend. I told you the mistake I made with Kenny Stabler. I should have disciplined him, and I didn't, and we went downhill from there. The other players had to realize I'd relented, and I could feel control slipping away.

Age had nothing to do with it — you can be out of touch at any age. And you're never too old until you think you are. People thought I was getting pretty old in 1969 when we lost to Vanderbilt and Tennessee in succession, the only time we've done that at Alabama. But I wasn't in the mood to examine the subject.

I said, "There are two sets of alumni. A large set, to which I belong, and a small set, composed of Mary Harmon and me. That small set will decide when I get too old, too fat or too ignorant to coach. There won't be any need for the other set to mouth off about it."

As I said, campuses across the country were going through a rebellion in those days. It hadn't seemed to touch us at Alabama and I suppose I got complacent. It wasn't until I was up to my nose in it, and discovered that at least part of our trouble was drugs, that I snapped to attention.

I had one boy during that time that I felt real close to. A tough little linebacker from Florida, named — well, call him Danny. He was such a good kid, and so talented he could have made All-America. He had an I.Q. of almost a genius.

His home life was sad. His daddy had been a millionaire, but quit his wife and went broke. When Danny got to Alabama he was in the middle of his parents' problems. I personally saw his daddy cry in front of him.

Danny said he wanted to go to another school, for architecture. Four of his high school teammates were signed to go there. The school was buying them, but, according to Danny, the recruiter didn't offer him anything.

He asked the recruiter, "What am I going to get?"

The recruiter said, "You're too hot. Alabama will catch us if we give you anything." Danny told me that himself.

So he came to our place empty-handed, and as a sophomore he was great against the easy teams. The next spring I was gone most of the time, which was my worst mistake during that period. I spent over a month in California alone. When I got back Danny was in every kind of trouble. Mostly just doing the opposite of what he was supposed to.

I brought him in and we talked, and he could con me good. He'd smile — a cute little red-headed kid with freckles and big thick glasses he couldn't see across the room without — and he'd scrunch up his little eyes, and before I knew it I'd be saying, "OK, Danny, OK." And he'd be off scot-free.

Two weeks later it was something worse.

I took him off scholarship.

The next fall I gave him a chance to come back. One of our first drills in the fall requires a player to run a mile in six minutes. It's so easy I could do it. But Danny couldn't.

I said, "For heaven's sake, get yourself straightened up and come back when you can make it. This is the easy part." I told him he could stay in the dorm and we would help him make it. "We won't feed you, but we'll help you get back."

He was there for about six days. I didn't know this until after he left, but he didn't take a bath the whole time. And one day he just disappeared.

He wound up at another school, and finished out his eligibility. But that didn't relieve the hurt any. I felt this way. He was a good kid when he came to Alabama and we didn't help him. I don't know what kind of job his daddy did, but I did a sorry one. It goes right back to communication. If I had been communicating I'd have known, and I would have stopped it before it started, I guarantee you.

Well, I brought narcotics experts in to talk with the boys. To tell them what they were letting themselves in for, how bad it could be. And there were other kids who talked to them, kids who had gone the drug route and had some pretty chilling things to say. But it didn't completely sink in.

One of my real good ones, Johnny Musso, the All-America running back, came to me during that time and told me that no matter where they went they were running into it.

He said, "What are we going to do, Coach? Sit in the room all the time?" Not long after that we built the annex to the dorm, a big playroom where they could bring dates and enjoy themselves. But that wasn't the total solution.

When it got so bad that I knew I had to do something I talked with them myself. Gave them an ultimatum. I said if you're doing it, stop. If you've got any of it, get rid of it. That there would not be another chance.

And at five that afternoon we descended on the dorm. We searched every player's room and found seven of them who were apparently using it.

I called the parents of each one. I said we were having a meeting to discuss their boys' taking drugs. Two of the parents said, "What's wrong with that?" They didn't even come.

So we told the seven that they could withdraw from school, or we would just turn it over to the president and let the law handle it. They all withdrew.

I suppose I could say that never happened here, because nobody knew it. But it happened. And we faced it. And I think we made an impression. We haven't had any trouble since, and the next year we won eleven straight.

I'm not completely satisfied with the changes we've allowed in conduct the last few years, but I wasn't hardheaded about it. I did some accommodating during that time. I told you about the hair. I remember my little grandson, Mae Martin's boy, used to get his cut short because of me, white sidewalls and all, and it nearly killed him. Jimmy Hinton's boy was suffering the same way and I began to realize that even at that age they wanted to be stylish.

I still draw the line on facial hair. I made a mistake on that because traditionally the black boys wear those little pin-striped mustaches. But I let them all wear their hair longer, as long as it was trimmed and neat and not dangling over their shoulders.

One boy I told to get a haircut last year said, "Coach, let me ask you something. Why do you get after us about hair?"

I said, "To tell you the truth when it's straggly like yours it's unsanitary. I can't tell if you got bugs or what, and I don't know how that little girl you go with even wants to touch you. It must be important to you, your hair. But if it's more important than football then I don't want you."

I tell them now when they come out I want them to look like athletes, not girls. And I don't want them to miss a day's practice because I have to send them to the barber.

I know the reason, of course. The girls like long hair, and they like the girls. Athletes don't have to look the way we did when I was in school to be athletes, so I'm not archaic about it. David Bailey, one of my former players, told me I was wrong, and that woke me up some.

But I tell my players they're special. They're something everybody should be proud of. They're not like the other students. I say, "If you were we'd have 15,000 out for football. You've got to take pride in being something special."

I had one come in and tell me after that talk that he just wanted to "be like the other students."

I said, "Well, you go on away from here then, because you can't be a winning football player and be like the others. There's no way."

It boils down to this. What do you come to school for? I told one the other day, "You must have thought you liked the way I did things. You wanted to play here. You could have gone to any school in the country. Well, you're going to do this my way or not at all." I feel I know enough now not to get myself into one of those binds again. I won't take a kid when I think he might be a problem. There was a good-looking blond halfback from another state who wanted to come to Alabama recently. Ran the hundred in 9.8 and was big and tough. His coach said, "Take him, Bear. You can straighten him out."

I told him I didn't want to straighten him out. The biggest mistake coaches make is taking borderline cases and trying to save them. I'm not talking about grades now, I'm talking about character. I want to know before a boy enrolls about his home life, and what his parents want him to be. And I want him to know the criterion at Alabama is up on my office wall in those four-color pictures — the four National Championship teams we've had.

I don't think you could play any more interesting football than we did in the early and mid-sixties, and again the last three years. I said that coaches talk to one another. They also listen. When John McKay and I play golf together at the Hope tournament or someplace, we visit and we talk football. And I listen. You better believe I listened when Bud Wilkinson said anything, and Bobby Dodd.

When I was at Kentucky and Bud was winning so much and we upset him in the Sugar Bowl, he invited me to speak at his clinic during spring practice. He assigned a bright young man to take me around. We hit it off immediately. It turned out to be Darrell Royal. Through the years, I suppose Darrell and I talked more than anybody. He's a great telephone guy. I probably talk $10,000 a year with him.

Five years ago Darrell called me about his new offense — the wishbone. (He called it that because the backs line up in the shape of one.) He told me what it was, and how he was going to use it. He said, "Don't say anything. We're going to pull it on Houston."

Houston tied Texas 17–17, but Darrell wasn't discouraged. He kept adding to it and adding to it. Making it better. And we would talk about it on the phone, or at clinics, and I was listening pretty good.

Then three springs ago, when I knew we couldn't win with what we had, doing what we were doing, I told our coaches, "What we could win with is the old split-T. We may be dull as hell, but we'd win."

You go one step further and you got the wishbone.

I went to see Darrell. And we put it in. That was 1971, when we went eleven and zero.

Don't misunderstand. Formations don't win football games, people do. But they can give you an edge, and that's what coaches look for. That's why we change so much.

When I first started everybody was using the single wing. Matty Bell and Dutch Meyer and Rusty Russell started spread formations out in Texas, throwing the ball on every down, and that changed some thinking. Don Faurot and Bud and Jim Tatum came out with the split-T, which changed football, and changed me.

That's what the wishbone is today, a glamorized split-T. After that there was nothing significant until the so-called pro offense, drop-back passing and reading defenses. Now the wishbone. And I've gone with all of them.

Most coaches do. They go with the trends, what is successful, what looks good on TV. I do it, everybody does.

But we've had the players who could make them go. The players' abilities dictate what we do. I've had more great quarterbacks than all the other coaches put together, and half of that was pure luck. Babe Parilli at Kentucky was luck. Joe Namath was luck. I inherited Blanda. And one of the greatest was one nobody heard much of, Roddy Osborne at Texas A&M. I inherited him. Of course, he was a fullback when I got him.

There's still a lot we don't know about the wishbone, but it's the best formation I have ever seen. In the first place, the fullback is always in the same spot, and it's easy for the quarterback to get the ball to him. In the old split-T, with the irregular line splits, the quarterback was reaching a lot of the time. Some of the best plays in the split-T were missed handoffs, when the quarterback had to keep it and confused everybody.

Too, in the old split-T, when the quarterback moved out to option on the defensive end he had to pitch the ball blind, or blind *behind* him, to the trailing halfback. With the wishbone the halfbacks line up a little deeper and closer in to the fullback, and their weight is back in the stance and not forward like it was in the split-T. As a result it measures out that the halfback winds up about 4 yards wider when the quarterback makes his pitch, and the quarterback can *see* him. It's so much easier. And the big plus is that the whole thing is that much ahead of the pursuit.

The thing about the wishbone that I've worked hardest on is passing. The advantage there is unbelievable. We're still discovering how good it can be.

Here's what happens if you've got any kind of team at all. You make them take five men to defend against the fullback. That's basic. It takes five to keep the fullback contained, with all the routes he can run. That leaves three defensive players on each side — one to take the pitch, one to take the quarterback, and *one* to cover the pass.

You get one-on-one coverage *every* time. Then it's just a matter of whether you can hit the receiver.

Now, if you can't make them take five to cover the fullback you don't have an offense. They're better than you are. But try to picture what it means to us to get one-on-one every time instead of all that double coverage, and sluffing off, and zones that converge on the receivers.

For four or five years we used the dropback pass. We did everything the pros do — we read, we did it all. Scott Hunter did a heck of a job for a college quarterback, and Steve Sloan as a coach on the field was probably the best we ever had for picking something up before the ball was snapped.

But we'd have to work all week to figure a way to read the defenses and get our best receivers one-on-one against the coverage. It took us until Thursday to have our game plan. That meant every coach on the staff studying movies till all hours, trying to spot whether this

313

guy lined up with his feet one way or the other, or if they did this or that, trying to get something before the ball was snapped.

Now, with the wishbone, you get what you want automatically. I *know* our game plan, and I know it for every game, basically. I don't give a hoot what *they* do, I know what *we're* going to do. We're going to walk out there and read 'em and go. You can't imagine the difference that makes. For you, for your coaches, for the kids. The confidence it gives them.

In 1973 we threw for a touchdown one of every seven completions. We averaged 24.8 yards per completed pass. If you don't know what that means, I can tell you it's fantastic.

The one major difference in lining up a wishbone is that you should have your best athlete at quarterback. He has to run, he has to pass. We had Johnny Musso, our best running back, ready to play quarterback about ten times in 1972. I knew sooner or later they were going to start making our quarterback keep the ball, which you can do with the wishbone, and which is why the pros won't risk it.

But we didn't have a Richard Todd quarterbacking then, and we were afraid we'd be vulnerable if they made our quarterback keep the ball. We kept going and they didn't do it, and we kept winning, and finally LSU — old Charley McClendon — made us do it on national television. We had Johnny ready to play quarterback that night. But he got hurt. And he never did. Terry Davis went all the way and was super. Musso got in and made a key block on a Davis touchdown and we won, 14–7. Davis was our first wishbone quarterback and in those two years won every regular season game except one. But I made up my mind that in the future we would have that all-around athlete at quarterback.

Well, I said we're still learning about the wishbone. We played VPI last year at Tuscaloosa and the last thing I wanted to do was embarrass young Charlie Coffey, the VPI coach. He's a nice fellow, and I sure wasn't trying to run up the score. The first team only played twelve minutes, and we were shoving in the reserves as fast as we could. We won, 77–6, and set a national rushing record of 748 yards and a total offense record of 833 yards. I couldn't do anything to stop it. We played seventy-four men.

By the time we got to Notre Dame in the Sugar Bowl I about had myself convinced that it was the best offense I ever had, no matter what the formation. I'd have said it was the best, period, but Notre Dame beat us, 24–23, coming from behind three times to do it, and since we didn't win I can't call it the best anything.

But if you saw that game you had to believe you were seeing football the way it ought to be played, college, pro or whatever. I understand people had heart attacks watching it, and one Alabama sportswriter died in the pressbox right after. We sure don't ever want football to be *that* exciting, but the comments I heard were mostly how good the game was for college football, having two fine teams with great traditions play to such a thrilling finish. It was the first time Alabama had ever played Notre Dame, and it won't be the last. I have to think we gained a mutual respect.

It wasn't so thrilling for me because we lost. I thought if it were close in the second quarter we'd run away with it in the second half. For a while it looked that way. Once we got everything sorted out and knew what they were up to we handled them pretty convincingly.

But we got down there twice before the half without getting anything out of it, and after we went ahead we let their man get away on a 93-yard kickoff return that was the only one returned for a touchdown on us all year. Our people ran around their blockers and watched him score.

At the finish Notre Dame was the one that made the big plays, not us. The one that everybody talked about, though, was our punt that rolled dead on the Notre Dame 1-yard line late in the fourth quarter. A roughing-the-kicker penalty was called on the play and a lot of people didn't understand why we took the punt instead of the penalty.

Well, the rule doesn't call for an automatic first down. We'd still have had fourth and 5, on our own 45. I would much rather let them have it on their 1, trying to dig out, than us trying to make 5 yards in one try, with the goal still 50 yards away.

There's so many ways to win in that position — Notre Dame on its 1-yard line. A fumble. A good defensive play to force a safety. A blocked punt. The main thing was to hold them and make them kick out. We were sure to have good field position and plenty of time to score. We also had two time-outs left.

It all fell into place. In two downs they made only 2 yards. Then on third down their little quarterback, Tom Clements, made a great fake and threw a play-action pass to the end, who was so close to me on the sidelines I could have knocked the ball down myself. None of our backs did, however, and it saved the game for Notre Dame.

I got a letter from Ara Parseghian shortly afterward, the only one I ever received from a coach who beat me. He said how much his group had enjoyed playing us, how wrong the impressions were beforehand. (They pictured us as a bunch of rednecks, and we had some thoughts about them, too.) He said how much everybody got out of the game, and how great it was for college football that we now had a series going. It was very gracious, Ara's letter. One I'd loved to have written him.

Like I said, though. I don't really consider it a loss. We just ran out of time.

— Thirty-Three —

I probably get more kick out of the game now than ever. I'm more fired up than I was twenty years ago. I have been fortunate, I've had honors. But if I couldn't stay in it I'd probably croak in a week. I don't have as much fun as I used to because I'm not as close to the kids, not coaching as much. But still. Today, tomorrow. When I walk out on that practice field cold chills run up my back. A new day. And it's something I wouldn't swap for anything.

I don't work as hard. I'm not as tied up. I don't bleed inside like I used to. I take more time to enjoy it, and I get a lot of that attention I craved so much as a kid. I sure don't object to that — the Coach of the Year awards, the other honors.

I am a big enough ham to love it when I see that Bryant Field sign on old Sloan Bashinsky's sandspur patch on the Keys, or when I walk into the Green Turtle Inn and see my old tennis shoes hanging from the ceiling, or to know that men like Henry Forrest, Kuaii King's trainer, and Jones Ramsey named their sons after me. I understand that more than a hundred poor little babies have been named after me. Lee Roy Jordan's is another one.

But sitting back and being petted and catered to isn't my idea of enjoying success. They used to say I walked behind a mule so long I became one, but I genuinely enjoyed the hard work, and I miss it. My teams don't work as hard, either, of course. We rarely scrimmage once the season starts. We have to have partial scrimmages occasionally, in order to pick up stunts and things and to have an idea what they'll do when the game starts. It's like batting practice. But there's so much more to learn that we don't have the time.

I enjoyed being physical with my players because I think it drew us closer. And it used to be I was with them all the time, on the field and off. We could communicate. I could preach my sermons. Lee Roy was interviewed once and flattered the dickens out of me. He said, "If Coach Bryant said wear green shoes I'd have green shoes." It's not that way anymore.

First, with two-platoon football we have too many people. In the days when players went both ways you could take two assistants and coach *nine* teams. When Lee Roy was playing I'd be out there grunting and butting with 'em, and they believed what we were doing would win. I don't do that anymore, and miss it, and consequently I don't do as good a job.

Oh, occasionally I get the old urge and let loose a little. After we lost to Florida one year at Denny Stadium — my first defeat there — we were down in the old meeting room on Sunday morning, with the players sitting at those little desks. I had gotten pretty exercised by the films, seeing how sloppy we were.

I was tossing a ball when I got up to make my talk, and I said, "Gentlemen, this is the way you tackle," and I pitched the ball to Bebs Stallings and plowed into him. Must have knocked over half a dozen desks.

Then I said, "And here's the way you hold the ball when you run," and we did it again, knocking over a few more.

You say, well, that was childish, you could have wound up in the hospital. But I enjoyed it and so did Bebes, and I know we got those boys' attention.

I have rules for myself that I abide by now, and they make everything a lot more pleasant. For one, I have a rule that no player can do anything wrong during a game. Just me. He comes off the field and I'm going to be there to greet him and tell him that's fine and just forget it, because if I had been on the ball he wouldn't have done something poorly or made a bonehead play.

I made up my mind a long time ago that I wouldn't let the players take the rap for losing. At Texas A&M Elwood Kettler was our quarterback, and led the conference in total offense the year we won one out of ten. Against Baylor in a 20–7 loss we had a first and goal on the 1. Four plays later we were on the 9.

After the game nobody had asked me who called those plays. So I got Mickey Herskowitz aside and asked him to, and he did.

"Coach, who called those plays on the goal line?"

I said, "Me. I did. What of it?"

When I correct them in a meeting it's always "we" or "our" mistake, so they know it's a team deal, that we're responsible as a team. If I have to criticize, I like to start with something positive, like, "Fellas, I've never seen us tackle so good," or, "John, you're breaking better for the ball." Then when I've got their attention — they're always going to agree with you when you're telling 'em something good — I come back and say, "But boys, we are covering kickoffs like we're trying to live forever."

Or, "Now here's what you need to do, Crow. You need to concentrate a little more on keeping your head up on your block."

I always make it a point to correct the outstanding players. There's no use fussing a boy who doesn't have any ability.

There's no easy way to win, and the tougher it is the more they have to believe in you, and to trust you. Communication. It's the key to everything. You have to have it to win, and when you lose, too, so you can hold them in your hand.

My players don't talk to me as much or come to see me now unless they've got a real big problem. It used to be they'd come with any kind of problem, big or small. John Crow, Lee Roy, Charlie Krueger would come by just to visit. We're closer now than we were three or four years ago, though, and sometimes it's almost as good as it was.

We played Florida one of the greatest games any team ever played in 1972, winning 38–0 in Gainesville. When we got out to the airport afterward, the plane wasn't there. Our kids could have been home and out enjoying themselves, but there we were standing around in that heat, and I was mad.

Well, I don't know why — it was Mary Harmon's idea, really — but I went around and said, "When we get back, if you don't have anything better to do, bring your wives or your dates and come over to our house. We got a new pool with AstroTurf all around, and Mary Harmon will cook up something."

I expected a handful. Half the team came. I was inside having a drink and listening to a game on the radio and they were around the pool with their girls.

And one by one they started slipping in there until they were all inside, laying around on the rug like little pigs, listening to the game with me. The girls still out by the pool. I think it was one of the best times I ever had.

I had a young coach at my place at Lake Martin one summer. He wasn't on my staff, but he wanted to be. He had a lot of ideas he was trying on me, and one thing led to another and I got my dander up a little, which was stupid, but he backed off.

Then he started oohing and aahing over my house, and the way I lived. He said, "Coach, what does it take to own a beautiful place like this?"

And I said, "Some points on the scoreboard, son."

Well, I've said it a jillion times at clinics. If you want to coach you have three rules to follow to win.

One, surround yourself with people who can't live without football. I've had a lot of them.

Two, be able to recognize winners. They come in all forms.

And, three, have a plan for everything. A plan for practice, a plan for the game. A plan for being ahead, and a plan for being behind 20–0 at the half, with your quarterback hurt and the phones dead, with it raining cats and dogs and no rain gear because the equipment man left it home. What are you going to say? You'll know if it was right by the scoreboard.

On the field I try not to make any decisions unless they have particular significance — I don't mean I sit there on my fat fanny, like I have done in some games, thinking or praying *they* would do it when I knew *I* should have — but I try to have a plan and the guts to stick to it no matter what happens.

All right, so what about those "winners." How can you tell when you've found one?

You can't, not always. It'd be nice if you could see into a boy's mind, see how much football means to him, but nobody can do that. I think I can tell a pro team more about my players than any scout or any computer they use, but almost anyone can recognize great talent. The one that makes you proud is the one who isn't good enough to play, but it means so much to him, he puts so much into it, that he plays anyway.

I have had a lot of those, and I can coach them better than most. The ones who have ability and don't use it are the ones who eat your guts out. I've messed up my share of those.

Players can be divided, roughly, into four types. Those who have ability and know it, those who have it and don't know it, those who don't have it and know it, and those who don't have it but don't know it. The great ones — Bob Gain, Steve Meilinger, Joe Namath — anybody could coach. But I don't think one coach will do as well as another with an average guy like Jimmy Sharpe because you have to reach him.

Sharpe had no ability, but he sure thought he did. He was a winner. Ray Perkins was a winner. His freshman year he had a serious head injury. The doctors put a plate in it. Not many would have come back after that, or even tried.

When they operated it was more a question of whether Ray would live. He stayed out for a year and then came back as a receiver. He had been a tailback and a defensive safety, with terrible hands. Catching passes wasn't his strong point. But just on pride and determination he *became* a great receiver. He is coaching now for the New England Patriots.

There are a lot of guys like Perkins who have made it worthwhile for me. Fun people. I warm to them. I always said if I needed Jordan or Crow or Krueger, they'd start walking. But some wouldn't.

I've made a lot of mistakes with a lot of players, and some still hate my guts, I'm sure. I can understand that. A football player has to make a lot of sacrifices, and if he's been put through the mill and didn't do much and doesn't have much to look back on that's pleasing, I'm not sure he has any reason to think kindly of me. But at the time it was the only sure way for me, and if I was starting again, betting my life on it — which you're doing when you're a young fellow — I would have to go the same sure way.

Today the premium is on getting the top athlete. When we played both ways we could take a guy like Sharpe, 194 pounds, hone him down, have him so quick, and he'd go out and beat a guy who weighed 240. They used to ask me what I thought about little players. I said they looked as good to me pitching the ball to the official behind the goal as the big ones do.

But we're not kidding anybody. We have to have ability *and* size now. A guy 6–5 to rush the passer, and a guy 6–4 to block him. You can't win with the good little guy anymore. No chance. Not since the two-platoon.

Bud Wilkinson told me what to expect before we played Nebraska in the Orange Bowl in 1972. We were talking about who we wanted to play, about this team and that one, and Bud said, "I'm going to tell you. Nebraska has more great athletes than have ever been on one team."

And after what happened to us — 38–6 — I believe him.

But it's still a coach's game. Make no mistake. You start at the top. If you don't have a good one at the top, you don't have a cut dog's chance. If you do, the rest falls into place. You have to have good assistants, and a lot of things, but first you have to have the chairman of the board. Then you have to recruit, and then you have to get them to play. On the field it's a player's game.

Another rule I believe in: I don't have any ideas, my coaches have them. I just pass the ideas on and referee the arguments. If we have had a bad practice, I don't have to chew out my assistants. I whistle the team in early, and when they're gathered around I say, "Gentlemen, I want to apologize to you for the lousy coaching job we did today. You didn't get anything out of it, and I promise you we're going to have better coaching tomorrow."

If that doesn't wake up my coaches then I have hired the wrong men.

I don't get real close to my assistants socially, except those who have been with me so long, like Sam Bailey and Carney Laslie. But you sure have to know what motivates them, because that's the first rule in the book, motivating your coaches so they can motivate the boys they're responsible for.

I try not to be buddy-buddy with any assistant because I don't want the others to think I have pets. Bum Phillips, who was with me at A&M, said I never had jealousies on my staff because nobody could say, "Well, no sense suggesting that idea to him. So-and-So's with him all the time and he'd just veto it."

That doesn't mean I don't get to know them. I'd take Pat James to lunch one day, or get Bum Phillips to drive me to Houston, and now I have coffee with two or three at a time, just working my way through the staff. Visiting, getting to know one another. But there is never any doubt who's in charge.

Bum still talks about his first practice with me at A&M. He was supposed to be out fifteen minutes early to work with the quarterbacks and the centers, and when he came out I was already there.

He looked around and there were no footballs. He figured somebody knew to bring out the balls, but he didn't want to start a period without them, so he said, "Coach Bryant, you reckon the managers will have those footballs out here on time?"

I gave him kind of half a grin and said, "I don't know, Bum, but I'll tell you one damn thing. I ain't gonna go get 'em."

He says on the way back in to get the balls he realized the difference between a head coach and an assistant.

The thing is, they have got to believe what you say, and you've got to make them say what they believe, too. In the old days — and sometimes now — if some coach brought up a point on a halfback's stance, say, or a way to block a specific play, I'd jump out of my chair to challenge him.

"What the hell do you mean you'd rather do it this way? Do you think that's better than what we've been doing?"

I'd get right in his face, and if he believed it he would stand by what he said. I might have believed it from the beginning, but I wasn't going to change something unless I knew he believed it, too. I don't want ideas just thrown out, I want them thought out.

So many of them — former players, former assistant coaches — are now head coaches that if I tried to name them all I'd forget a few, but it can't help but make me proud the way, say, Charley McClendon has done at LSU, Jerry Claiborne at Maryland, and Jim Stanley at Oklahoma State. Jimmy Sharpe's at VPI now, and Steve Sloan at Vanderbilt, and they'll win. What worries me is that some of them will win at the wrong time. In the 1974 season I have to coach against four of my former players — Sloan, Bill Battle at Tennessee, Claiborne and McClendon — and one former assistant, Bob Tyler at Mississippi State.

They got to be so numerous we had to quit having our "closed clinic" every year. We had all the coaches and former players in, and we'd talk football and get up some terrific golf matches during the week, and then we'd have a big party at our house.

Parilli and I were playing Blanda and Charlie Mac one year at Indian Hills, and of course I made all the rules. Blanda was on me for giving myself the "Eisenhower treatment," which was making them up as I went along.

On the last hole I lucked in a putt to win. Namath was there and he said, "Pick you a partner, Steve and I'll take you next time." Sloan is a great golfer, and Joe could be.

So I picked Bebes Stallings and we agreed to play handicaps. On the first three holes Steve and Joe had five birdies. But I did better than that before we even started — I got eighteen strokes.

After a while it began to look like somebody was guiding my ball. On the 14th I was in the woods, and up near the green there were some telephone lines between me and the hole. Bebes was out of it; they knew they had the hole won. I hit a wood shot out of the rough and the ball hit the telephone wire and dropped down and rolled two inches from the pin.

I sank another putt with all the guys standing around the 18th, and we won. Joe and Steve wrote out checks for us — I think it came to about $70 apiece — and I wouldn't take anything for the satisfaction. But I told Bebes I was going to send Joe his check back.

"The hell with that." Bebes said, "I'm keeping mine."

I don't make a lot of rules for my players. I expect them to act like gentlemen, to have good table manners, to be punctual, to be prayerful. I expect them to be up on their studies, and I don't expect them to be mooning around the campus holding hands with the girls all the time, because that comes later, when they're winners. In a war, what do the losers get? I heard a coach say one time he'd rather have a whore kick his player out of bed and say, "Go get me some touchdowns," than for some little old sweet gal to say, "Be careful, now, and don't get hurt." That's a little salty, I suppose, but the message is plain.

I don't know any other way to say this, but I love my players. Love them as if they were my own. I was telling one the other day, a black boy from Montgomery, how proud I was of him, and was planning on telling his mother how proud I was the next time I saw her. I said, "And don't forget to come around if you have any problems." I meant it. And he knew it.

The next day he was back in my office.

"Coach," he said, "I got a problem."

"What is it?"

"I'm going to get married."

I used to be against that, but I'm not anymore.

I said, "Well, two can live as cheaply as one."

He said he was going to try to set her up in a place in Montgomery. I said, "If you're going to get any help from me you're going to bring her here and be with her. I'll put you on married scholarship" — which means $150 extra a month if they live at the dorm — "and you can be together."

I didn't always go for that. But I learned.

I talked with the wife of one of my former players one time, after she had separated from him. And she gave me the lowdown on their sex life, before and after marriage. And what she said made a lot of sense. I decided it would be a lot better if the boy went ahead and married the girl if she was a good one. And if they were in love and could afford it.

It's better for a lot of reasons. For control, it's better than being footloose. If they can handle it financially it's better, because when she works she has something to say about what's going on. Chances are they'll be home at night instead of running around being tempted by drugs or something.

This wife of my former player set me straight on one postnuptial point, too. I used to let the wives come to the hotel with the married players the night before a game. She said, "Coach Bryant, there's something about a hotel room. . . ."

Now when we're on trips we separate them the night before.

The thing is, a football player at Alabama has two full-time jobs. He doesn't need extra burdens. If my players are putting forth maximum effort in their studies and in football, they won't have time for much else. And I always say this: because of our program they'll wind up better people in the three important areas of life — mental, physical and spiritual.

I used to go along with the idea that football players on scholarship were "student-athletes," which is what the NCAA calls them. Meaning a student first, an athlete second. We were kidding ourselves, trying to make it more palatable to the academicians. We don't have to say that, and we shouldn't. At the level we play the boy is really an athlete first and a student second.

He's there as an emissary of the school, paid with a scholarship to perform a very important function. He represents the students, the administration, the alumni, everybody. Sometimes before millions of people. The fact that he's a student, the second part of the deal, is the only meaningful way we have to pay him.

There's absolutely nothing wrong with saying he's an athlete first, and we've got to quit choking on the idea. If you measured the effort he has to make to perform that dual role, as I have, you'd appreciate it more.

The fact that we don't lose sight of the second part is to our credit, and to professional football's for not invading the campuses to hire away players before their class graduates. Baseball's record isn't as good. Bill Murray of Duke made a study of something like nine hundred kids who signed professional baseball contracts before graduating from high school. Twenty or twenty-five made it to the big leagues, and only five got in the necessary five years for their pension.

And a very small percentage — only a handful — of the original nine hundred ever got their college degree. That's disgraceful. It shows a total lack of concern for the boy.

I want to be as close as I can with a boy without destroying the coach-player relationship. I remember so well, after I played my last game, how alone I felt, and I want my boys to always feel they can come to me. And I'll say this, you can learn as much from them as you can teach them.

We have had a lot of Christian boys on our squads, and one year at Texas A&M, my first year there, in fact, Marvin Tate came to me and said they were very resentful, all the swearing and cussing I was doing on the field. That really upset me.

I called a meeting, and I apologized to the squad and told them it was a lack of vocabulary on our part, that it showed a weakness, and from then on it would cost me $10 for every swear word I used on the practice field. It would cost the assistant coaches a dollar and the players a quarter, and we would put the money into a fund and buy something for the dorm or have a Christmas party.

As far as techniques and tactics are concerned, they are overrated. The greatest technicians I've known weren't always the toughest guys to beat. I don't mean you can be technically unsound, but if you can't get your boy to play any more than 80 percent of his ability on Saturday, a field coach, a guy that gets it done, will beat you every time.

Nearly everything you do has been done at one time or another. Trap blocking, for example. I remember Coach Thomas was doing that when I played at Alabama, and I know he was the first in our area to try it. Matty Bell was talking about stunting when we were in the service, and I know Red Sanders was doing it at Vanderbilt in 1948.

About the only thing we have ever done that we thought was original was stunting the secondary, keying everything and reading. For example, if you're in a four-deep defense, you might use any one of the four as a free man, play the others in a zone or man-to-man. Or you might read on key offensive men and support inside-out or outside-in.

All else being equal, the same things still win. You just got different excuses nowadays. You're still going to win with preparation and dedication and plain old desire. If you don't have genuine desire, you won't be dedicated enough to prepare properly. It's a coach's job to get those things across.

It doesn't take a genius for that. The best coaches, *most* coaches I've known, weren't Phi Beta Kappa in the classroom.

I better watch what I say, though. We were having our meetings in Dallas one time, and playing golf, and I said, "Show me a football coach who shoots good golf and I'll show you a horseshit coach."

About that time somebody came running into the little lounge there, hollering, "Hey, Bud Wilkinson just shot a 71, and Paul Dietzel a 72!" Unh-oh.

Well, for me it's still true. I was out at Lubbock for the All-Star Game a couple of years ago playing with Chuck Fairbanks, who was then at Oklahoma but now coaches the Patriots and is a warm friend of mine. Every day he was shooting par and just loving it. I had to think, if I were his age, I'd be out recruiting and figuring out some way to beat somebody. I couldn't do it any other way. At my age, what difference did it make, playing golf?

In terms of hours on the job, at Kentucky and Texas A&M and those first few years at Alabama, I would say it took every hour other than about three in a twenty-four-hour day. The other three I just wasted. Taking a little nap.

My approach to the game has been the same at all the places I've been. Vanilla. The sure way. That means, first of all, to win physically.

If you got eleven on a field, and they beat the other eleven physically, they'll win. They will start forcing mistakes. They'll win in the fourth quarter. I don't think any coach has a monopoly on how to win, but that's my approach.

Somebody asked me, "Don't you consider yourself an innovator? A stylesetter?"

"No," I said. "I ain't nothing but a winner."

I am a student of the game, sure. I think anybody is if he's making a living at it, or had better be. But formations won't win if you don't have good players. And if you do, you have to have the defense to start with, because you have to keep from losing before you can win.

And defense starts with the kicking game. The first thing in the book. That hasn't changed very much. Coach Wade, Coach Thomas, Bob Neyland. They all won on their kicking game.

I'm talking about all of it — kicks, kick coverage, returns, field position. Take Coach Wade. Alabama was playing Tennessee, and I forget the exact figures but Tennessee had a kicker who averaged, say, 45 yards a punt. The kicker was also the star runner. Coach Wade decided to put a strong rush on every punt, to cut the average down.

Alabama almost blocked the first one, and for fourteen punts the kicker's average was cut 5 yards. He ran from scrimmage for 70 yards, but the punts totaled a net loss of 70 yards. The two canceled out.

I'd like to know how many games Johnny Rodgers broke open for Nebraska returning kicks his two years there, either for touchdowns or to put his team in good field position. And some of the things you never see in statistics are so important. Like fielding a punt. Do you realize how many games are lost not just because a guy doesn't return the ball but because he doesn't field the punt? How many times have you seen a guy run up to catch a punt, then back off and have it bounce 30 yards past him? If he catches it every time he is going to save a lot of yards.

Field goals have changed the game, too. Everybody has a field goal kicker now. You have to play a little different defense out of respect, depending on the other kicker's range. I remember one game we played Auburn and they had Ed Dyas, and we went into a goal-line defense at midfield. Beat 'em, 3–0.

It might not be a bad idea to adopt the new pro rule — to bring the ball back to the point of a kick on a missed field goal. That could cut down on some of those shots in the dark that field goal kickers try, and restore a little flavor to punting and goal-line stands. On offense it has gotten to the point where you've got to take chances to get away from your goal line to keep from giving up the ball in field goal range.

But passers are better, too, and they've got more room to throw in that area. It's probably the easiest place to complete a pass, and not as risky as it looks. For example, the Notre Dame pass that got them out of the hole against us in the Sugar Bowl.

Every conference now has two or three great passers, and some great receivers. Even with the wishbone and the triple-option offenses. I remember Bud Wilkinson saying years ago that in his entire career at Oklahoma Bobby Layne and Babe Parilli were the only two great passers they played against. This was before he saw Namath in the 1963 Orange Bowl.

Now there is talent in every area, and it gets better every year because people like Joe get all that publicity, their faces covered with shaving cream on television, and it's fun to practice being Joe Namath because it's not hard work. Playing pitch and catch. A kid can start early.

So there's more talent, and that makes it tougher to excuse yourself when you lose. I know even lately there were games I hurt us, games we won in spite of me or lost because of me. Win or lose, if you don't recognize the mistakes — mistakes in preparation, mistakes during a game — you're hurting yourself. I've been outcoached, too, and I sure don't forget those times.

Do they live as long as the big victories?

No. They live longer.

— Thirty-Four —

There has been a lot of speculation and gossip in the past few years about me quitting and going into politics, and I have to admit I have thought about it. If movie stars can make it, football coaches ought to be able to. I've been around so many politicians all my professional life, really, that I'd be surprised if some of it hasn't rubbed off.

When I first went to Kentucky I got real close with Happy Chandler and his family. Happy was a U.S. Senator then, and became governor. Mary Harmon and I used to get whipped regularly at bridge by Happy and Mildred. Later on, when Earl Clements was governor, we got to be close, and my warmest friend during that time was Governor Wetherby, old X–1. He and I were duck hunting together when Arkansas made me that flattering offer to come home to coach.

George Wallace was on the school boxing team when I was an assistant coach at Alabama, and we have seen him off and on over the years. George is a very knowledgeable person, and has turned out to be right about so many things, things I didn't agree with at the time. He's got guts coming out of his ears and I was glad to see him come back after being shot and paralyzed.

A couple of years ago I was trying to recruit a black quarterback down in Mississippi. The boy was worried about what Wallace would say or do. So I called George, and he got on the phone and told me he wanted good people at Alabama, and he didn't care if they were black, green or purple. He said anything he could do to help he'd do, and to call on him.

I have already told you about my friendship and feeling for the Kennedy family, how impressed I was with Jack and Bobby. When we had our coaches' convention in California one year Bud Wilkinson, Duffy Daugherty, Charlie McClendon and I went out to the racetrack and lost some money, and the next day Richard Nixon invited ten or twelve of us to lunch. He was the vice-president then. We passed up the invitation to go try to win our money back at the track. We lost again. And I've always regretted it. Both ways.

When Mr. Agnew was vice-president he came down to present us the Governor's Cup after we beat Auburn. I joined him and his wife at the airport, and sat between them on the dais. I asked Mrs. Agnew if the vice-president had a sense of humor and she assured me he did.

When I got up I said, "Pardon my nervousness, folks. But I'm not used to sitting next to vice-presidents. I'm used to sitting next to presidents."

Mr. Agnew about busted a gut laughing.

It's so flattering that people in your own state think you could make a good governor, or a good something. Ryan de Graffenreid's people called me in February 1966, after he died in that plane crash. De Graffenreid was the number one Democratic candidate in the primary.

Governor Wallace had told me he wouldn't run if de Graffenreid did. I had run into George at a banquet in Montgomery honoring David Ray. Politicians are always ready to help honor an outstanding athlete, and Ray had been our star placekicker. He's with the Rams now.

I knew if George ran he would beat me to death. He'd beat anybody in Alabama. But if he didn't run (as it turned out, Lurleen Wallace did), I thought I could win, and I agreed to sleep on it. I was down on the Keys, at Sloan Bashinsky's place, when a couple of de Graffenreid's people came and asked me to run. A serious offer.

And after a couple snorts that night I got real brave and said, "OK, I'll do it."

But the next morning I had lost the glow. I realized I couldn't do it. You get wrapped up in yourself when you have offers like that, to run for some office. People make over you a little, and you get taken with the idea of all those folks voting for you, and before you know it you're hooked.

When I realized it was just an ego trip I knew I couldn't do it. A few years later it was almost cut and dried that I could have won the U.S. Senate race, with Jimmy Hinton backing me. I would have run as an independent, but I wasn't interested enough to try.

I'm confident enough to believe I had a chance at any office in Alabama there for a while, but the thing that has always turned me away is this: football has been my life. I know football. If I need an assistant coach to work on my defensive line I know where to go to get one and who to get. If I need a publicity man, a ticket manager, anything, I know where to go.

But if I were governor and needed somebody for this job or that one, I wouldn't be so sure. Besides that, I control our football program, and if I do my job I know we're going to win. A Miami writer once wrote that I stare down most of my critics and sue the others, and though I think that's a little harsh it tells you the difference between my position and a politician's. I couldn't control the levers in the polling booth.

I think you can get an ulcer in any profession, you can kill yourself in any profession if you go at it hard enough. Here our kids had won three national championships, and the morning it was announced we had won the third I got over to the dormitory at 3 A.M. and pinned up that sign about going for number four.

And when we won it last year I immediately set my cap for number five, because that's the way I am. I'll want one every year.

At this point, though, I'm a lot older, and if we started losing I would probably retire from coaching, because I wouldn't take the abuse that goes with losing. I know that doesn't sound like me, but look at it another way. I'm not planning for it to happen, either.

I have to laugh. One SEC coach was quoted as saying, years ago, "Under Bryant, Alabama will win some the first year, go to the Sugar Bowl the second, and go on suspension the third."

Well, we did, and we went, and we haven't, so maybe he has learned something about me, and maybe I've learned a lot too.

Since then many good things have come my way, and I don't mind saying it's nice for people to think well of you, and it's nicer if a *lot* of people think a lot of you. I even get a kick out of those corny Bear Bryant jokes that make the rounds.

The worst one — and my preacher friends will have to pardon me — is about the guy who goes to Heaven and sees this very impressive figure with a white beard walking around a football field that has platinum stripes. The figure is wearing a cap with an A in red rubies on the peak.

The guy says, "Who's that?"

And Saint Peter says, "It's God, but He thinks He's Bear Bryant."

Bob Devaney was always after me on the banquet circuit. He told the story of losing to us in the 1967 Sugar Bowl, how he moped around for several days until his grandson came to visit. He brightened up a little then, and one of the kids said, "Grampa, tell us the story of the three bears."

And Bob said, "Oh, no! You mean there are two more?"

I could have said the same about him, after what he did to us in that 1972 Orange Bowl game. I was glad he retired.

Me, I have no reason to retire. None at all. Besides, I have to get out of debt first.

We've done pretty well, Jimmy Hinton and I. We've got part ownership in a meat-packing firm, Zeigler's. And I have a small piece of a yarn-treating firm, Olympia, and a Volkswagen distributorship, and I'm on the board of the First National Bank of Tuscaloosa, Federated Guarantee of Alabama, a development company in Huntsville and one in Houston. And I have a few stocks that keep me in debt.

But most of my money is tied up, and I'm always scrambling. I'll show you how stupid I am. I had been turning down raises almost every year. My salary is $29,000 annually, but they would have paid me twice that if I'd wanted. But I kept saying no.

Then one day President Mathews said, "Paul, you got to have a raise."

I said, "I don't need a raise."

He said, "But *I* do."

He said it was easier if he gave me one, too. He explained that my retirement benefit at the salary I was getting was only worth about $7,000 a year. That I needed to make more in order to have a decent retirement. Well, it's too late now because I would have to be making it over a period of time, so I blew that one.

So *I'm* the one who'll decide when my career is over. They won't have to ask me to quit the way they did Adolph Rupp. I'll know the time. As long as I'm getting those chills up my back, as long as I *know* I'm contributing toward another National Championship, I'll be around.

And the only way you can measure that is by winning. There's no other way.

I want to make it absolutely clear at this point that the only reason I can talk about National Championships is people — people who have made thirty years of coaching worthwhile, people who taught me and played for me, and people who didn't have a thing to do with football but stuck by me and pulled me through when things were going bad. Like Niel Morgan of Tuscaloosa. Niel's an Auburn man, but I guarantee you he was right beside me every minute of the way during that business with the *Post*, having me at his dinner table almost every night, watching out for me, flying me places. He actually cried with joy when Wally Butts won his suit.

There are so many people who have made it all worthwhile, and I'd be sure to miss somebody, so I'm not going to even try to name them all. People like Niel and Frank Moody and Billy Sellers and Julian Lackey and Jimmy Hinton, people outside of football. And the coaches I've worked for and with — Thomas, Drew, Crisp, Sanders, Paul Burnum, Glenn Killinger — were nothing less than inspirational.

I'll tell you something else, too. I got a lot of help and learned a whole lot from the other side, from great coaches like Bill Alexander and Bobby Dodd of Georgia Tech, Wallace Wade of Alabama and Duke, and General Bob Neyland of Tennessee. General Neyland beat us so much I *had* to learn something.

A lot of them were there when I was inducted into the Arkansas Hall of Fame in 1964, and I guarantee you I had a full throat that night.

Bill Dickey was on the dais, and George Kell and Lon Warneke.

Somebody said I had left thumbing a ride, and had come back in a Cadillac, and I said that was right and I had a lot to be thankful for.

I said, "I have more to be thankful for than anybody," and I had to stop. I am a big crybaby, anyway, but this was tough.

I said, "I am thankful to God for good health, so that I could work hard. I'm thankful to my mother and father and my wonderful family. I'm thankful to Dan Walton and Bob Cowan for starting me in football. I'm thankful for the opportunity to play for a great coach like Frank Thomas.

"I'm thankful for my teammates. I'm thankful for my beautiful wife and my children. I'm thankful I could work under Red Sanders, and have such great players as John Crow, and the ordinary ones who made themselves great. I'm thankful to all of you."

Well, we're supposed to be living in a very sophisticated time. With sophisticated young people. All worldly-wise and knowledgeable. How can a game of football still be important in that context?

I'll tell you how I feel. I feel it's more important than ever. What else have we got to tie to? Where else can we walk out there even, same everything, *even*, and compete?

I think it's ten times more important. Let me ask you this. Have you taught your children to work? To sacrifice? Have you taught them self-discipline? Hell, no. They don't get it in the home, they don't get it in the schoolhouse, they don't even get it in the church the way they used to.

But I guarantee you this. You send your boy to Steve Sloan at Vanderbilt — I use Steve as an example because he's right up the road, and he's one of mine — and he'll teach him those things. Check up. Look around. Maybe the football field's the only place left. We may have already lost it everywhere else.

But why football? Why does it have to carry such a burden? That's hard for me to say because football is my life. No in between, no compromise. It's my life.

Football is different things to different people. For everybody I know it's something to tie to. Everybody can't tie to an English class. Everybody can tie to a football team. And the results are right there to see, and a lifetime of work comes down to that.

Every football game you see represents a whole lot of preparation,

335

all the way back to the parents, when a player was a boy, on into high school and beyond, and a lot of people have had something to do with it. The equipment man, the man who mows the grass, the fans, everybody.

It touches so many people. I don't know why — whether it's because it's a contact sport or what — but it gets hold of people. Students and alumni go wild. Everybody talks about it. Presidents call to congratulate winners in the dressing room. Newspapers devote more space to it than anything.

In Alabama, you better be for football or you might as well leave. I have been in Europe, thinking I was the only American left, and had people stop me and say, "How's Alabama gonna do this year, Bear?"

The beautiful thing about it, for me, is this. Four years ago when I accepted that offer from the Dolphins and tried to resign Dr. Mathews wouldn't have any part of it.

He said, "Paul, I'm a young guy, and I've got all these young administrators. You're the last guy I've got to hang my hat on." You know, the old man. The significance of it didn't hit me then, when it did I realized a few things.

Administrators who aren't enthusiastic about football aren't part of my experience. They are ones I don't run into, though I'm sure they're around. But you can put this down: at Alabama, they are *never* going to mark football down, whether I'm there or not. Certainly not as long as I'm living and have something to say about it.

I used to have that plaque on my wall: Winning Isn't Everything, But It Beats Anything That Comes In Second. When Benny Marshall wrote his little book about me in 1965 that was what he called it.

That sounds a little stern to some people, a little narrow-minded, but when you're committed to a winning effort there's nothing more gratifying in the world. I wrote it down for something Bebes Stallings and I did years ago, and it applies today:

That there is no sin in not liking to play, that it's a mistake for a boy to be there if he doesn't want to. But if he loves it it's an opportunity to make himself a part of a big thing. To be associated with the best group of kids in the world.

It doesn't have to be at Alabama. If the system is right, no matter where he plays he's with the best group he'll ever be with. His teammates.

He has been accepted by an institution and has been given an alma mater, something to tie to. He is going to go a lot of places, firstclass, and perform before thousands of people, even millions, including his family and people he loves.

He'll be getting his foot in the door for the future, gaining recognition, learning lessons about living. There will be times when he'll hate that smelly uniform, and times when he gets mad at his best friend, and times when he's cussing his coach under his breath. He's going to have to work hard.

But when it comes down to those Saturdays, and the band's playing and the cold shivers are running down his back, he'll *know* how much it means to him. If he loves it, and gives it everything he has, he's one of the luckiest young men in the world.

Well, like I told Benny and he put in his book. When I was little we raised pigs, and one morning Daddy told me to hitch up the wagon and take ten of them to town to sell. He said I could keep a dollar if I sold 'em all. I was no more than eleven years old.

Halfway from Moro Bottom to Fordyce, on a lonely stretch of road, the wagon got stuck in the mud. No matter what I tried I couldn't get it loose. Time was flying by. I could see my sale going out the window. Finally I just sat there and cried.

But I got lucky. Somebody came by and helped me out, and I drove on to Fordyce and sold those pigs, and made my little fortune.

I've had that kind of luck all the way. I was lucky to have stumbled onto football. Lucky to have gone to Alabama to play. Lucky to have played under Coach Thomas, and to have found Mary Harmon, and to have gotten the jobs I did. Lucky to have had the players I've had, who put up with me, and the coaches, and the people around me.

Shoot, I've said it a jillion times. I've been lucky all my life.

337

— Appendix —

THE BRYANT RECORD

Winningest Active Coach

Coach of the Year,
1961, 1971, 1973

SEC Coach of the Year
Four Times

All-time SEC Coach

Coach of the Decade, voted by
the Football Coaches
Association of America

Past President, American
Football Coaches Association

Career Record of 231 Victories

Best Record for Past Decade

Four National
Championships

Eight Conference
Championships

Twenty Bowl Teams

Twenty-one College
Head Coaches

Forty-seven All-Americans

Forty-two Academic
All-SEC Players

Seventy-six All-Conference
Players

Four Jacobs Blocking
Award Winners

Fourteen Teams in
Nation's Top

Second Total Defense
Past Decade

Third Rushing Defense
Past Decade

National Scoring Defense
Champion for Past Decade

Teams on Television 32 Times

BRYANT'S RECORD AS HEAD COACH:
WON 231, LOST 70, TIED 16

Year	School	W	L	T	Year	School	W	L	T
1945	Maryland	6	2	1	1960	Alabama	8	1	2
1946	Kentucky	7	3	0	1961	Alabama	*11	0	0
1947	Kentucky	8	3	0	1962	Alabama	10	1	0
1948	Kentucky	5	3	2	1963	Alabama	9	2	0
1949	Kentucky	9	3	0	1964	Alabama	*10	1	0
1950	Kentucky	11	1	0	1965	Alabama	* 9	1	1
1951	Kentucky	8	4	0	1966	Alabama	11	0	0
1952	Kentucky	5	4	2	1967	Alabama	8	2	1
1953	Kentucky	7	2	1	1968	Alabama	8	3	0
1954	Texas A&M	1	9	0	1969	Alabama	6	5	0
1955	Texas A&M	7	2	1	1970	Alabama	6	5	1
1956	Texas A&M	9	0	1	1971	Alabama	11	1	0
1957	Texas A&M	8	3	0	1972	Alabama	10	2	0
1958	Alabama	5	4	1	1973	Alabama	11	0	0
1959	Alabama	7	2	2					

*National Champions

BRYANT AS A PLAYER, ASSISTANT COACH AND HEAD COACH

As a Player

1933	Alabama	7	1	1	.833
1934	Alabama	10	0	0	1.000
1935	Alabama	6	2	1	.722
	Totals	23	3	2	.857

As Assistant Coach

1936	Alabama	8	0	1	.938
1937	Alabama	9	1	0	.900
1938	Alabama	7	1	1	.833
1939	Alabama	5	3	1	.611
1940	Vanderbilt	3	6	1	.350
1941	Vanderbilt	6	1	2	.778
	Totals	38	12	6	.732

As Head Coach

Maryland, 1 year	6	2	2	.722
Kentucky, 8 years	60	23	5	.710
Texas A&M, 4 years	25	14	2	.634
Alabama, 16 years	140	30	7	.811
Totals	231	69	16	.756
Composite Totals	292	84	24	.760

Coach of the Year Honors

National Coach of the Year — 1961, 1971, 1973. SEC Coach of the Year — 1961, 1964, 1971, 1973

MARYLAND ERA
1945 (6-2-1)

60	Guilford	6
21	Richmond	0
22	Merchant MA	6
13	Virginia Poly	21
13	West Virginia	13
14	Wm. & Mary	33
38	VMI	0
19	Virginia	13
19	South Carolina	13

KENTUCKY ERA
(8 years, 60-23-5)
1946 (7-3)

20	Mississippi	7
26	Cincinnati	7
70	Xavier	0
13	Georgia	28
10	Vanderbilt	7
7	Alabama	21
39	Michigan State	14
35	Marquette	0
13	West Virginia	0
0	Tennessee	7

1947 (8-3)

7	Mississippi	14
20	Cincinnati	0
20	Xavier	7
26	Georgia	0
14	Vanderbilt	0
7	Michigan State	6
0	Alabama	13
15	West Virginia	6
36	Evansville	0
6	Tennessee	13

Great Lakes Bowl

24	Villanova	14

1948 (5-3-2)

48	Xavier	7
7	Mississippi	20
12	Georgia	35
7	Vanderbilt	26
25	Marquette	0
28	Cincinnati	7
13	Villanova	13
34	Florida	15
0	Tennessee	0
25	Miami	5

1949 (9-3)

71	Southern Miss.	7
19	LSU	0
47	Mississippi	0
25	Georgia	0
44	The Citadel	0
7	SMU	20
14	Cincinnati	7
21	Xavier	7
35	Florida	0
0	Tennessee	6
21	Miami	6

Orange Bowl

13	Santa Clara	21

1950 (11-1)

25	North Texas St.	0
14	LSU	0
27	Mississippi	0
40	Dayton	0
41	Cincinnati	7
34	Villanova	7
28	Georgia Tech	14
40	Florida	6
48	Mississippi State	21
83	North Dakota U.	0
0	Tennessee	7

Sugar Bowl

13	Oklahoma	7

1951 (8-4)

72	Tennessee Tech	13
6	Texas	7
17	Mississippi	21
7	Georgia Tech	13
27	Miss. State	0
35	Villanova	13
14	Florida	6
32	Miami	0
37	Tulane	0
47	Geo. Washington	13
0	Tennessee	28

Cotton Bowl

20	TCU	7

1952 (5-4-2)

6	Villanova	25
13	Mississippi	13
10	Texas A&M	7
7	LSU	34
14	Miss. State	27
14	Cincinnati	6
29	Miami	0
27	Tulane	6
27	Clemson	14
14	Tennessee	14
0	Florida	27

1953 (7-2-1)

6	Texas A&M	7
6	Mississippi	22
26	Florida	13
6	LSU	6
35	Miss. State	13
19	Villanova	0
19	Rice	13
40	Vanderbilt	14
19	Memphis State	7
27	Tennessee	21

TEXAS A&M ERA
(4 years, 25-14-2)
1954 (1-9)

9	Texas Tech	41
6	Oklahoma State	14
6	Georgia	0
7	Houston	10
20	TCU	21
7	Baylor	20
7	Arkansas	14
3	SMU	6
19	Rice	29
13	Texas	22

1955 (7-2-1)

0	UCLA	21
28	LSU	0
21	Houston	3
27	Nebraska	0
19	TCU	16
19	Baylor	7
7	Arkansas	7
13	SMU	2
20	Rice	12
6	Texas	21

1956 (9-0-1)
(SWC Champions)

19	Villanova	0
9	LSU	6
40	Texas Tech	7
14	Houston	14
7	TCU	6
19	Baylor	13
27	Arkansas	0
33	SMU	7
21	Rice	7
34	Texas	21

1957 (8–3–0)

1	Maryland	13
1	Texas Tech	0
8	Missouri	6
8	Houston	6
7	TCU	0
4	Baylor	0
7	Arkansas	6
9	SMU	6
6	Rice	7
7	Texas	9
	Gator Bowl	
0	Tennessee	3

ALABAMA ERA
(15 years, 129–30–7)

1958 (5–4–1)

3	LSU	13
0	Vanderbilt	0
9	Furman	6
7	Tennessee	14
9	Mississippi State	7
2	Georgia	0
7	Tulane	13
7	Georgia Tech	8
4	Memphis State	0
8	Auburn	14

1959 (7–2–2)

3	Georgia	17
3	Houston	0
7	Vanderbilt	7
3	Chattanooga	0
7	Tennessee	7
0	Miss. State	0
9	Tulane	7
9	Georgia Tech	7
4	Memphis State	7
0	Auburn	0
	Liberty Bowl	
0	Penn State	7

1960 (8–1–2)

1	Georgia	6
6	Tulane	6
1	Vanderbilt	0
7	Tennessee	20
4	Houston	0
7	Miss. State	0
1	Furman	0
5	Georgia Tech	15
4	Tampa	6

3	Auburn	0
	Bluebonnet Bowl	
3	Texas	3

1961 (11–0–0)
(National Champions)

32	Georgia	6
9	Tulane	0
35	Vanderbilt	6
26	N. C. State	7
34	Tennessee	3
17	Houston	0
24	Miss. State	0
66	Richmond	0
10	Georgia Tech	0
34	Auburn	0
	Sugar Bowl	
10	Arkansas	3

1962 (10–1)

35	Georgia	0
44	Tulane	6
17	Vanderbilt	7
14	Houston	3
27	Tennessee	7
35	Tulsa	6
20	Miss. State	0
36	Miami	3
6	Georgia Tech	7
38	Auburn	0
	Orange Bowl	
17	Oklahoma	0

1963 (9–2–0)

32	Georgia	7
28	Tulane	0
21	Vanderbilt	6
6	Florida	10
35	Tennessee	0
21	Houston	13
20	Miss. State	19
27	Georgia Tech	11
8	Auburn	10
17	Miami	12
	Sugar Bowl	
12	Mississippi	7

1964 (10–1–0)
(National Champions)

31	Georgia	3
36	Tulane	6
24	Vanderbilt	0
21	N. C. State	0

19	Tennessee	8
17	Florida	14
23	Miss. State	6
17	LSU	9
24	Georgia Tech	7
21	Auburn	14
	Orange Bowl	
17	Texas	21

1965 (9–1–1)
(National Champions)

17	Georgia	18
27	Tulane	0
17	Ole Miss	16
22	Vanderbilt	7
7	Tennessee	7
21	Florida State	0
10	Miss. State	7
31	LSU	7
35	South Carolina	14
30	Auburn	3
	Orange Bowl	
39	Nebraska	28

1966 (11–0–0)
(SEC Champions)

34	La. Tech	0
17	Mississippi	7
26	Clemson	0
11	Tennessee	10
42	Vanderbilt	6
27	Miss. State	14
21	LSU	0
24	South Carolina	0
34	Southern Miss.	0
31	Auburn	0
	Sugar Bowl	
34	Nebraska	7

1967 (8–2–1)

37	Florida State	37
25	Southern Miss.	3
21	Mississippi	7
35	Vanderbilt	21
13	Tennessee	24
13	Clemson	10
13	Miss. State	0
7	LSU	6
17	South Carolina	0
7	Auburn	3
	Cotton Bowl	
16	Texas A&M	20